ComputingFailure.com

ISBN 0-13-091739-7

90000

9 780130 917393

Other books by Robert L. Glass:

Computing Trends:
The Universal Elixir, and Other Computing Projects Which Failed, 1977, 1979, 1981, 1992
Tales of Computing Folk: Hot Dogs and Mixed Nuts, 1978*
The Power of Peonage, 1979*
The Second Coming: More Computing Projects Which Failed, 1980*
Software Soliloquies, 1981
Computing Catastrophes, 1983, 1991
Computing Shakeout, 1987
Software Folklore, 1991
Software 2020, 1998

Prentice-Hall and Yourdon Press:
Software Reliability Guidebook, 1979*
Software Maintenance Guidebook, 1981*
Modern Programming Practices: A Report From Industry, 1982*
Real-Time Software, 1983
Software Communication Skills, 1988*
Measuring Software Design Quality, 1990?
Software Conflict: Essays on the Art and Science of Software Engineering, 1991?
Building Quality Software, 1992*
Measuring and Motivating Maintenance Programmers, 1992*
Software Creativity, 1995
An ISO 9000 Approach to Building Quality Software, 1996
Software Runaways, 1998
Computing Calamities, 1999

IEEE Computer Society Press:
In the Beginning: Recollections of Software Pioneers, 1998

* Out of print
? May be out of print

Computing Trends books are available from:
1416 Sare Rd., Bloomington, IN 47401

ComputingFailure.com

War Stories from the Electronic Revolution

Robert L. Glass

To join a Prentice Hall PTR Internet mailing list, point to
www.prenhall.com/register

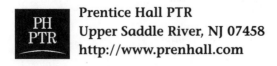

Prentice Hall PTR
Upper Saddle River, NJ 07458
http://www.prenhall.com

Library of Congress Cataloging-in-Publication Data

CIP data available.

Editorial/production supervision: *Mary Sudul*
Acquisitions editor: *Paul Petralia*
Manufacturing manager: *Alexis R. Heydt*
Composition: *FASTpages*
Marketing manager: *Debby vanDijk*
Cover design: *Nina Scuderi*
Cover design direction: *Jerry Votta*
Editorial assistant: *Justin Somma*

 ©2001 Prentice Hall PTR
Prentice-Hall, Inc.
Upper Saddle River, New Jersey 07458

Prentice Hall books are widely used by corporations and government agencies for training, marketing, and resale.

The publisher offers discounts on this book when ordered in bulk quantities.
For more information, contact: Corporate Sales Department, Phone: 800-382-3419;
Fax: 201-236-7141; E-mail: corpsales@prenhall.com; or write: Prentice Hall PTR,
Corp. Sales Dept., One Lake Street, Upper Saddle River, NJ 07458.

Printed in the United States of America

10 9 8 7 6 5 4 3 2 1

ISBN 0-13-091739-7

Prentice-Hall International (UK) Limited, *London*
Prentice-Hall of Australia Pty. Limited, *Sydney*
Prentice-Hall Canada Inc., *Toronto*
Prentice-Hall Hispanoamericana, S.A., *Mexico*
Prentice-Hall of India Private Limited, *New Delhi*
Prentice-Hall of Japan, Inc., *Tokyo*
Prentice Hall (Singapore) P.T.E., Ltd.
Editora Prentice-Hall do Brasil, Ltda., *Rio de Janeiro*

Contents

Foreword

by Tom DeMarco

I know this sounds weird, but success in our business is inextricably tied up with failure. The days of achieving anything important without risk-taking are over forever. Today you need to positively flirt with failure in order to achieve meaningful success. The projects that are really worth doing lie at the hairy, scary edge of feasibility. Your intimate understanding of the potential failures that may await you is surely your most potent weapon for avoiding them. You need to become an expert on failure.

But focusing on failure is something that goes against the grain. Our cultures guide us to think only of success, to concentrate on winning, not losing. That all sounds good, sounds positive. The Plan For Success mentality sounds great, but it makes risk management almost impossible. And risk management is your most effective tool in a risk-intensive world. To do real risk management, you have to develop a deep understanding of the factors that have undone those who have gone before you, understand how these factors acted and what measures proved insufficient to contain them. If such factors proved fatal to your predecessors, they may prove equally fatal to you.

Maybe you're willing to accept this idea with no more said, but (never a master of understatement) I have chosen to hammer it home anyway with a grisly word-picture: If you find yourself proceeding over a battlefield that is littered with fresh corpses and you don't know what killed them, you are in trouble. You better be thinking furiously, What did they learn at the end that I may still have to learn in the near future?

This is exactly the situation most software project managers find themselves in. They need to learn quickly about failure. Of course, the classic way to learn about failure is to make all the mistakes yourself and guide different projects to a great selection of awful conclusions. If you had already done that, you would now be a relative expert on the failures that characterize these projects. Your reputation would be in the dumpster, but your understanding of risks would be excellent. However, the cost you would have paid for the experience is too high. The trick is to gain a useful understanding of project failure mechanisms without actually failing yourself.

That's where Bob Glass's long and careful study of project failure mechanisms comes in. Over the past decade, Bob has been a keen observer of our industry and has turned his particular attention to the patterns that characterize failed endeavors. In ComputingFailure.com, he sets out for you a series of failure scenarios anchored in real and recent fact. Read them and profit from them. It is your understanding of these past scenarios that can help you build a future scenario for your project that has a chance of leading to success.

Tom DeMarco
The Atlantic Systems Guild
Camden, Maine

"The paradox is that you have to experience failure to have success."
—Tore Dyba, Research Scientist, SINTEF
(Norwegian Institute of Technology), in
"Improvisation in Small Software Organizations,"
IEEE Software, September 2000

"The world is becoming a software world. There is no aspect of life that does not have software in it these days."
—Paul Maritz, V.P. Development, Microsoft, in an
interview in Crosstalk, September 2000

Introduction

This is a book about computing failure. It is largely about the failure of dot-com, Internet/Web, companies. It uses a "war stories" approach, consisting largely of in-depth failure anecdotes. I think you're going to find them fun and fascinating reading.

But before we get to those stories, let's set some context.

Something odd is happening in the world of computing failure. Actually, two something odds.

The first odd thing is that the rate of failure in traditional computing software projects is dropping. The organization that collects data on these kinds of things, the Standish Group, says that its latest, hot-off-the-presses data, as we go to press with this book, shows a "dramatic" fall in failure rates.

The second odd thing is the rise and fall and rise again of dot-com enterprises. Cruising along like world-beaters at the turn of the millennium, dot-com companies fell on really hard times come the spring of 2000, with spectacular flameouts and massive (for dot-com companies, at least!) lay-offs. But as summer, 2000 evolved into fall, the death rate dropped again, and the dot-com future appeared, for the moment, assured again.

Before I go on to discuss the whys and wherefores of this failure information, I suppose I have to confront a basic problem. You the reader may not care very much about such failure trends at all! Well, rest assured, if that is the case (or even if it's not!), this book really is full of failure war stories. You know, the kind of stories that make interesting reading because everybody loves to read abut the dumb things that someone else did? These are in-depth stories full of learning experiences and human pathos and all those other good and readable themes as well. They are not stories full of dry-as-dust data on how many companies are failing, and why that is.

Dry-as-Dust Data!

But in this chapter of the book we will, indeed, explore some dry-as-dust data. Why? Because I think that data sets the stage nicely for all those stories that follow. This data-focused chapter, coupled with the final chapter of the book (the wrap-up), represents the bread of the sandwich. What follows after this chapter, the stories themselves, is the meat of the matter.

I hope you'll agree with me, by the end of this chapter, that even this data is not really dry as dust. I think numbers show, with sometimes fascinating clarity, trends that may not be observable if a string of facts is presented only as anecdotes. Let me give you an example.

Traditional Computing Software Failures

Standish—you know, the organization that gathers data on failed computing software projects?—has been gathering and presenting failure data since 1995 now. When they first presented their data, they called the report that surrounded it the "Chaos" report, because their feeling was that the failure rate of computing projects demonstrated that the field was truly chaotic. What was that rate, according to the Standish data? Thirty-one percent of all computing projects, they said then, were canceled. Another 53%, they went on, were "challenged" (completed, but behind schedule, and/or over budget and/or without all features desired). Only 16% were listed as "successful."

This was damning data. The software field, at least according to this data, failed much more often than it succeeded. Other reports, from other sources, chimed in with comparable numbers. Interestingly, the numbers were not by any means equivalent—some reports showed 80% and even 98% failure rates!—but the overall message remained the same. The software field is a troubled field.

The term "software crisis" had been used for a couple of decades already, and this data tended to support the claims of crisis. Many in the software field, especially gurus and academics, had been claiming that there was indeed a software crisis, in that most projects were "over budget, behind schedule, and unreliable."

Now, before I go on and bring that data up to date (remember, at the outset I said that "something odd" was happening to this failure data)—I want to interject myself into this story. I am a professional software specialist who is also a software failure nut. I have been studying software failures almost ever since there was a software discipline. I have written and self-published informal, anecdotal, stories of software project failure. I have published previous, edited collections of in-depth failure stories by investigative journalists. I have read and sometimes written academic studies of failure episodes, and failure trends. I have steeped myself in failure so much that, if I didn't realize the not-so-hidden message in the term, I would call myself "Mr. Software Failure"!

The reason I want to interject myself into this story at this point is that I, personally, do not believe that there is a software crisis. Now that may strike you as odd, since (a) this chapter of the book is chock full of data that seems to support the notion of crisis, and (b) how could I possibly have created a career studying and writing about failure if there weren't plenty of failures to fuel those fires?

Here's my (very contrarian) reasoning on this subject. Most of our lives, now, are supported and surrounded by computing and software. We travel using software reservation systems. We use software word processors to write our letters. We communicate increasingly often with software email programs. We invest and buy and research and study using software-driven web applications. We bank using banking software systems, either at our ATM (especially at our ATM!) or at the teller's cage itself. Our cars are computer-software controlled, and so our most of our appliances. In one of the opening quotes of this book, we see that "the world is becoming a software world." And, the most amazing thing of all is, this software works correctly nearly all of the time. When was the last time your car broke down because of a software problem, or your reservations were botched because of a software problem? In our day-to-day lives, perhaps to some extent unbeknownst to us all, software is doing its thing—and our things—in a hugely successful way. Given all of that, I find it hard to see this as a field in crisis.

Couple all of that success with the fact that there is little consistency in the oft-quoted software failure numbers, and my own personal conclusion is that the software crisis is partly real, but mostly bug-a-boo set up by people who have something to gain if everyone believes there is a crisis. Gurus with methodologies or training courses to sell. Academics who need funding for research projects. Anyone who relies on the claims of crisis to convince you—or someone—that money should be spent on what they are doing.

OK, enough self-interjection. Back when I began that personal aside, I promised you that hot-off-the-presses computing software failure data.

Standish, in its year 2000 data, has numbers directly comparable to those failure rates I quoted earlier for the year 1995:

- 23% of all software projects were canceled (vs. 31% in 1995)
- 49% were challenged (vs. 53%)
- 28% were successful (vs. 16%)

These are very nice improvements. Not as good as we software folk would like, of course, but improvements nevertheless. I especially like that rise in successful projects—from 16% to 28% means an improvement of 75% in five years!

But there's more to this year 2000 data from Standish:

- The percentage of applications completed 200% or more over the original schedule has fallen from 12% in 1994 to 2.5% in today's report.
- The cost of failed projects decreased from $81 billion in 1995 to $75 billion today.
- There was a "dramatic" shift in cost overruns from $59 billion spent in 1994 to $22 billion today.

Something is clearly happening in the field of computing and software. This may not be a field in "chaos" any more. The cries of "crisis" ought to be diminishing in a way comparable to these numbers. There are still troubled projects, to be sure, but there are not as many as there have been in the past.

What does all of this have to do with this book? Well, much of this book is about computing dot-com failures, and we will return to that subject shortly. But Chapter 5 of this book is about traditional computing failures, and this data provides some important background for those Chapter 5 stories. There are still fun and fascinating and frustrating traditional computing failure stories to share with you, of course, but they are fewer in number than they have been in the past.

Shout it from the rooftops! Computing and software are maturing into amazing, useful, and—hooray, hooray!—dependable disciplines.

Dot-Com Failures

And now, back to those dot-com failures. When last we spoke on the subject, I promised that most of this book would be about dot-coms. You know, the companies that make a presence on the World Wide Web, offering you information, products, and services in ways that a decade or so ago might have seemed inconceivable?

How about some dry-as-dust data on dot-com failure? Let me start with some data that shows that dot-com failure is not only a recent phenomenon, it's one that exploded onto the scene.

I've been collecting computing failure stories, as you've already seen, for some time. I chuck stories about failure into a folder, later coming back to revisit the folder to see what I have accumulated there. Prior to the year 2000, there was virtually nothing about dot-com failure in my folder. What that means is, in my—reasonably extensive—reading of the computing and general press, I simply hadn't come across any significant stories about dot-coms that didn't make it.

Part of the reason for that, of course, is that the dot-com revolution is relatively new. There would have been no dot-com failure prior to, say, 1995, because there were no significant dot-com companies then. And, for another thing, dot-com companies were the darlings of investors until recently. Your dot-com isn't turning a profit? Just spend some more of our venture capital money, please—the sky's the limit on where your company may go, and we don't want to inhibit your thinking by worrying about mundane things like profit.

Tick, tick, tick. All of that was about to change. That change is reflected in the publication dates of the material I gathered for this book. Prior to the year 2000, I collected only six relevant stories. In the first quarter of 2000, I gathered two more. It would be a long time, I guessed, before I would be able to publish a book like this one, judging by the slow filling of my failure folder.

Wrong-oh! In the second quarter of the year 2000, April through June, suddenly 19 more stories fell into my folder. In the third quarter, there were another 17. What on earth was happening?

As you probably know by now, and will soon know from the chapters that follow if you don't know already, the venture capitalists finally slammed on the brakes. That lack of profit, the problem that had been overlooked for so many quarters, suddenly became vital. Dot-com after dot-com fell out of business, and into my folder. Others teetered on the edge of failure, and also fell into my folder.

That riches to rags story looks like it is turning back to riches again. The venture capitalists, as far as I can tell as of this writing in late 2000, have stepped on the gas again. I have collected only a few failure stories so far in the fourth quarter of the year 2000. The shakeout at the middle of the year, the VCs seems to be saying, has done the job. The weak have been culled from the herd. Now, they seem to be saying, onward into the future. We shall see.

But before I turn you loose to proceed on into our failure stories themselves, I want to present one more collection of dry-as-dust data. With all of this riches to rags to riches rollercoastering, you may be wondering how you can spot another rags trend if one appears on the horizon.

Here's one way. Dot-com corporate layoffs can be a huge clue. E-Commerce Times, in its July 25, 2000 issue, reports that large layoffs often "signal the end for dot-coms." "Of the 122 companies that have laid off workers in the past eight months," they say, "24 . . . subsequently ceased operations." It's a small clue, to be sure—20%—but still, in a world of this kind of uncertainty, any clue is a good clue.

How has their layoff data worked out? Remember that, above, we noted a spike in dot-com failure stories in the middle of the year 2000? In that same period, E-Commerce Times reported in its Sept. 26 issue, layoffs doubled in September vs. the preceding July. There were over 4800 layoffs in September, vs. 17,000 for the whole year to that point (and roughly 2200 in July). Sure enough, there was a layoff spike—just like that failure spike—in the third quarter of 2000. (The numbers, E-Commerce Times says, are probably under-reported because (a) they collect data on large dot-coms only, and (b) there are tons of one, two, and five-person dot-com companies). Why all these layoffs? E-Commerce Times says "dot-com companies are cutting superfluous positions with an eye toward profitability."

Let me close this chapter by summarizing one more time what I am trying to do here. I have collected in-depth, human-interest, investigative journalist reports on computing failure stories from the general and computing press, periodicals like the Wall Street Journal and Computerworld and the Industry Standard. I have received permission from those publications to republish their stories in this book. I have focused on dot-com failure stories, but there are some traditional computing/software failure stories here as well. Chapter 2 contains overview stories, a step-back look at the phenomenon of "the sky's the limit" followed by "the sky is falling" in dot-com land. Chapter 3 is the meat of the dot-com material, over a dozen tales of dot-com failure, some spectacular. Chapter 4 is about some key people involved in dot-com failures, people who ranged from some pretty nasty sinners to some near-saints. Chapter 5, as mentioned before, is about non-dot-com failures— a section on top-down failure (companies and leaders that failed), and another on bottom-up failure (projects that failed). In Chapter 6, we do something completely different. Here are a few fascinating stories about viruses— failure of yet another kind. And in Chapter 7 we have the inevitable wrap-up, looking at what happens after the smoke of failure clears away (with, as background music, the song "Zorba the Greek" (you'll have to read it to understand!))

One of the key phrases here is "in-depth" stories. If you're a failure fanatic like me and want a quick fix on computing failure stories, there are web sites—believe it or not!—that cater to that need! (Why not? Web sites seem to try to cater to every need!) These tend to contain one- or few-liners about who hasn't made it, and what their status is. DotcomFailures.com was one such web site, but, ironically, it added itself to its list of failures back in September and I suspect that you'll find the site vacant all too soon! The more famous one is the unfortunately-named FuckedCompany.com, which uses outrageousness and a sort-of tongue-in-cheek approach to cover computing failure stories. (My view on four-letter words such as the one used by this company is that there are times when one desperately needs to use a four-letter word, and that usage shouldn't be cheapened by using them willy-nilly in totally inappropriate contexts). Even this latter web site is up for sale, so it's hard to tell how much failure will be left in the web failure world by this time next year!

And one more very personal bit of housekeeping. As I have already said, most of the stories in this book are being used with permission from other publications. For each of those stories, the author of the story is named at the beginning of the article. The material I have written—the "glue" words at the beginning of each chapter to set context and hold the material together—have no byline whatsoever. That's how you can tell they are mine.

Ah, enough of these preliminaries. On to the failure stories themselves.

Robert L. Glass
Fall 2000

CHAPTER 2

Overview

I believe it was the famous philosopher Chicken Little who is reputed to have run about proclaiming "The sky is falling." I don't recall precisely what Mr. Little believed was causing the sky to fall, but whatever it was, Mr. Little was extremely serious about it. But besides being serious, Mr. Little had a colossal emotional involvement in his proclamation. You couldn't have heard Mr. Little without becoming convinced that something truly bad was in progress.

I can't help believe that Chicken Little, in the Internet era, would have suffered from a sort of bipolar disorder, been a little schizophrenic. There would have been the early Chicken Little, who would have run around proclaiming "The sky's the limit" as the stock value of companies involved in the Internet and/or the Web shot skyward like a Space Shuttle from its launching pad. "Jump on this bandwagon (space vehicle?) now," Mr. Little might have cried, "or you'll miss the opportunity of ten lifetimes."

And then there would be the latter-day Chicken Little, reverting to type. "The sky is falling, the sky is falling," he would have proclaimed. Probably holding up today's copy of the *Wall Street Journal*, and pointing to the stock listings, as he ran about in many directions. "I really mean it," Chicken might have added, trying to grasp a bit of credibility. "The sky really is falling."

And doggoned if Mr. Little wouldn't have been right. On both counts. Not too long ago, the sky really was the limit for any company that had stepped aboard the Internet/Web bandwagon. The world really went mad, to paraphrase one of the articles that follows. If you weren't investing in a web company (that same article refers to it as "catching the Web wave"), you weren't participating in a giant escalation of paper profits. You might even have been castigated by other investors for sticking with a measly 6–20 percent traditional growth in investment value.

Should you have listened to Mr. Little? Well, of course, at this point in history—and remember, after all, that history consists of a series of snapshots taken while pushing on the pause button of life—you should not have. Those who caught the web wave have by now, for the most part, fallen off their investment surfboards and been gobbled up in a voracious surf.

And Mr. Little is up to his old tricks. "The sky is falling" once again, and Mr. Little is crying it with all the vigor and emotion of his previous cry. You can imagine, of course, that it would be a good idea to listen to Mr. Little now(*). If the sky really is falling, then your best personal strategy is probably to dump all your web wave attachments and sit on the shore to see how the storm turns out. Right?

There's a fundamental problem here, one that is also one of life's most important messages. Both of Chicken Little's cries are correct. The sky really was and still is the limit. The sky really was and still is falling. It's what you do about all that sky action, and not the cries themselves, that determines how successful you will be at your chosen goals.

In one of the stories that follows, the author mentions a stock broker who says that even if an investor loses all of his/her money on a major portion of his/her investments, if the investor manages to score a major win on the remainder, then the investor comes out ahead. Not just ahead, but potentially WAY ahead!

Try it out yourself. Let's say you put $10,000 into a collection of carefully chosen investments (which either your broker, your Uncle Fred, or your dartboard suggested to you). If you lose a sort-of worst case 80 percent of that, you have $2,000 left. But if that $2,000 escalates in value by a sort-of best case 1,000 percent, it becomes worth $20,000. Subtract the $8,000 loss, and you still have a net worth of $12,000. More than you started with. Not by much, but more. The trick, of course, is to NOT choose those 80 percent losers, and to CAREFULLY choose those 1,000 percent winners. Not an easy task, mind you, but it's all conceptually possible. So Chicken Little's "sky's the limit" and "sky is falling" cries can coexist.

But we digress. The point of this chapter is to set the stage for what follows. The meat of the book, in subsequent chapters, will be to tell failure stories. In this chapter, we want to establish a context for those stories.

The first article takes an investment-oriented view of that world gone mad that infected the stock marketplace when Chicken Little first saw the sky moving upwards. It goes on to point out that those soaring Internet plays quickly tanked. "Almost half of all Internet companies now trade below their Initial Purchase Offering (IPO)" stock price, the author soberingly notes. He calls it "the Great Internet Bubble," and goes on to call it "one of history's greatest bubbles." You soon come to realize that, in the investment world, a bubble is a bad thing. You have this image of a soap bubble so beautiful, just before it bursts before your very eyes!

There are other views of what has happened to the Internet/web wave besides an investment view, of course. The second article in this chapter's collection takes an academic view of the business aspects of this bursting bubble. The author speaks of wave companies having a tendency to ignore the traditional business benchmark of the price/earnings ratio (a number derived by dividing stock price by annual corporate earnings), and notes that all too many Internet companies have invented a faulty new replacement concept he calls the "price/vision ratio" (which, unfortunately, is based on that easy-to-imagine, difficult-to-quantify "vision" thing).

How else can we look at these failures from an overview perspective? There was to be a next article in this chapter, through which we would have taken a how and why look. But the publisher, *Red Herring* magazine, declined to give permission to reprint it here (the article is "The Anatomy of Failure," by Geoffrey Moore, from the October 1999 issue). However, we are free to abstract the article's essential points. The author identifies four failure modes that can be derived from today's collection of failure stories. Some enterprises fail, he says, too slowly to spot the problem until it's too late (he calls it the "Slow Fail"); some get caught in the gap between building an early success and building a mainstream product (the "Chasm Trap"); some leap into a market that has not yet arrived (the "Tornado Dive"); and some build products that allow their customers to achieve modest success that isn't quite large enough to overcome the modest pain of achieving it (the "Dead Zone").

And while we're summarizing rules regarding this whole failure flap, here's another set from a British publication called *ECompany.* In an article titled "ePocalypse Now" in the September 2000 issue, David Kirkpatrick lists six rules for avoiding e-failure:

- The CEO has to drive the bus
- Make sure everyone takes a nice, long swig of Kool-Aid (everyone has to row in the same direction)
- Get your marketing and tech departments to quit bickering
- No matter what, your (old economy) salespeople will hate you
- Redo those organizational charts (most companies find they need a separate e-business organization)

- Money makes e-commerce believers of us all (fund e-efforts adequately)

It would be possible for a book on failure to become quite depressing, of course. I would like for that not to happen to you, dear reader. So I close this overview chapter with a couple of humorous views of the Internet bubble bust. In the first of those, the author wistfully describes the banal failure of Internet companies, which are going under simply because they didn't make enough profit. Why, he laments, couldn't these failures have been "a horrible economic cataclysm," where the companies were "crushed by deep-pocketed bricks-and-mortar rivals, or hacked out of existence by maniac crackers bent on destroying capitalism on the web"? Why, indeed? He ends his lamentation with the mundane, oh-so traditional view that "failure is still just failure . . . If you can't make money at it, you can't keep it going." Pity, he seems to be saying. Dying with a whimper, not a bang.

And the other, final, humorous article of this chapter? How about a 10-best look at how to identify a sickly company? Or, to make it even better, how about a 15-best look? Like, for example, "there are more going-away parties than there are days in the week." Or "the receptionist now doubles as CFO." And what do you do about it, once you've spotted the problem? The author presents his strategies for bailing out, and closes with the uplifting thought that most Internet company survivors can quickly move elsewhere: "In the gravity-defying Internet Economy, there's no such thing as dead weight. Everybody falls up."

* No less a pundit than IBM CEO Lou Gerstner recently articulated Chicken Little's "the sky is falling" message, referring to dot-coms as "dot-toast" during IBM's semiannual meeting for stock analysts.

Author's Note: In case you think the Chicken Little analogy is a little labored, you should be aware that there's a book called *The Coming Internet Depression: Why the High-Tech Boom Will Go Bust, Why the Crash Will Be Worse Than You Think, and How to Prosper Afterward* (by Michael J. Mandel (*Business Week*'s economics editor), published by Basic Press, 2000). The author presents the Chicken-Little-Like premise that the Internet boom is heading toward a depression bust, that policymakers will fall into the same traps that exacerbated the Great Depression of the 1930s, and that the general economy—and all of us—will be dragged down with it!

Well, so much for ending this chapter introduction on a cheery note!

The Color Green

The Internet Bubble Broke Records, Rules and Bank Accounts

By Wall Street Journal staff reporters Greg Ip, Susan Pulliam, Scott Thurm and Ruth Simon

"The world has gone mad."

The thought flashed in the mind of Internet analyst Lisa Buyer one morning in November 1998, as she and colleagues at Credit Suisse First Boston stared at a stock-quote machine. They were, Ms. Buyer recalls, agog at the trajectory of the initial public offering of theglobe.com, a collection of community Web sites. Theglobe.com had puny revenues and heavy losses. CSFB bankers did not think the company was ready to go public. Yet theglobe.com's stock, offered at $9 a share, instantly soared to $97, briefly giving the company a market value of nearly $1 billion.

Crazy—but there was a message to the madness. CSFB soon scrapped some of the rules it had used to gauge whether a company was ready for the big time, and took public no-profit Internet plays Audible Inc., Autoweb com Inc., Career Builder inc. and others arguably just as slight as theglobe.com ever was. Today, Audible trades at 54% below its offering price, Autoweb is down 69% and CareerBuilder is off 86%. Theglobe.com closed yesterday at $1.8125, or $3.625 before a split. Theglobe.com declines to comment on its IPO but asserts that the company is "committed to achieving profitability." Its underwriter, Bear Stearns & Co., very much believed in theglobe.com at the time, a spokesman says, noting that it traded above its offering price for months.

The Great Internet Bubble may be starting to fade from many memories, but the fallout blankets the landscape. This craze, after all, ranks among history's biggest bubbles. Investment bankers, venture capitalists, research analysts and investors big and small, through cynicism or suspension of disbelief, financed and took public countless companies that had barely a prayer of prospering. Rarely have so many people willingly put prudence on hold to enter a game most were sure could not last. "We all knew we were going to get a big kahuna correction at some point," says Jay Tracey, former manager of the Oppenheimer Enterprise Fund.

Murky Realms

While the Nasdaq Composite Index has clawed back half of its 37% plunge between March 10 and May 23, Internet stocks as a group, valued at $1.4 trillion at their March peak, have lost 40% of that—erasing almost as much paper wealth as the 1987 crash. Even former stalwarts like Amazon.com trade at a third of last winter's highs. Though investors are slowly warming again to Internet IPOs, almost half of existing Internet companies now trade below their IPO price.

The question is: What brought on the mania? Some answers lie in the murky realms of mob psychology, the human capacity for denial, the get-rich-quick mentality—factors in speculative frenzies since the days of the tulip. But to an unusual degree, the Internet bubble was a product of basic avarice and tactics that smacked of the boiler room. From Wall Street pro to fledgling day trader, all joined hands in a giddy game of lowering standards, pushing out IPOs and trumpeting prospects, with little regard for a company's true long-term—that is to say, more than three months'—outlook.

"People were throwing money at businesses that wouldn't pass simple due-diligence screens five years ago," says venture capitalist Jim Breyer of Accel Partners. "People overlooked almost all business fundamentals and drove valuations into the stratosphere."

Drenched in Warnings

Many investors have made good money, but many got clobbered. And the pros? They made billions, and most of them wound up winners even after the bubble burst.

People were certainly warned. Every IPO prospectus was drenched in warnings and risk factors, but most investors breezed past them. When the hype crossed the line into manipulation or other wrong-doing, the Securities and Exchange Commission usually stepped in. But most of the time, regulators could only stand by and warn investors about the risks of playing a completely legal game.

There is no denying the enormous business opportunity or the huge changes represented by the Internet and information technology. Some of the companies that emerged from the Internet upheaval will almost certainly mature into enduring, valuable enterprises, as the rebound in a handful of Internet leaders in recent weeks seems to bear out. Yet with the true potential came some truly cynical actions driven by a willingness to see what the market would bear and the investor buy—i.e., a bubble.

Here's how some of the pivotal players stoked one the hottest stock-market crazes in history.

These have been heady times for investment bankers. Just since theglobe.com's IPO—an event many cite as a line of demarcation between raging bullishness and outright bubble – Goldman Sachs Group Inc., Morgan Stanley Dean Witter & Co. and Credit Suisse Group's Credit Suisse First Boston each pocketed more than $500 million in IPO or secondary offering underwriting fees, according to Thomson Financial Securities Data. It was the most lucrative hot streak investment bankers have ever seen in a single sector.

It wouldn't have happened if bankers hadn't changed their rules. For instance, way back at the beginning of 1999, CSFB had a rule of thumb that a company needed at least $10 million in revenue in the 12 months before its IPO. (Profits were no longer critical; Netscape Communications and Amazon.com, two early IPO meteors, had proved that.)

Flying over Thailand on his way to meet a client in January 1999, CSFB Internet analyst Bill Burnham piped into a regular Monday morning teleconference during which a spirited debate had emerged over whether the rule should be canned. The bank was losing clients—and fees—to competitors. "Everyone realized the entire market was doing deals like this," Mr. Burnham, now a venture capitalist, recalls. "Companies we had relationships with but didn't have any intention of taking public anytime soon announced, 'Hey, if theglobe.com can go public, we can'."

No formal decision on relaxing the guideline was taken at the time, but soon CSFB's bankers concluded that if they really liked a company, they could take it public with $10 million in annualized revenues—in other words, just $2.5 million in the previous quarter, regardless of revenue in earlier periods. "It was emblematic to me of the competitive devaluation of underwriting standards that went on and reached a crescendo in the first quarter of this year," Mr. Burnham says.

One company that wouldn't have fit CSFB's old standard was CareerBuilder, an online recruitment firm. Before CareerBuilder's IPO in May 1999, its prior 12 months' revenue was just $8.8 million. But revenue in its last quarter was $2.8 million, or $11.2 million annualized. After CSFB took CareerBuilder public at $13, it traded as high as $20 but has since fallen to $4.0625.

Bill Brady, CSFB's head of global corporate finance for technology, says CareerBuilder remains a great company that is meeting expectations. He says he doesn't regret any of the deals CSFB has done in the past 18 months. Some, like Commerce One Inc. didn't fit the old standard either, but were successes. Still, he acknowledges that he thought that the prices many stocks hit after their IPOs were irrational, even as CSFB brought similar companies to market.

Other investment banks were priming the IPO machine, of course. Alan Naumann, chief executive of Calico Comm., Inc. says that for nine months before the business-to-business e-commerce software company went public last October, he had 15 different investment banks courting him with regular phone calls.

"The pitch to Calico was, 'Other companies are going public with smaller revenues and fewer customers—we think you're ready. You've got $2 million in sales, go for it,'" he recalls. Calico held off and eventually picked Goldman Sachs as its lead underwriter. It went public at $14, shot above $62 on the first day, but has since slid back to $17.375 a share.

Mike Yiu, a software developer in Los Angeles, paid an average of about $58 a share for 1,100 shares of Calico between late October and early January. Mr. Yiu sold about 900 of his shares in April at about $19 a share and the remaining 200 last month at about $16 a share, for a total loss of more than $43,000. The timing of Calico's IPO was "perfect," Mr. Yiu observes. But "we got burned."

The stock price notwithstanding, Mr. Naumann says Calico's business remains on track. Its revenue grew 66% to $35.6 million in the fiscal year ended March 31—but its loss widened by 82% to $27.8 million.

Goldman's Brad Koenig, head of the firm's technology investment banking, says Goldman had good reason to believe early-stage companies could be winners. He points to the debate proceeding an early Internet IPO in April 1996. "There were a certain number of people who were highly skeptical of this company named Yahoo! with its yellow-and-purple logos," he says. Even with the recent 51% decline in its price from early January, Yahoo! Inc. is up more than 100-fold since its IPO.

The risks Goldman took on Yahoo went from being the exception to the norm. In 1997, of the 24 domestic companyies Goldman took public for which data are available, a third were losing money at the time. Of the 18 it took public this year through mid-April, 80% lose money. A Goldman spokeswoman says this trend reflects the growing number of IPOs of Internet companies, which typically are unprofitable.

Some were companies that its arch-competitor, Morgan Stanley Dean Witter Inc., had decided were too speculative to underwrite. Mary Meeker, Morgan's star Internet analyst, says the firm passed on taking the TheStreet.com Inc., the Internet financial-news site, public because it wasn't ready. (An official at TheStreet.com says Goldman was its first choice.) After Goldman took it public in May 1999 at $19 a share, TheStreet.com shot above $70 on its first day, but has since slumped to $6.

Goldman officials deny that their standards slipped, and contend that the firm also passed on deals that rivals chose to underwrite. Mr. Koenig adds that the criticism of underwriters is off-target. If an Internet start-up with losses exceeding revenue "goes public and goes to a $22 billion valuation, whose fault is that? It's a tough philosophical argument . . . Is it an underwriter's responsibility to determine whether the market is overvalued or undervalued? Investment bankers wouldn't be making a good living if that was required."

The bankers got help in feeding the furnace from a new breed of mostly young securities analysts who presented themselves as pathfinders in the uncharted terrain of the Internet.

The best-known is Henry Blodget, famous for forecasting in December 1998 that Amazon.com would hit $400 a share. At the time, Amazon.com was trading at $240; within four weeks it blew past $400 on its way to a high of more than $600. Mr. Blodget was celebrated as a seer and left his job at CIBC Oppenheimer for Merrill Lynch & Co. Amazon.com? It closed at a split-adjusted $35 yesterday, equivalent to $210 at the time of Mr. Blodget's big call.

Mr. Blodget, 34, has regularly predicted that 75% or more of Internet companies will fail, and he stands by his general belief that Amazon.com and many of his other picks will be winners over the long haul. Mr. Blodget adds, "If AOL, Yahoo, Amazon, eBay, a few others we recommend as core holdings, go down 70% and stay there for four years, I will have been wrong. No argument. But a 50% pullback is still in the line of how this industry performs."

Still, to critics, Mr. Blodget epitomizes the change in the analyst's role during the overheated market in tech stocks: more cheerleader than detached observer. And the buzz—and career opportunities—that Mr. Blodget did draw may have encouraged other analysts to make similarly adventurous forecasts, the critics add.

Despite Mr. Blodget's 75% caveat, his recommendations on individual stocks, like those of many Internet analysts, got more bullish even as they led the Nasdaq Composite Index to ever-more-dizzying heights. Today, he rates 12 of the 27 stocks that he follows as "buy" (the rest are "accumulate"), compared with just one buy rating for the 10 stocks he followed a year ago, says Bob Kim, a former Merrill Lynch supervisory analyst whose Web site, Restex.com, monitors Merrill technology research.

Consider Pets.com Inc., which Merrill took public at $11 in February. It slid to $6.125 in a month, when Mr. Blodget initiated coverage with a prediction that it would soar to $16 a share, or 160%, in 12 to 18 months. A major justification: Despite the pet-supply seller's continuing losses, he noted that it was trading at five times this year's estimated revenue, a discount to Amazon.com at eight times revenue. Since Mr. Blodget's prediction, Pets.com has been a dog, falling 70% to $1.8125.

"Out of one side of his mouth, the message of caution," says Mr. Kim, "the other side, buy the leaders." He describes the Blodget message as: "The risk isn't losing 100% of your investment now, it's giving up 10-times gains in the future." But, says Mr. Kim, "it seems that so far little of that has panned out except for the downside part."

As lucrative as the bubble has been for investment bankers and analysis, their profits pale compared with the money venture capitalists and other early-stage investors have made. The journey of eToys Inc. shows why.

The online retailer went public on May 20, 1999, at $20 a share, and soared to $76.5625 on its first day of trading. On Oct. 11, it closed at a high of $84.25—and has since plunged 93%, closing yesterday at $5.625 a share.

A disaster for eToys' early-stage investors such as idealab, an Internet incubator that invests in and nurtures start-ups? Not exactly. Idealab paid just half a cent a share—a total of $100,000—for its eToys stake in June 1997. In late 1999, idealab sold more than 3.8 million shares at prices between $47.50 and $69.58, for a profit of $193 million. It still holds a further 14.5 million shares, so idealab has seen its paper profits dwindle. But even idealab's remaining stake in eToys is still worth roughly 1,000 times what idealab paid for it, while anyone who bought at the IPO price is down 72%. (Idealab, which itself is trying to go public, declined to comment, citing its quiet period.)

And plenty of investors fared worse than that. On Dec. 2, Daniel Sperling, a 35-year-old technology consultant in the Detroit area, bought 200 shares of eToys at $70. "Our goal was to ride the tidal wave of Christmas shopping and get out," Mr. Sperling says. But in early December, it became clear that big Internet sales weren't materializing, and eToys skidded. Mr. Sperling bought more: A hundred shares at $58.50 on Dec. 6. A hundred more at $47.50 on Dec. 14. A hundred more at about $20 in January. Today, his $26,000 investment in eToys is worth $2,800, a paper loss of $23,800.

Some venture capitalists' profits were truly astounding. Benchmark Capital's $5 million early stage investment in eBay Inc. grew to $4.2 billion by the time Benchmark distributed the shares to its investors late last year and early this year. If Benchmark's partners kept a typical 25% to 30% of the firm's investment profits, five of its partners would have split more than $1 billion when cashing in eBay stock.

Venture capitalists say they deserve big rewards because they take big risks. Many investments go bust. During the early stages of the Internet frenzy, however, it appeared that venture capitalists couldn't lose. They threw more money in earlier stages at start-ups than ever before. Often they pushed the companies to go public as quickly as possible to cash in on their investments faster than ever.

Even some who benefited from the feeding frenzy agree. "You could invest in a company, take it public and cash out before you proved your business model," says Michael Barach, a former venture capitalist who is now chief executive of Mothernature.com, an online health-products seller. Mothernature.com received its first venture-capital investment in June 1998 and went public last December.

The Internet craze set off an "Oklahoma land rush," says Roger McNamee, general partner at Integral Capital Partners in Menlo Park, Calif., which manages both private and public investments. "In a land rush, you suspend rules because your perception is that time is of the essence."

All told, venture capital invested in start-ups jumped to $36.5 billion last year from $14.3 billion in 1998, according to San Francisco market researcher VentureOne Corp. The number of deals increased to 2,969 from 1,972.

Mr. Barach of Mothernature.com attests to the craziness. Two investors gave him $10 million apiece after hearing him give a speech at an investment conference. Investment bankers told him they could take his company public when it reached $750,000 a month—an annualized $9 million—in revenue, and they did. "No one ever mentioned or talked about how much money we'd lose in 2000 to get to that revenue," he says. The company, which Bear Stearns took public, reported a loss of $59 million last year on sales of $5.8 million. Its stock trades at 81.25 cents, down 94% from its IPO price of $13.

IPOs can't soar without big buyers—and mutual funds are among the biggest.

As tech stocks roared, mutual-fund managers faced powerful incentives to ride the rocket, trying to boost their funds' returns—which can mean higher compensation for fund managers. Their voracious appetite for tech shares expanded the bubble.

Between Nov. 1, 1998, and last March 31, investors poured almost $72.5 billion into technology and small-cap-growth mutual funds, according to Financial Research Corp., a Boston-based financial-consulting firm. It says that about $11.4 billion of that total flowed into funds specializing narrowly in the Internet. Six of the 14 Internet-only mutual funds tracked by Lipper Inc. had gains of 100% or more last year.

Sometimes the tactics driving the action in mutual funds have raised questions. When business-to-business Internet player Ariba Inc. went public at $23 (pre-split) share last June, it shot to a first-day high of more than $90, thanks to people like Gary Tanaka, a founding partner of Amerindo, a growth-oriented mutual-fund group.

On most IPOs, Mr. Tanaka would get 50,000 to 70,000 shares. On Ariba, he got 100,000, in part because he informed underwriter Morgan Stanley that he would buy an additional 100,000 in the after-market once the company went public. His agreement to buy shares in the after-market "probably helped boost us to the top bracket for allocations," he says. Internet IPO allocations helped juice returns of Amerindo funds; its Technology Fund, for instance, posted a 249% gain in 1999. After-market orders also contributed to a big first-day run-up in the stock price—more than ever the mark of a successful IPO.

Some market experts say agreements to buy stock—and thus support the price in the after-market—raise regulatory questions depending on how explicit the arrangement is. Mr. Tanaka says he believes his arrangements are both appropriate and a natural results of his firm's role as "long term investors. If we are buying one million shares, we feel we should get a better allocation." Mark Hantho, managing director of equity capital markets at Morgan Stanley, says the firm doesn't use after-market bids to allocate IPOs, although "it's common to hear feedback as to how investors value the company . . . and we listen carefully to that."

Funds' appetite for IPOs also super-charged the market in another way. "On a hot deal, everyone would put in for 10% and the bankers could tell how hot a deal was by the number of guys who were circling 10% on the deal," Mr. Tanaka says. None of the institutions really expected to receive a full 10% allocation of a red-hot IPO, many of which involved only 10 million or so shares. But the idea was to get a bigger piece of the pie.

The overstated "order book" from institutions, as it is called, was then sent to research firms that rate IPOs based on their interest from institutions. "Sure, that artificially inflates demand. But that's how you rate a deal," says Vinnie Slaven, with Cantor Fitzgerald, whose job it is to rate IPOs based on investor demand. So the process itself helped to create an aura surrounding certain deals of vast enthusiasm among other institutions. This in turn helped to whet the public's appetite for shares of hot IPOs, often leading individuals to buy shares during an IPO's giant first-day run-up.

To catch the Web wave—and keep up with peers' performance—many fund managers loaded up on Internet stocks even though many in their hearts believed the shares to be overvalued. Twice last year, Mr. Tracey, until recently manager of Oppenheimer Enterprise Fund, thought a mammoth correction was coming and sold many Internet stocks. Both times he was wrong. So, after the second time, he jumped at the chance a few weeks later to buy into the

IPO of an online industrial auctioneer called FreeMarkets Inc. It was valued at
$1.8 billion based on its IPO price, despite 12-month sales of just $16 million
and steep losses. But Mr. Tracey figured that similar companies were trading
at far richer levels, and as to whether those valuations were ridiculous: "I said,
'I'm going to suspend judgment for the moment.'"

That proved profitable for Mr. Tracey, who watched FreeMarkets rocket
from its IPO price of $48 in December to $280 the first day of trading. He
held on as it roared to $370 in January, then dumped it in February at $215. It
now trades at $55.0625 a share. This strategy helped Mr. Tracey's fund post a
105.8% return in 1999, though it's down 4.1% so far this year. Mr. Tracey
recently moved to Denver fund manager Berger LLC to become chief investment officer.

The tech bubble had one thing no past manias had: the push from online
brokers, who made speculating on stocks easier than ever and advertised
heavily to encourage people to chase riches.

In September 1998, employees at online broker E*Trade Group Inc. hit
TV viewers with a barrage of commercials in an effort to add one million customer accounts to its total of 500,000 in the coming year. Some ads suggested
that trading stocks over E*Trade was a better route to wealth than waiting to
win the lottery, others that it was better than waiting for a rich relative to die.
All promised a fast, cheap, powerful way to play the stock market.

As new accounts poured in, E*Trade kept upping its ad spending, says
Michael Sievert, chief marketing officer. E*Trade spent $321 million on mar-
keting in the fiscal year ended last Sept. 30, and surpassed its goal, with 1.6
million accounts—but with a loss of $54.7 million. It has already spent an
additional $307 million on marketing in the six months through March 31,
helping to boost the number of accounts to 2.6 million.

The astonishing growth made online brokers a powerful force in the
market, as their customers drove the stocks of newly public and established
companies to unprecedented levels. By some estimates, individual investors—
most of them trading online—accounted at the peak for 65% of the volume
on Nasdaq.

E*Trade's Mr. Sievert says the firm's ads tell investors they won't get rich
quick, and that they should take charge of their finances. He notes one of
E*Trade's commercials warned against being carried away with a profit that
could quickly disappear.

But critics say the Internet brokers did indeed encourage many unsophis-
ticated investors to trade aggressively in the belief they could get wealthy and
failed to adequately disclose the risk. "The marketing campaigns by these
Internet brokers encouraged novice investors, who had no business trading

securities, to short-term trade stocks, and they in many instances ended up losing a major portion of their net worth," charges Douglas Schulz, a Westcliffe, Colo., securities-fraud expert who advises investors with complaints against their brokers.

Jay Kiessling, a physician living near Mobile, Ala., had been trading through E*Trade for about 16 months when he heard about theglobe.com. "I wasn't quite sure if it was a good stock for the long run, but I was almost sure it would have a terrific first day," he says. He put in an order for 5,000 shares, expecting to get the stock at the IPO price of $9 a share.

But because the stock rocketed at the opening, he ended up paying between $84 to $88 ($42-$44 split-adjusted), more than $420,000 in total. He finally dumped most of the stock a few days later at $42 a share, and had to liquidate about two-thirds of his retirement investments to cover the loss.

Dr. Kiessling and his wife filed an arbitration claim against E*Trade, saying it allowed them to "buy an unsuitably over-concentrated position," according to his attorney, James Eccleston, and that E*Trade should have alerted customers that the stock would open up so much higher. In a statement of answer filed last year with the National Association of Securities Dealers, E*Trade said that the Kiesslings "could and should have minimized their risk" by immediately selling the shares and that the couple is responsible for the loss. The case if pending.

Mr. Kiessling hasn't made a single investment since theglobe.com. But though such stories are commonplace, it's hard to say whether the bubble mentality is dead. Just yesterday, two new technology companies went public. Neither is a pure Internet play and one actually is making money. Still, the prices of both more than doubled.

Kara Scannell contributed to this article.

For Dot.Coms, It's The Vision Thing

By Avi Shama

It is by now a foregone conclusion that most Internet companies will fail, and sooner rather than later. What's important for the future of the industry is how the strategies helped them fail. The answer: Dot.coms have been failing because they regard sales revenues and profits as distractions. In fact, many such companies have entered the market without fully developing and market-testing their products and services, and the fact that 80% of even systematically developed and market-tested products fail does not seem to concern them.

This is the chief conclusion of a recent study conducted by my students and me when I was on the faculty of the University of New Mexico's Anderson School of Business. We looked at 136 recently public companies selected at random from a roster of new public firms listed on www.inernetnews.com/stocks/list. The selected companies include more than 50% of all companies listed on the site.

The study examined the history of the companies as well as their sales, profits, products and services, target markets, distribution, promotion and international operations.

Most surprising, we learned that the companies, instead of concentrating on improving their revenues and earnings—many viewed such things as distractions—concentrated instead on capturing the largest share of a market vision. As a result, they have been replacing the widely accepted valuation measure of price to earnings, or P/E, with a boundless price-to-vision, or P/V, ratio, in which the larger the vision, the higher the stock price. Meanwhile, of the 136 companies studied, fewer than 10% reported any profits.

The reason most of these dot.coms are losing money is that, in their chasing a large share of their market vision, they had entered the market prematurely. To cope, many have been taking different measures to stay afloat. Some have changed their business model by, for example, adding a business-to-business, or B2B, activity to their B2C—business to consumer—operations. Some have bought up or merged with other companies to improve their competitive advantages.

Premature market entry and the ensuing frantic efforts to adjust can be traced to a lack of business experience at many dot.coms, the easy access to venture capital and the need to establish market leadership quickly.

Dot.coms are characterized by very rapid product development, forgoing the traditional multi-step development process. Because of competition, real or imagined, they have been forced to try new methods of discovering user need and launching new products rapidly.

Such methods are particularly suited for online products. Nevertheless, dot.coms vary widely. The companies we surveyed included 46 that provide Internet services, 15 electronic retailers, 14 Internet software providers and 12 providers of Internet infrastructure.

Internet companies throw the traditional distinctions among the consumer, industrial and public sectors out the window. Their stance is that they serve multiple markets. However, when pressed, the firms specified main target markets.

In a vision-driven business with numerous "strategic alliances," which serve to further inflate the vision, why worry about pricing and the profit built into it? Of the companies studied, only 37% use cost-plus pricing. The remainder determine their prices based on demand, or negotiates their prices, or use a combination of those pricing methods. Normally, such methods would produce superior profits. However, given the lack of profits, one must surmise that such an approach has been producing losses because pricing is based on high "visionary" future demand, not realistic estimates.

It depends on the market

The pricing methods used by dot.coms depend on their target markets and sectors. B2C companies tend to price their products using the cost-plus method, B2B firms tend to negotiate their prices with their customers, and B2P—business to public sector—companies tend to use cost-plus.

There is a clear and statistically significant relationship between the promotional tools used and the target market or sector. Eighty percent of B2P firms and 68% of B2C companies rely mainly on advertising to reach their target consumer, and 41% of B2B use personal selling.

For all the globally enabling Internet technology, most sales of dot.coms are made to U.S. customers. This may be attributable to the wider use of the Internet in the U.S., to a deliberate strategy to capture the more familiar U.S. market first, and to the nature of the service or product (delivering groceries and fast food, for example, is more appropriate for a local strategy).

The picture that emerges from this study is of a technology-induced industry that began running on its technical success and is now facing a stark reality: To succeed, its companies must couple technical know-how with business savvy as exemplified by such success stories as Intel, Microsoft and Dell. In fact, as may be inferred from the strategies developed by Intel's Andy Grove and Microsoft's Bill Gates, a savvy business strategy may be more important than technical know-how.

The Banality of Failure

By Kevin Fogarty

You know what disappoints me about the recent flameouts among the dot-coms? Not that it's happening—everyone knew it was coming. Having *dot-com* as part of your company name is practically an advertisement that you plan to live fast and die young.

No, it's the banality of the failures. They're not dying in horrible economic cataclysms or being crushed by deep-pocketed brick-and-mortar rivals or hacked out of existence by maniac crackers bent on destroying capitalism on the Web. They're just running out of money. And customers.

Sure, that happens to normal companies. That's corporate evolution, right? Survival of the fittest.

But the dot-coms weren't normal companies in any sense. From the beginning, they were Something Different.

They broke all the rules. They had more cash than they had any right to have. Their stock prices were stratospheric, based more on faith than analysis. They took over Wall Street and turned it into a yo-yo. They made a lot of people rich.

They defied the laws of physics.

They defied Alan Greenspan.

They were superstars.

They should have died like those movie stars of the '50s: foot on the gas pedal, wind in their hair, daring Deadman's Curve to live up to its name. Not like Elvis, in a lonely bathroom with their pants around their ankles.

But that's what's happening. Glamorous companies are going down the tubes for reasons that they were supposed to have overcome while inventing the New Economy.

Toysmart CEO David Lord tells a dramatic story about trying to pull his company back from the brink. After hitting a low point, he and his top execs worked around the clock to hammer out a new business plan that would convince majority partner Walt Disney that they were still on the road to success. They celebrated the brilliant solution the night before the presentation. In the same meeting they presented the plan. Disney shut them down.

Time, Lord says, was a problem. Lack of faith from Disney, he says, was a problem. A culture clash with Disney, he says, was a problem.

But ultimately, he says, the problem was that Toysmart couldn't attract enough customers.

That's not a New Economy kind of excuse. In the New economy, smart companies are supposed to succeed anyway.

But even smart New Economy companies are failing. A study from Chicago outplacement company Challenger, Gray & Christmas found that almost 5,400 employees from 59 Internet companies have been laid off since January. Toysmart is gone. Boo.com is gone. New Economy pioneer CD-now is trying to sell out but can't find a buyer. Even Amazon.com is coming under fire.

E-commerce isn't easy. Even traditional companies with existing bases of customers to exploit have trouble making it work.

Online, historical return-on-investment criteria don't work, so developing e-commerce projects have to be funded as a leap of faith—more on an R&D basis than a traditional commercial one, according to Kathy Britain White, CIO at $26 billion Cardinal Health Care. And companies with real-world revenue streams can afford to keep that up longer than start-ups.

But there's a limit even to leaps of faith. Among the dot-coms, it was an article of taith that the old rules of business no longer applied.

Some of the old rules, maybe, but not all. If you're smart enough, agile enough and offer enough value to customers, you can build a customer base from nothing.

But if you can't make money at it, you can't keep it up. No matter how crass that is, no matter how mundane, no matter how banal, that rule still applies.

And it's taking its toll. Even though there really should be a more stylish, more spectacular, a more New Economy way to go, failure is still just failure.

Take It and Leave It

By Carl Steadman

Successful startups are more or less all alike, but every unsuccessful venture fails in its own inimitable way. It might begin when your new CFO speeds away in his signing-bonus Boxster . . . or when the unsustainable European office becomes increasingly unsustainable. Be on the lookout for the warning signs—so you can trade those golden handcuffs for a golden parachute before your dot-com is dot-gone.

Sure Signs of a Sickly Startup

- To call long distance, you need to dial 10-10-220.
- The receptionist now doubles as CFO.
- More managers. Less staff.
- The self-service kitchenette is now full-service vending.
- Your new deadline coincides with the end of the quarter.
- "Good news! We'd like to double your stock options."
- More going-away parties than days in a week.
- Your waste basket? It's under that trash heap somewhere.
- Headhunters have you on speed-dial.
- "New" PCs are Mac Classics donated by local schools.
- Your boss can most often be found under his desk.
- The two-year anniversary bash is BYOB.
- You've gone from intern to VP—in three weeks!
- Your name is on the "war room" whiteboard . . . crossed out.
- You're leaving the building with a fax machine under your coat.

Preparing for the Fallout

Don't wait until there are no more envelopes, or staplers or pretty pieces of colored paper. You need to prepare for the lean times—those desperate two weeks when you're wrestling with the difficult choice between another early stage startup or the startup that is pre-IPO.

Make no sudden moves. Just tuck a few folders under your arm at the end of each day, announcing to anyone within earshot that you'll be "finishing up a few things" at home. (You should be doing this already—not the working at home, just the loud announcement part.) Don't walk out with anything too obvious, like the Pikachu on top of your monitor. Save that for last. Stick to the confidential memos and product plans. Nobody will miss those.

Beat the Rush

Here's how the dismal day unfolds: An executive assistant goes from desk to desk, quietly informing the staff that your acting CEO has an important announcement. Attendance is mandatory.

At the all-hands, your brave chief will explain how they ran out of quarters and couldn't feed the meter. He'll look down at his shoes as he mutters something about "highly volatile markets." And then someone from editorial will burst into tears and there will be *hugging*. It goes on like that for hours. "It was unbelievable working with you people, you were like family to me . . ."

Avoid the long lines! Toss your few remaining personal effects into the shopping bag that's stuffed in the back of your file drawer for just such an occasion. Then grab anything that's not bolted down on your way to HR. (To assuage guilt, you can always leave an "IOU—1,000 shares" in place of the Aeron chair.) Keep the exit interview short, and cash out your vacation time while you still have the chance.

Failing Up

Repeat as necessary: It's not your fault. OK, so maybe it was. After all, you never did manage to work out exactly what you were hired to do. And that, in some way, might just have been related to your startup's demise. But even though you may feel like you've hit rock bottom, it's worth remembering that in the gravity-defying Internet Economy, there's no such thing as dead weight. Everybody falls up.

Now it's not precisely true that startup culture *rewards* failure. If that were the case, we'd have retired long ago. Win or lose, it's all counted as experience. So treat each new failure as an opportunity—and not just to update your resume with a dewy-eyed account of your struggle against the inevitable. (It's hard to check references when the company no longer exists.) The theory goes that you learn more on the way down than on the way up. Which makes you quite the catch: Your next startup's investors can benefit from the mistakes you made with someone's money, in the dubious hope that you're unlikely to repeat them. The only drawback: You'll have to try harder to fail better next time.

CHAPTER 3

Who Put the Duh
in Dot-Com?

This is the part of the book where we demonstrate that the latter-day Chicken Little was right. In this chapter, we provide the stories of over a dozen dot-com debacles. Many of these stories, in fact, were published during the late spring and summer of 2000. For a little while there, the sky really was falling—rapidly—on the dot-com world. Troubles continue, of course, to this day, but the falling sky was a deluge back then.

Why? The answer is scattered through the stories that follow, stories that tell in heart-breaking directness about the pain of failure in a rapid-growth world. But it is worth pausing for a moment here at the beginning of the chapter to see if there are lessons to be learned from all of that carnage you're about to encounter.

For openers, the *Wall Street Journal* provides us with a wonderful/awful overview of what happened (I admire the WSJ for its accurate and timely reporting, but more than that for putting a human face on its stories). In this first story of our chapter, the WSJ story takes a May 2000 snapshot view of the sky falling all around it. The principle problem, according to this article, is that the momentum of the dot-com revolution finally was caught up short. There'd been too many promises, too much excitement, too much spending of capital resources—and too little to show for it. The mantra that profit was an artifact of the bricks and mortar era finally came acropper in this here and now. Venture capitalists, the WSJ tells us, got tired of funding financial losers. They warn "get ready for a pileup of corpses in the land of the dot-coms." They report that venture capitalists wonder "which of our progeny do we just let die?" They tell us "bankruptcy-law firms are staffing up to handle an expected rise in business failures." The article names several companies whose stories are told in more depth in later articles in this chapter of our book.

The remainder of the stories make for good reading—or at least we hope you'll agree that they make for good reading. But before we turn you loose to read them, let us take one more stab here at answering that question we asked a couple of paragraphs back: why did so many dot-coms fail in such a short time? What follows is the result of a little research done on the articles that follow, extracting from all of them the reasons given in the individual failure stories.

It's hard to see an industry sector answer to the dilemma of failure. That is, we can't point to any one sector and say that's where the dot-coms tended to fail most frequently. In fact, there's an astonishing variety of kinds of dot-coms in our failure stories. Industry sectors include medicine, retailing (of several flavors, ranging from pet stores to audio-visual), wholesaling (the food and drink exchange company that failed would, in today's terms, be called "business to business," or "B2B"), banking, and entertainment. It seemed, then and now, that there is no sector of our economy that isn't a candidate for dot-comming. Win or lose.

It's when we get into specific business reasons for failure that we find consistency in the answers derived from these stories. **"We grew too fast"** seems to be the number one wail, with four of the stories citing something specifically related to that. One company tells the story of how it began in Sweden, but, urged on by its enthusiastic venture capitalists, quickly went international. The story ends plaintively with the note that, as the company failed, it was having its best month ever in Sweden.

Close behind is **"our management was inadequate."** That reason took on several different facets, ranging from the naiveté of dot-commers who had never managed anything before (and were sometimes not yet dry behind the ears), to the problem of traditional managers with no Internet experience trying to run a dot-com ("management decisions required too many meetings and to much hierarchy").

That lack of management ability played directly into the third most common problem, the **lack of a workable business model**. Several companies, in fact, report major tinkering with their business models as time passes, a sort of Nero fiddling while Rome burns. If you don't know where you're going, any road will get you there, of course; but you may never get there at all.

There were also several stories where the problem was the clicks (Internet) companies **were too closely tied to bricks (traditional) parents**. You might think, based on the prominent failures of dot-com startups, that independence was something of a curse, and that some apron strings to hold onto might not be such a bad thing. Not so. Those apron springs are all too often too tightly attached to the past.

The next pair of reasons make a fascinating juxtaposition. In an Internet startup, is it better to have **more business savvy or more technical savvy**? The answer, at least from the point of view of these stories, is that either extreme can be a part of failure. One company lamented that it had all appearance and no actuality. Another spent six months on technical development "when all we needed . . . was a slide show heavy on business development." In other words, you pays your money and you takes your choice. Probably the correct answer for avoiding failure is to have a nice blend of tech and biz.

Our final story in this chapter takes a broader view of dot-com failure. Vultures are constantly circling these dying dot-comers, in the form of liquidator companies that sell off the assets of companies that are ceasing their struggle. Where do they hold these sales? On the web, of course. They, too, are dot-com companies! (Perhaps the life cycle of a dot-com company could be said to be from vulture capital to vulture liquidation!)

Let me give you one more interesting clue. In one pair of stories not included in this book because they were made obsolete by on-rushing events, one dot-com spokesperson says, in the first story of the pair, that they are not "shopping the company around." In the very next story, published two weeks later, they have been gobbled up—almost literally—by a competitor. What's the lesson here? Perhaps it's a generic one, one to watch for in all of the stories that follow. When it gets close to failure time, it's all too frequently true that the participants check their honesty at the door.

Angels of Death

Reality Bites Hard As String of Dot-Coms
Sees Funding Dry Up

By David P. Hamilton and Mylene Mangalindan
Staff Reporters of the Wall Street Journal

Get ready for a pileup of corpses in the land of dot-coms.

Just months ago, when the Internet seemed to promise untold stock-market wealth, web companies could count on their backers to keep pouring in more money whenever the coffers ran dry. Now that party is suddenly over, and Web investors are in brutal triage mode, on the lookout for losers and cutting off their cash.

Violet.com, an online retailer in San Francisco, learned the new rules the hard way. The company got $3 million in an initial round of fund-raising last October to help build a Web boutique stuffed with fancy beaded purses, orchid-oil lamps and other retail rarities. Founded two years ago by former Apple Computer Inc. engineer Amy Barnett and marketing specialist Bonnie Cohen, the site also featured a search engine that claimed it would let shoppers pick gifts based on their mood.

Shrinking Violet

The initial funding didn't last long, and by March, as the Internet-stock selloff was under way, Violet was asking venture capitalists for more. No way, said its backers, who tried to arrange a sale of the company to another retailer. When a promising deal fell through, the company's lead investor stepped back and let Violet fold.

It closed its doors last month. Today, all that's left on its Web site is a short note thanking visitors and urging them to "continue to seek out unique and interesting items that bring inspiration to the things you do every day."

In just the past week, nearly a half-dozen dot-com ventures have imploded, many of them quite suddenly. High-end fashion retailer Boo.com collapsed last week after spending much of its $135 million in seed capital on lavish marketing and advertising campaigns promoting its plan to dominate global online sales of Donna Karan, Helly Hansen and the like. Its investors, which included French entrepreneur Bernard Arnault and Italy's Benetton family, failed to find a buyer for the company, and instead put it up for liquidation.

Toys and Crafts

Earlier this week, Walt Disney Co. shut down Toysmart Inc., an online toy start-up in which it owned a majority stake. Craft-Shop.com, a Connecticut-based retailer of craft supplies, sought bankruptcy-court protection on Monday after its backers, led by Brand Equity Ventures of Greenwich, Conn., decided to withhold a promised second round of funding.

And one of the most closely watched experiments in online entertainment, Digital Entertainment Network, shut its doors last week after a long stream of bad publicity—including the resignation of a co-founder amid allegations of a sex scandal—soured investors on its prospects. That co-founder, Marc Collins-Rector, has denied the allegations.

Could some big-name Internet high-filers be next in line? Auditors at both CDNow.com Inc. and drkoop.com Inc. have expressed doubts about the companies' viability. CDNow says it expects to sign a merger or investment transaction by the end of the second quarter. Drkoop.com says it has slashed expenses and retained Bear Stearns Cos. to help it explore strategic financing options that could include the sale of the company.

In the meantime, even relatively successful Internet companies are postponing their initial offerings, following the stock-market slump. AltaVista Co., a unit of CMGI Inc. that operates a popular search engine, postponed its IPO until September or October, when the company expects to be closer to profitability. Others are doing some vigorous cost cutting. Living.com, an Austin, Texas, furniture e-tailer, on Monday laid off 50 people, or 13% of its staff, to streamline its operations.

Natural Shakeout?

Some venture capitalists see the spreading turmoil as a natural shakeout of marginal Internet companies—many of whom, they say, would never have been funded without an overheated IPO market that made cashing out early investments far too easy. The fallout could easily continue through the Christmas season and into next year.

"As those companies are locked out of money, they're faced with the challenge—they either shut their doors, find a buyer, or take cash at any price," says Michael Linnert, a general partner at Technology Crossover Ventures, a Palo Alto, Calif., venture-capital firm.

For Silicon Valley venture capitalists it comes down to this question: Which of our progeny do we just let die? In an April memo e-mailed to his investors, Ron Conway of Angel Investors LP warned that because the IPO window has closed for many Internet companies, his primary focus would be to steer the fund's resources to its "top-tier" companies. The remainder, he wrote, were being encouraged to obtain additional funding from corporate partners.

"There are several of our portfolio companies that we have chosen not to fund in these market conditions," Mr. Conway wrote. "While we have not had one of our investments fail yet, we predict that five to 10 may fail in the next 60 to 90 days."

Mr. Conway was traveling and unavailable for comment, but Angel partner Bob Bozeman confirmed the authenticity of the memo. "You have to hit people on the head with a two-by-four to get their attention," Mr. Bozeman says of the memo. "Even now, we have companies that don't have enough cash, and they're doomed unless they get an infusion."

That doom befell Violet, which was one of Angel's portfolio companies. Many investors in Violet thought highly of Ms. Barnett and Ms. Cohen, and believed it was meeting the financial benchmarks used to judge a company's performance, says Angel's Mr. Bozeman. "They were a victim of circumstances and timing more than you should be," he says. "In a capitalist world, you shouldn't be subject to that hysteria."

Gamely, Violet's founders agreed to consider a buyer, and started soliciting interest among prospective "white knights." The company quickly narrowed down its choices to several prospective partners, one of whom was eStyle Inc., a Los Angeles-based online women's retailer. But none of the deals worked out. One investor in Violet, who declined to be identified, argues that the deals ultimately failed because one of Violet's chief assets was its brand, which would inevitably be submerged after a merger. "At the end of the day, the value wasn't worth the transaction cost of relocation," the investor says.

EStyle's founder and CEO, Laurie McCartney, says that "multiple factors" nixed her company's potential acquisition of Violet. She adds that eStyle ultimately "didn't see enough of an opportunity to make it worthwhile."

Violet's lead venture capitalist, Neil Weintraut of 21st Century Internet Venture Partners, looked for new investors. But other venture capitalists were reluctant to sink more money into online retailing. When that failed, Mr. Weintraut pulled the plug, Mr. Bozeman says. Mr. Weintraut couldn't be reached for comment. Ms. Barnett, Violet's CEO, declined to comment.

Law Firms Staff Up

Like venture capitalists, Silicon Valley lawyers expect many more such failures. Bankruptcy-law firms are staffing up to handle an expected rise in business failures, although some of that reflects a rise in interest rates and fears of an economic slowdown, says Ken Klee, a bankruptcy attorney in Los Angeles. While many start-ups have few assets beyond their domain name, some will possess technology licenses or real estate that other firms will want to acquire, "and the best way to do that would be through bankruptcy court," Mr. Klee says.

And woes for one Web start-up create opportunity, naturally, for another. Traffic is heavy at Startupfailures.com, a fledgling, self-described "philanthropic for-profit" Web site founded earlier this month by Nicholas Hall, himself a three-time failed entrepreneur. The site, which features an active chat board in which failed and failing entrepreneurs vent their frustration and share tips, has been overwhelmed with requests for "coaching" from on online adviser Mr. Hall brought on to pep up visitors.

Mr. Hall has been forced not only to seek out more coaches, but also to hire five part-time assistants who help maintain the site. He is in the process of arranging sponsorship for the site, and also plans an online marketplace where failed entrepreneurs can market their equipment and intellectual property to others.

Fallout from the Internet-stock turmoil has extended even to some would-be dot-com landlords in Silicon Valley. Real estate agents who not long ago demanded start-up equity for office space are now instead asking Internet companies for six months of advance rent, a three-month security deposit and a one-year letter of credit. Many even want to see extensive documentation, including executive biographies, profit-and-loss statements and recent bank statements, says Roark O'Neill, a sales associate for Emerald Real Estate Brokerage & Investments Inc. in San Francisco.

Looking for 'Partners'

At the next level of triage are those companies forced to look for corporate buyers, often euphemistically dubbed "partners." Angel has even hired Tracey Ford, a former research analyst at Credit Suisse First Boston, as a dedicated mergers-and-acquisitions expert who advises portfolio companies on their options, helps them compile a list of potential suitors and acts as an intermediary.

Ellen Pack, senior vice president and general manager of Women.com Networks Inc., says the company now receives about twice as many calls from companies promoting themselves as potential acquisitions than before the stock-market slump began—many from firms in the crowded online beauty-products sector. But Women.com, a San Mateo, Calif., operator of a Web portal for women, hasn't taken any up on their offers.

"The audience was a good fit, but the business models weren't," says Ms. Pack. One problem was that because Women.com doesn't sell products, merging with an online retailer would set up conflicts with its existing commerce partners.

Perhaps the toughest blow for a Web start-up is when the drying up of venture capital also prevents the company from finding a buyer.

Consider Craftshop.com, which until recently sold both craft products and projects, such as pottery tool kits or a wood-and-copper birdhouse. It also ran online communities on topics such as sewing and quilting, fine arts and framing, and kids' crafts. Angus Mackie, who for five years had run a Web-design firm that built Internet sites primarily for craft-related organizations, says the idea for the site struck him in early 1999 after a meeting with an investor who wanted to buy craftsearch.com, a domain name Mr. Mackie had registered but never used.

Mr. Mackie hammered out a quick business plan, and with a small amount of funding from that investor in hand, he successfully won a $15 million commitment from Brand Equity Ventures and CMGI's @ Ventures. The venture-capital firms put up $4.5 million of that amount last August and promised to release an additional $3 million in February if CraftShop.com could meet revenue targets and other benchmarks. The remainder would follow later.

"That August, we started doing everything at once," says Mr. Mackie, since the initial investor's funding wasn't enough to build up the site. His technical team labored to procure digital images for about 40,000 products, and then had to rewrite thousands of product descriptions in the company's suppliers' databases, which, for instance, originally listed 'green thread' as "GRNTHD."

Getting Vanna White

While the team had hoped to launch by Thanksgiving, "we all agreed that if it wasn't our best shot we shouldn't do it," Mr. Mackie says. So the team labored through the holidays, even as Mr. Mackie made plans to relocate his technical team from San Francisco to a new headquarters in Norwalk, Conn. The site went live just in time for the Hobby Industry Association convention in later January, and won attention for Webcasting video clips, press releases and product reviews from the convention. CraftShop even snagged a video interview with famed crochet maven Vanna White.

As February rolled around, however, CraftShop fell short of its revenue goal, although Mr. Mackie says the site easily met other milestones. "If we had gone live in late October, we probably would have had two to three months of sales," he says. "As it was, we had three weeks. I had assumed there would be some leniency when it came to the milestones."

In the meantime, several other craft-related competitors, the biggest of which was Craftopia.com inc., had also jumped onto the Internet, and enthusiasm was waning for such "business-to-consumer" Internet ventures anyway. Mr. Mackie forged ahead, proposing a partnership deal with a brick-and-mortar craft retailer. But that also fell through, in part because the retailer was worried about CraftShop's dwindling cash reserves. With the firm's backers withholding its second round of $3 million, Mr. Mackie laid off most of his 49 employees and filed a Chapter 11 bankruptcy petition on Monday.

The @Venture spokeswoman says the firm doesn't dispute Mr. Mackie's account, adding only that its partners felt CraftShop faced too much competition in a relatively small market and that no buyers could be found.

Mr. Mackie credits @Ventures with helping many of his former employees get jobs, and adds that he was able to introduce several workers to Priceline.com, whose offices are also in Norwalk. Still, he echoes an often-heard complaint these days: "If CraftShop had had a different funding source with more tolerance for the growth curve, we'd still be in business."

Startup Meltdown

By Dan Goodin

In the final moments of 1999, the future of startup ePatients seemed bright. That summer the company's founders, a pair of Stanford University medical students, had secured the services of a seasoned CEO who brought an impressive track record and a zeal to execute their dream: an online community for the seriously ill. The company's Web site was just a few weeks from going live, and ePatients' cofounders needed only to sign the requisite paperwork to close $10 million in first-round financing from some high-profile venture firms, including New Enterprise Associates. EPatients was still small—it had only 27 employees at the time, but it was thinking big: Sitting on the CEO's desk was an unsigned lease for office space large enough to house well over 100 employees.

The idea behind ePatients was simple but compelling. The company would bring together people suffering from serious medical problems, and match them with others with similar ailments or backgrounds. For instance, the site could introduce a multiple sclerosis patient in Vermont to another in Hawaii so that the two could swap notes on the most effective strategies for coping with the disease. Or it could pair two African American women in their 60s who both face terminal diseases, even though their afflictions might be different.

There were plenty of health-related sites on the Internet when ePatients was founded that June, but as far as those behind ePatients knew, none had plans for creating such a grand patient-to-patient support network. EPatients would make money by selling various health-related products, from wheelchairs to books to government-sanctioned alternative remedies.

Little did anyone involved with the company know that only 10 days into the new year ePatients would cease to exist. Rather than being another success story about a pair of twentysomethings from Stanford worth improbable sums, the ePatients saga is a cautionary tale. On the one hand, it's about the pitfalls of operating too fast, of agreeing to things that you don't quite understand in the name of moving at Internet speed. On the other, it's about doing business with beginners. Human frailty played a role in ePatients' sudden demise, as did naivete, paranoia and greed. The story of ePatients is the anatomy of a failure, and like most failures, it's a tale replete with accusations and counter-accusations that has left all sides—the cofounders, the venture capitalists, the consultants and a highly touted CEO—feeling angry and miscast as villains. Yet the assigning of blame probably doesn't mean much to the angel investors, many of whom were company employees, who have been left in the lurch for roughly $1.2 million and have lost six months of their lives.

Sean Lin was in his second year at Stanford School of Medicine when his mother, a Taiwanese immigrant, fell ill with breast cancer. Lin's mother, who spoke little English, relied on friends and family for support and help in navigating the health care system. But none of them knew the first thing about living with cancer. Only after she befriended a Taiwanese-speaking breast cancer survivor did Lin's mother's condition improve.

"They connected at a level that even I, as a son, couldn't," says Lin, an ePatients cofounder. "There was so much knowledge that the patient knew that doctors don't . . . I really believe isolation causes premature death." Lin soon learned that what he had discovered anecdotally had been quantified by Stanford professor David Spiegel in a 1989 study of women with an acute from of breast cancer. Women who participated in cancer support groups, Spiegel found, on average lived nearly twice as long as those who didn't.

Another Stanford med student, Meetpaul Singh, was also thinking about the shortcomings of a medical establishment that, for all its attention to disease, failed to provide the emotional support necessary for the healing process. Singh, too, came to this understanding through personal experience. An ailing grandmother inspired him to establish a WebTV-based service he called Eldernet Link, which helped elderly people keep in touch with friends and family. Singh spoke about the program during a Stanford symposium that Lin attended in 1998. The two became fast friends, and the company that eventually would be called ePatients was born.

Lin, now 26, is a classically trained violinist who graduated magna cum laude from Harvard University. Singh, 24 immigrated from India to the U.S. when he was 14, his sophomore year in high school; a year later he became Berkeley High School's senate president. After graduation from Stanford, he was simultaneously admitted to Stanford's medical and business schools.

These two overachievers were soon imagining a company that would collect the stories of hundreds of thousands of patients suffering from every imaginable disease and make them available online. The site would be a community and an information clearinghouse, as well as the perfect portal for those with products to sell to the seriously ill. The problem was that both had virtually no business experience. (Singh had yet to begin business classes at Stanford.) They needed money and the help of seasoned pros able to turn what seemed like a good idea into a viable business. So in June 1999 the pair began pitching the idea to people who might be able to help.

That summer became one of these magical periods that entrepreneurs dream about. Singh and Lin approached Paul Yock, a respected cardiologist and a professor at Stanford's medical school. Yock handed the pair a check for $10,000 on the spot and offered to introduce them to Rich Ferrari, a well-regarded chief executive who had run two of Silicon Valley's more successful medical device companies. Ferrari was so enthusiastic about the idea for ePatients that when the pair told him they had scheduled an appointment with a lawyer to incorporation the firm, Ferrari grabbed Singh's cell phone and punched in the number of a friend who worked at Wilson Sonsini Goodrich & Rosati, a prestigious Silicon Valley law firm. Less than an hour later, as Lin and Singh drove down Interstate 280, a Wilson Sonsini layer called and invited them to come in that day to sign incorporation papers. Meanwhile, Ferrari began raising money for the pair through Saratoga Ventures, a small network of angel investors consisting of Ferrari and friends. This dizzying series of events made the two believe that ePatients was their destiny.

At the time, Lin and Singh were so wet behind the ears that they had to ask for an explanation the first time someone mentioned the term "NDA," the ubiquitous shorthand for nondisclosure agreement. Ferrari, by contrast, is a seasoned businessman who is as intensely competitive as he is successful. He's also a third-degree black belt and a former All American lacrosse player who regularly quotes from Sun Tzu's *The Art of War*. In 1991, he took the helm of Cardio Vascular Imaging Systems, a company cofounded by Yock that created equipment to diagnose heart disease. Ferrari took the company public in 1992, and sold it for $100 million three years later. When Lin and Singh met Ferrari, he was the CEO of Cardio Thoracic Systems, a company that pioneered a less-invasive form of heart surgery.

Fortune seemed to be smiling on Lin and Singh. In late August, Ferrari revealed to them that he would soon be looking for a new job. He was selling Cardio Thoracic to medical device giant Guidant for $313 million, and offered to become CEO of ePatients as soon as the merger was complete. Lin says they jumped at Ferrari's offer without hesitation. "When we heard about his track record, we were salivating," Lin says. It all happened so fast, and it was hard for the two to envision anything but success. They dropped out of medical school, and in classic startup fashion started to build their business out of an apartment that Singh and his parents lived in. Singh's mantra was "SOL," which he understood to signify moving at the speed of light. He and Lin were making it happen, moving at that most intoxicating of velocities,

Internet speed. They were unaware of the motto's more prosaic meaning: shit out of luck.

By early fall, ePatients had moved into a small Santa Clara, Calif., office, on the front door of which Lin hung a copy of the resignation letter he had sent to Stanford. He was new to the world of startups but already was displaying that unique brand of hubris that seems a part of nearly every Valley entrepreneur. The company went on an aggressive hiring binge aided in no small part by the laudable mission of helping the sick seek support outside the medical community.

Typifying that creed was Debbie White, who had worked as the human resources director for Ferrari at his prior two companies. She has just given birth to her second child and was planning to take time off, living off the money she had made from Cardio Thoracic's acquisition. Yet White found the ePatients idea so powerful that she decided to go back to work though her son was only a month old. She took him to the office with her, hanging him in a baby swing as she worked.

"I lost my mom to cancer when I was 21 years old, so I had a definite connection to what they were doing," White says. "It was a very emotional thing for me to make this decision." Of course, there also was the prospect of making a lot of money off a company run by Ferrari. "We teased that he has the touch of gold," she says.

Other employees offered similarly powerful reasons for signing on. For one executive, it was congenital heart disease. For John Santaferraro, ePatients' VP of marketing, it was his 13 years as a youth and family pastor, when he regularly attended to sick and dying congregation members. Most of the staff, from places such as E-Trade and Apple, shared the founders' conviction that they could become millionaires while making the world a better place. The typical ePatients employee felt he was on a holy mission. Says Santaferraro, "It was strange to talk about a business like that. I talk about the religious side of my life that way, but not the business side."

Beneath the euphoria, however, there were subtle warning signs. In August, a Wilson Sonsini lawyer asked Singh to stop by the office to sign what was described as a routine document. Only because Singh was careful to read the document prior to signing it did he learn, to his astonishment, that it would have granted Ferrari control of ePatients, making him the startup's sole director and allowing him to immediately begin acquiring company stock. By contrast, the document would have prohibited Lin and Singh (and also Paul Chilean, Singh's cousin and a third, mostly silent founder in ePatients) from acquiring rights to ePatients stock for a year. And not one of the founders would be company officers.

As Lin tells it, the first time the founders learned of these terms was during that meeting at the lawyer's office. (Ferrari says he had generally informed the founders that he would be in charge, though he acknowledges that he never specifically discussed these terms before the Wilson Sonsini meeting.) In response, the founders hired their own attorney, Robin Edwards, a partner in the San Francisco office of Sonnenschein, Nath & Rosenthal. Edwards drafted a counterproposal that named Ferrari the company's CEO and chairman at the same time it made Lin and Singh board members and officers. Ferrari proved accommodating by agreeing to the terms, but the episode, Lin says, left him and his partner with a lingering bad feeling. "(Singh) was asked to sign it without reading it," says Lin, obviously still bitter. "We just missed being shafted."

The next incident that aroused their suspicions didn't happen until early December, when Edwards phoned Lin to ask about recent changes to ePatients' certificate of incorporation, already on file with the secretary of state's office in Delaware. Among the changes were new procedures for voting in additional board members, which Edwards saw as an attempt to wrest control out of the founders' hands. "It definitely is a one-sided deal, but that is pretty common in these transactions," says Mike Jones, an attorney who counsels startups at San Diego-based law firm Higgs Fletcher & Mack. Though Lin and Singh were the company's majority shareholders, Lin says, neither were consulted about the amendment—and certainly neither had approved the changes, as required by Delaware law. While the amendments were by no means unfair, Jones says, "it rubs me a little wrong if they didn't know about it."

Ferrari does not take kindly to such accusations. He greets the charges with clenched fists and a raised voice but, a seasoned pro, he is quick to compose himself. "I frankly spent more time giving free advice to Meetpaul and Sean than I have to any other person," he says calmly. "I warned them of the paranoia they would feel, (but) they always had fears they'd be removed from the company, and I told them that wouldn't happen." Was he always careful to hold their hands as they digested each new document to sign? No. But he adds, "They really had no clue how a company is run, and they really should have." He also said the two were forever putting off the signing of documents, even as ePatients' need to sprint forward grew. "These guys have a consistent history of procrastinating," he says.

Whatever the circumstances, Lin and Singh had yet to approve the amendments when Debbie White, on Dec. 7, sent both undated approval documents known as unanimous written consent forms, which would retroactively finalize the changes. Edwards counseled both to sign the documents because she thought refusing to do so would appear too confrontational. Lin and Singh signed, but neither would fully trust Ferrari nor anyone from Wilson Sonsini again. Says Lin, "Something this important should be run by the shareholders and the board of directors."

Even as they harbored fears that they were being muscled out, Lin and Singh pitched ePatients to some of the Valley's best known venture firms— appointments that Ferrari had lined up. "There was not a lot of detail," says one VC who heard the pitch. "We thought it was going to need a lot of work and a team of people to execute." A month later, Ferrari returned to this VC's office—this time alone—to say he had fine-tuned ePatients' e-commerce opportunities. That apparently worked. By mid-December, three firms—Morgenthaler Ventures, New Enterprise Associates and Prospect Venture Partners—had agreed to a first round of $10 million.

"We were really backing the seasoned CEO, not the founders," says Robin Bellas, the Morgenthaler partner who had funded Ferrari's prior two companies.

Everyone inside ePatients should have been ecstatic. The deal gave the 6-month-old start-up a valuation of $14 million prior to the investment. Lin, Singh and Chilan maintained more than 21 percent combined of a company suddenly worth $24 million. Ferrari, meanwhile, held a little over 9 percent of the company, and the rest of the staff split roughly 10 percent altogether. But despite the pending infusion of cash, many of the company's younger rank-and-file employees were unhappy that the company, in search of larger office space, would be moving to nearby Campbell, Calif., close to the homes of Ferrari and several other executives. The younger, more junior employees thought ePatients should be headquartered in San Francisco, home to many Internet ventures. There also were complaints by startup veterans about a team that was top-heavy with managers, most of whom made around $150,000 per year, and a work ethic that permitted employees and executives to leave promptly at 5 each night. Then there was the rat maze of cubicle dividers that some thought were antithetical to an Internet company, where employee interaction is crucial. "It just didn't feel like a startup," says former ePatients employee Steve Lin (no relation). "People weren't sleeping under their desks."

The biggest blow to morale, however, was the sudden news that Singh, who had been experiencing back pain for months, had an extremely rare form of malignant cancer on his spine, and needed to begin aggressive treatment immediately. He would be unavailable for weeks at a time just when many employees felt he was needed the most. "He was the glue between Rich and the rest of the team," says Jim Lieu, another ex-employee.

It also meant that Lin would have to face the next big crisis by himself. The terms of the $10 million offer included the condition that the company create a seven-member board of directors that included neither Lin nor Singh.

The board would include Ferrari, ePatients' CFO Steve Van Dick (a longtime Ferrari colleague), a VC from each of the three firms and two outsiders to be determined—yet not necessarily a patient advocate. "The company was about bedside healing and community, and Rich lacked expertise in these areas," Lin says. He suspected once again that the priority wasn't the patient, but rather Ferrari and his allies wresting control of ePatients.

Lin recognized that he was in over his head, so he turned to Randolph Tom, a financial and strategic adviser for entrepreneurs at Dynasty Capital Services in San Francisco. After a series of e-mail messages in which Lin pleaded with Tom to act as his adviser and mentor, Tom agreed to a phone consultation. "When I told him a little about the deal, he said, 'You guys are getting screwed,'" Lin says. As Lin tells it, Tom told him that both he and Singh should have been promised a seat on the board of directors and granted greater equity in the company. And then he suggested that the founders find a new CEO. "I was completely blown away," Lin says.

Lin was shocked by the idea of firing Ferrari and eased out of the mentorship by saying that Singh couldn't agree. "Good luck," Tom responded in an e-mail addressed to Lin. "If your partner could not see the wisdom from our discussion, you are doomed to your inevitable destiny."

Lin was content to ignore the admonition, but a few weeks later, on Jan. 3, Ferrari dropped another bomb: The VCs had lowered ePatients' premoney valuation by 28 percent, from $14 million to $10 million, and whittled the founders' share of the company from 21 percent to 15 percent. At the same time, they funneled more equity to other executives and the employee stock-option pool, and granted more stock options to Ferrari. The company had less than a month's cash on hand—a fact Ferrari was careful to stress in talks with Lin and Singh—and was already late in signing the new office lease. Two days later, after hours of heated exchanges, Lin says Ferrari delivered the following ultimatum: "We either do the deal and build this company, or we don't do the deal and I walk out." The founders told him they would let Ferrari know the next day—but then avoided him over the next five days while they thought over their next move.

With Singh still focusing on his cancer treatment, Lin felt alone. Feeling desperate, he phoned Tom on the evening of Jan. 7, two days after Ferrari's ultimatum. Lin again pleaded for Tom's help. Tom says he reluctantly agreed, in part because he wanted to help a fellow Asian entrepreneur, but he stresses how reluctant he was to jump into a situation that already appeared dire. "He was looking for an emergency-room doctor and there's nothing like that," Tom explains. "It was more of a courtesy to calm down a very hyper individual." That touch of courtesy, however, cost Lin $4,000, according to a retainer letter written on Tom's stationary (Tom declined to comment on fee-related matters). The two met for three hours that weekend, and talked more in subsequent phone calls. As Lin tells it, Tom offered advice on firing Ferrari and the other top executives who had been hired.

"(Tom) kept saying, 'Attack the deal, not the person. Say the valuation is wrong,'" Lin says. What Tom failed to point out, Lin says, is the uphill battle two founders with no track record or business experience would face if they were to fire the CEO who had been instrumental in raising money and hiring employees.

Tom, however, remembers the meeting differently. "(Lin) gave me a set of facts, and I gave him several alternatives," Tom says. "I did not tell him to go kick out this guy." Still, Tom didn't mince words in warning Lin to be wary of Ferrari. "The concept was, 'You've got a very steep discount on valuation, you've got less stock and other people have more and you're being told if you don't sign it, the whole deal is going to go bust,'" Tom recalls telling Lin. "That smells, per se."

As Lin tells it, his conversations with Aki Hashmi, a recent addition to ePatients' management team, also helped embolden him to consider firing Ferrari. Formerly a top executive at Quote.com, a stock service that Lycos bought for $78 million, Hashmi was one of the few ePatients executives with bona fide dot-com experience. He criticized a number of provisions in the term sheet New Enterprise Associates had proposed, including a section that would allow the VCs to receive three times their investment in the event ePatients was sold for a low price, diminishing other stockholders' return. (It's standard procedure for VCs to receive twice their investment, and not unheard of to demand three times their investment.) Yet Hashmi's main criticism was that ePatients was an Internet company, and the VCs that Ferrari (who came from the medical device field) had secured didn't have enough Internet experience to make a good match. Hashmi, Lin says, agreed to talk with some his contacts in the VC community to see about alternative financing. Hashmi says he criticized terms of the offer but really didn't go beyond that. And why not? From Lin's point of view, when he pitched ePatients during the summer and fall, everyone seemed interested. What would be different now?

EPatients' end came on Jan. 10. The Monday began with a meeting of the three co-founders—Lin, Singh and Chilana—and Ferrari at a Starbucks close to ePatients' offices. Lin was the group's spokesman, presenting a speech he says Tom had helped him prepare: "Rich, when we spoke last week, you said we had to sign the deal or you'd resign. Well, we can't go along with the deal, so we accept your resignation." Ferrari, however, as savvy as he was ambitious, knew that if he resigned he'd receive none of the stock promised him. So he said nothing. Over the next two hours, Lin sat in his car in a McDonald's parking lot and left voicemail messages for each of the VCs that had offered to buy a piece of his company. His speech to each one was virtually identical: "The valuation isn't right. Rich decided to leave. I appreciate you took the time."

The tears and angry outburst would come later that day, during an all-hands meeting of ePatients employees that Lin called for 2 p.m. Ironically, most were expecting only good news; the big venture deal in the works had been a poorly kept secret, so most employees were expecting that they'd learn the final terms of the agreement. Instead, Lin stood before them, staring down at his shoes and shaking slightly, and delivered the news: They had turned down the offer from the three VC firms. Ferrari was stepping down as CEO. And Lin would take the helm in the interim. "Everyone was in complete shock," says Dean Lucas, ePatients' VP of Web development.

Understandably, people demanded an explanation. Among the reasons Lin offered was that under the new terms the lower echelon employees would receive less stock in the company—a miscalculation that demonstrated to every employee in the room that he failed to grasp even basic business concepts.

Ferrari had been silent up until that moment, but now the former All American saw his chance to take up the attack. "If you're going to be CEO, why don't you stand up straight and get these numbers right?" one person present remembers him saying. In fact, under the changed term sheet, employees would receive slightly more stock—3.3 percent, instead of 2.9 percent. White, a Ferrari loyalist, stood up to explain the confusion: This was to be a reverse stock split, which meant that though the number of shares allocated would be divided in half, their value would double. Some employees began suggesting that the founders had rejected the deal simply because they had lost 6 percent of the company. One clearly emotional executive cried out: "It's not about the money. I came here to help patients." Many were reduced to tears, including Lin, who was so badly shaken that he felt compelled to go outside and lie down in the parking lot next to his car.

"The meeting completely changed everything," says Lin. "I was completely crushed. All of a sudden they were accusing us of being money-grubbers!" Some employees chose to go home while others stuck around the office and drank beer, uncertain of the company's future, their confidence shaken by Lin's emotional performance that day.

Meanwhile, Lin and Singh huddled late into the night with Elliott Wolfe, an associate dean at Stanford School of Medicine and a mentor for both. Wolfe had known both Lin and Singh since they started med school in 1996, and he also had a vested stake in the company's future: Wolfe is a founder of a startup that produces videos for health care companies and was in discussions about a possible merger or partnership with ePatients. Wolfe convinced Lin and Singh to reconsider their decision, but at that point no amount of negotiating could convince the VCs to do a deal that involved Lin and Singh. "In my naivete, I said: 'If we could simply go back to the previous Monday and say we're sorry and just continue,'" Wolfe says. "I couldn't understand why that couldn't be done." Employees, when they went home that Monday, had no idea whether they would still have a job the next day. It turns out they wouldn't.

Only in retrospect is it clear that ePatients was doomed from the start. What was supposed to be the stuff of success ended up a case study in how business naivete, paranoia, hardball tactics and carelessness can fatally injure a fledgling business. In their devotion to move at Internet time, Lin, Singh and Ferrari made critical mistakes that ultimately cost two dozen people their jobs and left investors out $1.2 million. "It was a combination of typical youthful, idealistic founders who didn't handle the situation well confounded by a head-strong management team," says Lawrence Busansky, a former business-development employee at ePatients. Other staffers are not so sure. "There's no logical answer to what happened, and that's what makes it a bizarre story," says White.

No single reason can explain why ePatients came undone. There are only contributing factors: a pair of inexperienced founders negotiating Silicon Valley deals, Ferrari's distraction in wrapping up the merger of his old company while trying to launch a new one, Singh's bout with cancer, and the role of the lawyers and consultants.

Signs of trouble loomed everywhere, but those involved did a good job of collectively masking the mistrust and power struggle raging below the surface. If nothing else, airing the conflicts would have demonstrated that Ferrari and the founders were not a good match. "This is another sign of inexperienced entrepreneurs—when they focus on control instead of value," Morgenthaler's Bellas says. "Their goal should be to bring all the best resources to the company as opposed to control." In their haste to sign a deal, and enamored by the validation and money they were offered, the founders never took the time to learn what they were giving up.

"Entrepreneurs do this all the time," says Jad Duwaik, founder of Greenhouse for Startups, a networking group for Internet founders. "They gave up too much in the beginning. In a sense they sold their soul." Duwaik is also founder of OptInk, a startup that helps individuals manage confidential information. From the start, he says, entrepreneurs need to establish careful boundaries with investors. "When you see something happening, particularly an individual accelerating your value-accretion process, figure out what the cost is," he counsels. In particular, this means obtaining a written agreement upfront that clearly states who will sit on the company's board of directors.

You can blame Ferrari for aggressively treating ePatients as if he were a cofounder. But as Duwaik sees it, that's exactly what he was. Once Lin and Singh had asked Ferrari to put his reputation on the line to raise seed money and run a company that had no product or employees and was worth exactly zero, says Duwaik, "in effect (he) became one of the founders."

For his part, Ferrari is careful to credit Lin and Singh for their initial idea, but he saw them as founders who had outlived most of their usefulness. "Their role within the company was becoming less and less important," Ferrari says, noting that neither founder had any experience writing computer code or striking business partnerships. "Their talent really lay in their thoughts about where ePatients ought to be at a certain point. They didn't have a lot to offer in terms of work value, and I think they began to realize this."

Ferrari took missteps in places where he should have known better. It was bad enough that he allowed ePatients' cash supply to fall so low, but in demanding that Lin and Singh sign the revised term sheet so shortly after the deal was altered, Ferrari violated one of the prime tenets in his favorite book. *The Art of War* repeatedly states that an effective warrior never backs a potential opponent against a wall. Ferrari's time demands are made all the more poignant by a fax that shows the revised term sheet was sent to him on Dec. 23—two weeks before the founders say they learned of the change.

Ferrari can't be faulted for demanding control of ePatients. After all, the terms he imposed were no different than those he made for his previous two companies, and he was well past the point in his career where he'd give a line-item veto to two twentysomethings with no business experience. However, he seems not to have been entirely straightforward with Lin and Singh: Eager to clinch the ePatients deal before someone else got it, he revealed the less attractive terms of his deal only after the founders agreed to make him CEO.

Then there are the professionals the founders retained for advice. Attorney Robin Edwards charged the pair more than $21,000. Randolph Tom, Lin's strategic adviser, charged $4,000 for several hours of counseling. At least Edwards was instrumental in pressuring Ferrari to make major concessions in the founders' employment agreements. But neither told the founders what they most needed to hear: Their lack of business experience had caused them to make crucial mistakes that could not be undone. Edwards didn't respond to numerous requests for an interview. Tom, meanwhile, says he merely offered Lin a set of alternatives, even if what Lin remembers is that Tom clearly counseled him to take the step that ultimately destroyed the company: Fire Ferrari.

Reinforcing the founders' belief that a cabal of opportunists have been out to steal their idea, former ePatients employees are at work on at least two patient-related Web sites. Lawrence Busansky, the ePatients employee who worked in business development, has formed a patient-related startup that he declines to discuss in detail. John Santaferraro, ePatients' VP of marketing, says he and Ferrari have turned their attention to a 10-employee startup. Santaferraro declines to name the company, which he says has yet to receive venture capital, but according to domain-name records Santaferraro owns the rights to the patientsplace.com domain, which he registered on Jan. 12, two days after the catastrophic ePatients meeting. Santaferraro estimates that at least a dozen patient-centered startups are flying under the radar, and he says the activity is testament to the power of the ePatients idea. "There's so much passion behind this vision that the vision had to go forward," he says.

Still, the sense of loss felt by those involved with ePatients is inescapable. Many of the early employees were also investors. They're out tens of thousands of dollars and six months of their lives. Lin and Singh dropped out of medical school for ePatients. They also incurred enormous debts trying to get the business off the ground. More important, they face the very real prospect of being blackballed by Silicon Valley's tightly knit venture capital community. Ferrari has yet to transfer his success in the medical devices industry to the dot-com world. He, too wasted six months at a time when experienced CEOs were in hot demand. About the only players not to lose are the VCs, which fortunately learned of ePatients' meltdown before they had invested.

Perhaps the biggest loss is that the world will never know whether ePatients could have lived up to its promise of making the health care system more responsive to patient needs. Says Hashmi, "They had an opportunity that could have been huge."

An American Dream Gone Bad

By Keith Perine Washington

For better or for worse, Value America always was a pioneer. Born in Nevada in 1996, the company was one of the first to spot the promise of the Internet to streamline retail delivery.

Last December, it broke ground again—this time as one of the first big e-retailers to fall on hard times, laying off half its 600-person staff.

Now Value America is forging into new territory again. Just as the company was early to explore e-commerce, it's now one of the first to mine federal bankruptcy law as a strategy to save lucrative portions of the business, hoping to resurrect itself or get acquired.

On Aug. 11, the company, now based in Charlottesville, Va., filed for Chapter 11 bankruptcy protection and also laid off 185 of its remaining staff.

It's not at all what founder Craig Winn had in mind four years ago when he set up the company as an "inventoryless" virtual middleman. Value America was modeled after the Price Club, the general merchandise chain founded by Sol Price that in the 1970s revolutionized "big box" retailing, ordering products in bulk and cutting out resellers whenever possible. Value America promised to go one better: Customers placed orders through its site but received their products directly from manufacturers.

Winn pitched Value America's inventoryless model as a strength—the company would be nimble and efficient because it wouldn't be saddled with the overhead of warehouse stock and property taxes, and wouldn't have to anticipate demand. Physical order fulfillment and returns, too, would be somebody else's problem. Value America was simply the means to make the purchase happen.

The idea was novel enough to draw the attention—and the pocket-books—of some notable investors. FedEx titan Frederick Smith kicked in $5 million of his company's cash along with $5 million of his own, and took a seat on the company's board alongside Bill Savoy, president of Vulcan Ventures, who pitched in $65 million of Microsoft co-founder Paul Allen's money.

FedEx's involvement, in particular, seemed to prove that the company was onto something good. Things grew fast—too fast. Soon, Value America's product lines had mushroomed to include everything from computers to cheesecake to barbecued spareribs. And some of Winn's side deals seemed spurious, as if he hadn't thought through the broader ramifications.

In one gambit, for example, the company sat up a Web link for Visa cardholders that had Value America accounts offering 100 "value dollars" for the first $200 spent on Value America's site. But the deal was scrapped after cardholders opened multiple Value America accounts and attempted to sell the link to cardholders who didn't yet know about the deal.

By last November, Winn followed the path of many startup founders; he was pulled from the CEO position. Taking his place was Value America executive Glenda Dorchak, a former IBM manager charged with streamlining the overgrown company and improving its delivery system.

Dorchak acted fast: She slashed the company's staff and whittled down its product lines to computer hardware, electronics and office supplies. Some of the moves worked. By all accounts, Value America improved its back-end support system, which was once so shoddy that the company had pallets of returned merchandise scattered around Charlottsville. But Value America couldn't come up with a marketing plan to lure jaded customers back to its site. And aside from a $30 million infusion in May from Smith, FedEx and Vulcan Ventures among others, Dorchak's mission to raise critically needed capital bore little fruit.

"The management for Value America speaks for itself," Smith said in a statement. Savoy didn't return telephone calls seeking comment, nor did Value America return telephone calls and e-mail messages seeking comment for this story.

By early August, things had turned desperate. Value America shuttered its online retail operation and tersely announced that it had filed for bankruptcy and would concentrate on hawking its back-end infrastructure of order fulfillment and payment systems to other e-commerce companies. That may be wishful thinking. Former Value America employees say that the technical support staff that built that infrastructure has either quit or was let go.

In a statement issued after the company shut down its site, Dorchak didn't sound very enthusiastic about the future. "The decision to shut down our Internet retailing business was difficult," she said. "Despite tremendous efforts on the part of our employees and the loyalty of our vendors and customers, it has become apparent that the prospect for near-term profitability of a company engaged exclusively in the retail side of the electronic commerce industry is not assured."

Winn's original vision looked good on paper. But many of Value America's vendors weren't geared to ship just one computer or cheesecake, and naturally gave individual orders a low priority. Customers shunned the Web site after encountering billing and fulfillment errors. Ironically, computer hardware proved to be one of the most reliable product lines because it was often shipped by middlemen resellers.

In the past year, Value American's business practices have been investigated by both the Federal Trade Commission and the Marin County, Calif., district attorney's office, and the company also has been hit with shareholder class-action lawsuits. In June, the company settled FTC charges of deceptive advertising related to computer hardware sales.

Value America is fighting its creditors in a Lynchburg, Va., federal bankruptcy court so that it can survive in truncated form or sell off its assets. Value American's creditors include local utility companies and staffing firm InService America, which says Value America owes it $100,000 in employee compensation.

On the Web site, a short message declares that retail operations have closed, and that orders that were not shipped by Aug. 11 won't be fulfilled.

The Nasdaq has suspended Value America's shares, pending a request for "additional information" from the company. By Aug. 11, the shares were trading at around 70 cents, down from a high of $74 on the first day of Value America's April 1999 initial public offering.

The timing of Value America's Aug. 11 filing wasn't random: The company had been scheduled to unveil on Aug. 14 what former employees say are disastrous second-quarter sales figures. Now that it has filed for bankruptcy, those numbers may never see the light of day.

Pets.com's Demise:
Too Much Litter, Too Few Funds

By Pui-Wing Tam and Mylene Mangalindan
Staff Reporters of The Wall Street Journal

SAN FRANCISCO—In the end, not even the famous Sock Puppet could prevent Pets.com inc. from becoming one of the first publicly traded Internet companies to fall.

Yesterday morning, as employees trickled into its trendy warehouse headquarters here, they learned that the online pet-supply retailer was about to close. Of the company's 320 employees, 255 were laid off right away. The company said it would sell the majority of its assets, including the remaining inventory. Also up for grabs: intellectual property including its sock Puppet icon, a floppy-eared dog with a spot over one eye that starred in TV commercials.

While scores of dot-coms have folded this year, Pets.com is one of the highest-profile failures. It underscores how such business-to-consumer Internet sites haven't found sustainable business models—even with massive infusions of capital, dwindling competition and national ads that grabbed the public's imagination.

The closure of Pets.com, as well as rival pet-supply Web sites, "symbolizes the worst excesses of the capital market," said Matt Stamski, a senior analyst at Gomez Advisors in Lincoln, Mass.

"People were betting on ideas that were almost stillborn. It's almost unprecedented to see an entire sector go from an idea to heavily funded to defunct in just a year and a half."

The announcement came after a series of last-ditch attempts to raise capital. In the summer, Pets.com hired investment bank Merrill Lynch & Co. to help initiate sale or merger discussions with potential partners, including other pet Web sites. But of the 50 domestic and international prospects contacted, fewer than eight were prepared to visit with the company, according to Pets.com.

Pets.com's chairman and chief executive, Julie Wainwright, said closing the company she founded was the best option. "In the end, we thought it was the best thing for our shareholders, who are our primary concern, since we're a public company. Obviously, that's sad," Ms. Wainwright said in an interview.

While the company had enough money to last through April, it needed an additional $20 million to $30 million in funding, according to its business plan, and didn't feel it would be able to raise that, said a person familiar with the situation. Indeed, according to internal company projections, Pets.com wouldn't become profitable until 2002.

In 4 p.m. Nasdaq Stock Market trading yesterday, the company's stock stood at 22 cents, down 44 cents a share, far below the $11 the shares fetched in their initial public offering in February.

Even in a time when e-tailers have been falling by the wayside almost daily, Pets.com is among the first publicly traded ones to fail. Yesterday, MotherNature.com, a publicly traded online retailer of vitamins and natural produces, announced it will close. In August, retailer Value America Inc. filed for Chapter 11 reorganization, and Mortgage.com, an online mortgage site has announced plans to close. Several other publicly traded dot-com companies, including Drkoop.com Inc., Garden.com Inc. and Egreetings Network Inc., have announced large layoffs and seen their shares dip to or near the precarious $1 mark at which they could have the stock delisted from the exchange.

Pets.com's downfall was particularly swift and brutal. The company, conceived in February 1999, courted publicity and was at the forefront of a pack of pet-oriented dot-coms that burst into prominence as Internet hysteria soared last year. It coasted into the public's consciousness with a multimillion-dollar ad campaign centered around the smart-talking Sock Puppet. Venture capitalists, including blue-chip firm Hummer Winblad Partners, Bowman Capital and partners such as Amason.com Inc., poured money into the enterprise, raising nearly $110 million in four rounds of funding by December 1999.

Just a few months later, the company went public. But Pets.com's stock made an unspectacular debut—it never rose above the $11-a-share IPO price—and the fanfare that surrounded the company's advertising never spread to other parts of its business. The company spent more than an estimated $25 million on ads, including premium time during the Super Bowl.

In April, the company attempted to diversify and capitalize on the popularity of its mascot by licensing Sock puppet merchandise. In September, the company relocated a customer-service call center to Indiana from San Francisco to trim expenses.

Almost from the start, Pets.com was a losing proposition, despite its backers' talk about how much money consumers lavish on their pets. Many pet supplies are heavy and costly to ship—cat litter, cans of dog food—and the firm couldn't sell enough higher-profit items such as pet toys. Moreover, to attract customers, the company depended heavily on discounts, said Jupiter

Communications analyst Heather Dougherty. As a result, the firm was selling supplies below cost the entire time.

Even if the company had succeeded in selling at a profit, it would have faced a tough future, analyst say. In the bricks-and-mortar world, profit margins on pet products are a razor-thin 2% to 4% according to Gomez Advisors.

"Pets.com's fundamental problem was that its cost model would only have worked if it had had very high levels of sales," said Ken Cassar, another Jupiter analyst. "Pets.com didn't have the financial resources to sustain itself till it reached that level of scale."

Other pet sites also have suffered. Petopia.com recently laid off half its staff. And in June, Pets.com announced it would acquire key assets from Petstore.com Inc. Just one online pet store is left unscathed, PetSmart.com. The closely held company is backed by the PetSmart Inc. retail chain.

Venture capitalists who infused this sector of the e-tailing market with cash were tight-lipped yesterday. Pets.com's closure is a bust particularly for its main backers, none of whom sold their stock before the company's closure announcement, according to First Call/Thomson Financial. The biggest losses were felt by Amazon.com Inc., which invested $60 million for a 30% stake in Pets.com before its IPO. Hummer Winblad had a 15.8% stake, Bowman Capital Management had a 5.1% stake and Catalyst Investments LLC had a 3.7% stake pre-IPO, according to SEC filings.

Yesterday, employees of Pets.com were subdued. Many blamed the lack of funding for the firm's demise. "It was a very difficult decision for the board and the company," said John Cummings, Pets.com's investor-relations manager. "The company was executing plans on schedule, but the capital markets just weren't there."

In the Pets.com office, executives huddled in a conference room while security guards hovered to keep out reporters. Some of Pets.com's staff left immediately after finding out about the company's closure, while others stayed on to finish up paying employees and filing legal documents, said Mr. Cummings. "We still have obligations as a company, and there are still a lot of relationships that have to be unwound," he said. The Pets.com Web site will be up until the end of the week, he added.

As for the Sock Puppet, Mr. Cummings said "it still remains one of the signature brands on the Internet." The puppet's fate, however, "is unknown at this point," he said.

Kara Scannell and Kara Swisher contributed to this article.

The End of the Line

By Jennifer Couzin

There were four attendees at Audio-café.com's early strategy meetings in 1998, which were held around kitchen tables and on living room couches. Andrew Keen, the company's 38-year-old founder; Marko Suvajdzic, a 24-year-old Yugolsav emigre who left just before that country disintegrated; Keen's infant son; and Max, Keen's West Highland Terrier.

Keen, energized by his vision of a Web company covering high-end audio equipment, plotted strategy. Suvajdzic, chief creative and technical officer, warmed the bottle, fed the baby and spun design ideas to draw hip, young users to the homepage.

In February, 18 months, $1 million and 20 employees later, Audiocafe closed for good. Unable to secure venture capital funding and facing formidable competition in the online consumer electronics arena, the company emptied its San Francisco office and employees moved on.

Keen lost the most. A London-born historian who taught at several Boston universities before moving to the Bay Area, he had sold his San Francisco home for nearly $500,000 to find the company. Still, Keen, now 40, looks back on the experience with surprising good humor.

He recalls the "psychotic" Web developer who one day bolted for Thailand. And the Chinese Web engineer who spoke almost no English and skipped town for Canada. Keen, never enamored of material possessions in the past, says he caught himself fantasizing about the Jaguar he'd buy with the riches that would befall him—a notion his wife, an attorney and founder of a San Francisco pedestrian-rights group, regarded with skepticism.

Audiocafe fell victim to the common startup hazards. It lacked a coherent business model. It didn't bring on employees with extensive business experience until early 1999, months after Keen hatched the concept. It grew too fast. Worst, it had to scramble constantly for cash.

Keen admits that the pressure to present a boffo business plan to venture capitalists let him to overhype Audiocafe's potential. "All appearance, no actuality," is how he now describes his company.

Audiocafe's first year was relatively successful. The company developed strong content that advised shoppers on pricey stereos, amplifiers, speakers and more. Traffic was doubling every few months and by the end of 1998 the

Originally published in The Industry Standard, June 12, 2000. Used with permission. Copyright 2000 by The Industry Standard.

site was logging more than 1,000 unique visitors a day. Ads supplied most of its revenue.

The scene changed in the summer of 1999. Seed money, mainly from the sale of Keen's house, was running out. Audiocafe brought two seasoned businessmen aboard to clarify the business model and help attract funding. Jim Thompson, an independent financial consultant, became the company's COO and, later, CFO though he never got a salary. Eric Hall, who also received no salary, had worked at Yahoo and had run an Internet consulting business; he was appointed Audiocafe's president. Both men invested in the company. Hall put in $30,000. Thompson won't say how much he contributed.

Together, Thompson, Hall, and Keen formed a management triangle. It was perhaps not the best plan of attack, admits Charles Smith, who joined Audiocafe as director of business development shortly after he graduated from Stanford Law School. "The three of them had different backgrounds, different visions of where the company was going," Smith says. "It may have been best to have a final person who has complete authority."

The trio trooped to venture capitalists around the country, struggling to articulate their vision. They managed to impress one company, infrastructure provider Pandesic. Pete Wolcott, president of Pandesic and eventual Audiocafe board member, recalls that, when he first met with management, the company had respectable traffic and was targeting a potentially strong market. Pandesic provided Audiocafe with commerce infrastructure and money, though Wolcott won't say how much. "I remember the energy," Wolcott says about Audiocafe. "But," he adds, "this is an unbelievably competitive environment."

The competition hit a high note that summer. Amazon.com announced in July that it would start selling audio equipment, a few months after 800.com got $16 million in second-round funding (the company received another $57 million in November). Audiocafe was convinced all this activity validated the space, but vying with such well-financed, well-structured rivals proved difficult.

So in November, Audiocafe made the first of several changes in its business model: It began selling audio equipment online. In retrospect, Keen says this heralded the beginning of the end. Sales margins were razor thin and the ad budget was almost nonexistent. To compensate, management adjusted the business model almost weekly.

Shortly afterward the company told many of its employees it could no longer afford to pay them—they had to take equity instead. Most stayed, though many used their time at work to look for another job. In December, layoffs began in earnest; the company shut down completely in February.

Hall and Thomson insist Audiocafe failed due to bad timing, entering the market just as consumer sites were falling out of favor with venture capitalists. But Keen, while agreeing that Audiocafe might have fared better six months earlier, is adamant that no company flops—or flourishes—on luck alone. "You make your own luck," he says, "and you make your own timing."

Keen resigned himself to Audiocafe's demise in January, when management briefly flirted with a business-to-business model. He realized that simply riding the trends was no way to run a company.

Suvajdzic moved to another San Francisco startup, BigPrizes.com, and is determined to stay with startups as long as they last. "The Internet startup is a dying breed," he says. "I don't think it's going to survive for longer than another year or so."

Keen joined incubator Slomedia and says his career has "taken off" since Audiocafe failed. Would he lead another startup? Only with an experienced business partner. And without selling his house.

Back In the Saddle

By Steffan Heuer

Failure doesn't have to suck. At least that's what Alan Eyzaguirre and Daryl Michalik believe. Though they put their startup, MetaFinancial, on the block in late 1999, their nearly two years of work didn't go down the T1 pipe. Instead, a better-funded competitor acquired the company's skeleton staff.

"We misunderstood what attracts funding," says Michalik. "You need vision, communication skills and connections. [But] we were lacking a bit in all three—mostly contacts."

MetaFinancial never got beyond beta, even though Eyzaguirre was a successful entrepreneur. The 30-year-old had already started one company, Swell Software, in late 1995 and sold it within 10 months to Adobe for $8 million. "It was a pretty easy sell," he says of his first venture. "We had competing offers."

"His experience was that the Internet is such a hot space, you could just do it again," adds Michalik. "Go ahead, get people, build technology and get bought up. What we didn't realize was that the space had changed by 1998."

It all started in early 1998, when Eyzaguirre approached Michalik, who had gone to high school with Eyzaguirre's previous business partner. He showed Michalik a technology that an engineering friend had built for the Swiss bank UBS; Eyzaguirre told Michalik that he had a killer app on his hands. The idea was to tweak the XML-like interface, which was developed to automatically settle complex trades at the bank and to aggregate data from multiple accounts, and broaden its use. The end result would be a Web-based platform that would establish MetaFinancial as an infomediary, either as a brand of its own or as a technology provider to financial portals.

"It was [meant as] a marketplace for consumer financial services," explains Eyzaguirre. "We wanted to start off with brokerage and advice comparisons and then partner with sites like Financial Engines and Direct Advice." Both sites offer financial-planning tools and investment advice to consumers. Eyzaguirre incorporated MetaFinancial in April 1998; Michalik, a former McKinsey & Co. consultant, came onboard full time as CFO in August.

After the duo had completed a demo version and started looking for funding in the spring of 1999, however, they realized that their development work wouldn't translate into easy money. "The product was too complex to spin," says Eyzaguirre, who was the company's CEO. "We had started a technology company first. While we got away with that in '95, things were different in 1999. It was the year of the slide show. We'd spent six months on technical development when all we needed in that market was a slide show heavy on business development."

They also needed big names to attract big money. Venture capitalists looked at the startup and mostly saw the holes in the business plan, 29-year-old Michalik remembers. "A platform doesn't get funded. They wanted to see more senior management. It had been my understanding that they would help us recruit [management]."

By now MetaFinancial had grown to seven employees with offices in San Francisco's Multimedia Gulch. Eyzaguirre's savings and some angel money got it off the ground, but the two founders needed to raise another $8 million.

Publicity in a business magazine last summer brought interest from names like PricewaterhouseCoopers and McKinsey, but the free PR proved to be a catch-22. The people who read and heard the buzz wanted to know who was funding the venture and who its customers were. "We had no good answer to that," says Michalik. "It was a chicken-and-egg problem that affected everything—hiring people, signing up partners and renting space."

The duo entertained some offers from what they deemed second-tier VCs, but declined to take what they call "dumb money." Turning those people away, says Eyzaguirre, was a tough decision for a young company scrambling to stay afloat. By last fall, MetaFinancial's staff had dwindled to four; the startup couldn't pay salaries.

By then the business climate had shifted. "Technology had already been commoditized; the emphasis [now] was all on business-development strategy," Eyzaguirre recalls. "If you had leverage in that field you could get a VC's attention. I had discounted the importance of luck the first time around. To succeed we needed some deep business-development people."

When the startup failed to survive a venture firm's late due diligence in October, the two entrepreneurs started thinking about an exit strategy. Eyzaguirre and Michalik began peddling their technology as an acquisition target. They say they talked to a big brokerage firm and financial-services infrastructure provider Home Account Network. Then MetaFinancial's founders happened upon a competing startup called Outcome.com, funded by Draper Fisher Jurvetson. An e-mail to the VC firm led to negotiations that in late December cleared the way for Outcome to acquire MetaFinancial's team for an undisclosed price.

The two survivors felt relieved that the mad race to make connections had finally stopped. The experience cost Eyzaguirre and an unnamed angel $300,000, but everybody received cash and options from Outcome.

Eyzaguirre served as adviser to the CEO of Outcome for a little while, then left to work as director of strategic development for the Webby Awards. Michalik is still at the new company, whose product is slated to launch this summer. He's convinced they've got it right this time. "We were just too early with an ambitious plan," he says.

Failure, with a happy ending, taught Eyzaguirre a lesson: "I still believe in ideas with big potential, but the battles are in the marketing arena. When I see business plans friends ask me to review, I think, look at Company XYZ— you can fit in there with a great product-management position. I don't believe in garage shops anymore. I believe more in senior management fallout."

In Foundering Swedish Dot-Com, A Cautionary Tale

By Stephanie Gruner and Almar Latour
Staff Reporters of The Wall Street Journal

STOCKHOLM—European e-tailer Dressmart.com AB is about to prove that a dot-com can start with a solid business model and modest aims but still go down in flames.

Struggling to avoid bankruptcy, Dressmart is expected to announce this week that it will be acquired by Swedish fashion retailer New Wave AB. New Wave would guarantee 25% of Dressmart's debt in return for full control of the e-tailer, according to Dressmart's court-appointed lawyer. The two companies are still negotiating how much New Wave will pay for Dressmart's database and Web technology as well as liabilities for salaries and possible severance packages.

Once a darling among investors, Dressmart was sucked into the market downdraft that earlier claimed Boo.com Group Ltd. and dozens of other dot-coms.

In retrospect, says Mathias Plank, one of the founders, Dressmart should have focused on its home market of Sweden until it became profitable and then ventured abroad. "But it's easy to be clever afterward," he says.

When Dressmart launched its Web site 16 months ago, investors couldn't throw enough money at the company's founders, two Swedish entrepreneurs in their 20s, Mr. Plank and Markus Larson. Their initial 10-minute presentation at a venture-capital forum yielded more than a dozen offers for meetings. The pair ultimately raised 20 million euros ($18.1 million at current exchange rates). The press wrote fawning stories as the online retailer of Thomas Pink shirts, Mulberry bags and Fila underwear expanded to eight European cities in 12 months. Comedian John Cleese commemorated the launch of the company's Norwegian Web site by cracking jokes and performing silly walks. Former Swedish prime minister Carl Bildt joined the board.

What went wrong?

The company eschewed small investments in hopes of landing a massive capital injection. It hired a chief executive with limited operational experience. It wasted time and money by launching showrooms at airports and by developing technological wizardry such as "plasma mirrors," designed to show online customers what they look like in certain articles of clothing. The company also set aside its own better judgment by following investor's advice to expand at warp speed.

Until this past spring, many venture capitalists and investors were handing out money to Internet entrepreneurs on one condition: Expand as fast as possible. The more international the start-up, the reasoning went, the higher the market value at the time of the initial public offering. So Dressmart and other European start-ups rushed to plant their flags from Helsinki to Rome. These days, electronic retailing and international expansion are out; caution is in. That requires many start-ups to shift gears from aggressive expansion to belt-tightening.

Dressmart's sale marks the end of a long entrepreneurial adventure for Messrs. Plank and Larsson. After meeting as university students in 1993, they opened a hot-dog stand, then moved on to selling textbooks. A few years later they came up with an idea to sell no-iron shirts via fax. As Europe's e-commerce climate began heating up, the pair's ambitions grew. Their original business model for Dressmart called for selling shirts (and only shirts) online in Sweden until the operation became profitable, then branching out to other European countries. That didn't go over well with investors. Although Messrs. Plank and Larsson were only looking to line up 200,000 euros in capital, investors urged them to think bigger.

So they tore up their original blueprint and agreed to expand across Europe. Executives from Merrill Lynch & Co. said it would be a snap to raise 15 million to 30 million euros. In the meantime, Dressmart's founders say, they had offers of nearly 20 million euros from others, but turned them away because they weren't blue chip investors. "We didn't have the experience in this field," says Mr. Plank, "so the board listened to our advisers, and so did we."

Dressmart launched itself in the United Kingdom, Germany and France. In March, Merrill Lynch produced just nine million euros—and a bill for $280,000. Even so, in March, Dressmart appointed Gwendolyn Carrie-McGuire, a Merrill executive who had led the team advising Dressmart, to be its chief executive and lead the company to its planned IPO. Then, virtually overnight in mid-April, Internet stocks plummeted worldwide. One week before Dressmart's scheduled auditor meeting for its IPO, Dressmart postponed the offering.

With no IPO money, Dressmart's original investors coughed up another five million euros to tide the company over while it approached some 30 traditional retailers and mail-order companies looking for strategic investors. By now, Dressmart was burning through a million euros a month. Discussions with a few large European retailers—including New Wave—dragged on without resolution. "Of course they were taking advantage of the situation," Mr. Plank says. "They understand what's going on. They read the papers. The longer they wait, the cheaper it gets."

New Wave officials refused to comment on specifics of the negotiation, but confirmed that they hoped to wrap up negotiations this week.

By the end of July, fearing bankruptcy and personal liability. Dressmart filed for court protection from its creditors. Ms. Carrie-McGuire resigned a few weeks ago as CEO. She was unavailable for comment.

The company is closing all of its operations outside Sweden. The remaining 55-person staff is likely to be fired today. Meanwhile, the founders say, business is booming. In July, Dressmart had its best month ever in Sweden, selling 220 orders in one day.

Efdex Misses a Meal or Two

By Polly Sprenger London

Efdex was business-to-business before business-to-business was cool. Back in 1995, founder Tim Carron Brown had an idea for an Internet-based exchange for the food and drink industry. He said the site would be up in three months.

But now, five years later, the idea has yet to bear fruit: After spending some $65 million, the company is struggling against being a good idea whose time never came.

According to Carron Brown, the company plans to launch in a few weeks. Even if it does, it will enter the market with a troubled recent history: Efdex missed payroll in April and May; petitions for payment are piling up in British county courts. And amid an uncertain future, some 30 staffers, out of more than 200 people employed in U.K. and Connecticut offices, have left in the last month.

The highest-profile departure was of Ellen Marram, Efdex's CEO. Marram, former CEO of PepsiCo's Tropicana unit and former executive at Nabisco, brought Efdex into the international spotlight and gave it credibility when she joined in August 1999. But Marram resigned abruptly May 18, just 10 months after she started, saying in a statement that the move was "by mutual agreement." Carron Brown declined to comment on her departure, citing a confidentiality agreement, and Marram did not return phone calls requesting comment.

Employees who haven't been paid for the months of April and May filed a motion with the local Employment Tribunal last week to remedy that situation. Efdex spokesman Mickey Mandelbaum said Thursday that all employees would be paid by 5 p.m. Friday. But when that hour rolled around, the employees still had not been paid. The company did not respond to repeated requests for comment.

The staff departures are not "a walkout en masse by any stretch," says Mandelbaum, "just the usual attrition rate." He adds that the departures "shouldn't have any effect on the investment." Indeed, last week Efdex said it received a round of interim financing to cover the company until it can close further financing, which Carron Brown estimates at $110 million.

Carron Brown acknowledges that "it has taken longer to build this business than we thought," but insists the payoff will be worth it. "In the so-called business-to-business arena, the entry ticket is going to be pretty high," he says. "But the sheer scale of what we're doing means it's a substantial and complicated task."

Efdex has been in development since 1994, when it was first conceived as an interactive trading platform—then called the Food and Drink Index—in which restaurants, supermarkets and suppliers all over the world could buy and sell foodstuffs.

Carron Brown envisioned a news and trading system where subscribers could watch prices rise and fall, and submit bids, similar to the financial markets. In addition, Efdex built a broadcasting studio, where it hopes to produce around-the-clock news aimed at specific segments of the market.

The service has been in beta testing since mid-1999, and Carron Brown says that when it goes live, some 2,000 customers will already be using the site.

But the project is stumbling, as its aspirations have failed so far to result in a working product. "Due to their level of funding and highly visible management team, they were well known, and I think people bought into their concept," says Mark Allen, a director of Food Distributors International, a trade association based in Falls Church, Va. "However, for whatever reason, they never managed to become operational. With so many entrants in the food service e-commerce space I think they were behind the ball."

Food Distributors is among the stiff competition Efdex faces. It recently hooked up with the Food Marketing Institute and IBM to launch a food exchange. And they are not alone; all told, there are at least nine b-to-b food exchanges, including Foodhunter.com, Foodbuy.com, Instill and others—most backed by leading industry and technology partners. The idea, once unique to Efdex, is now central to all its rivals: to serve the global food industry—estimated at $800 billion in North America alone—by cutting through the mind-numbing inefficiencies of buying, selling and transporting food.

Although the concept Efdex promotes is fairly straightforward, the company's history is not. It has gone by four monikers and is backed by 85 investors.

In its first incarnation, as the Food and Drink Index, the project was owned by Mondial Business Systems and funded by a reported $1.5 million investment from two well-known London advertising executives: Chris Ingram, head of CIA Group, and Richard Humphreys, the former CEO of Saatchi & Saatchi. Early in its development, Mondial needed a cash injection, and found it in the form of the Argyll and Isles Enterprise agency, a community investment project in Scotland.

Argyll and Isles was trying to reinvigorate the small town of Dunoon, Scotland. Mondial was one of the companies that stepped in to fill the void, accepting $620,000 in grant money from Argyll and Isles, and promising to bring some 150 jobs to Dunoon, a boon to the depressed area.

By April 1996, the company employed 60 people in Dunoon, and said it would soon expand the staff to nearly 100. At about the same time, Mondial renamed itself Channel 11, and the company was rebranded as a broadcaster of real-time broadband video that would provide 24-hour news for the food and drink industry.

Amid mounting debts, Channel 11 pulled out of Dunoon altogether in 1997. More than 20 employees took their case to an industrial tribunal after their final paychecks bounced. The tribunal found in favor of the employees, and eventually all were paid.

Today, after another name change from Channel 11 to Efdex, Carron Brown's company finds itself in similar straits. In addition to missing payroll, Efdex has apparently fallen behind on payments to creditors, with some debts dating back to 1997. County courts in Britain have received 23 petitions for payment on the company's unpaid bills; four were filed this May. Company spokesman Mandelbaum says the company has settled all its debts, but Britain's Registry of County Court Judgements shows no record of payment.

Carron Brown insists that all is well with Efdex, and investors will soon inject another $110 million into the company. He also says Efdex will appoint a new CEO soon.

Humphreys says that he sees "nothing untoward" happening at the company. "It's a work in progress," he says.

Atomic Pop's Final Encore

By Hane C. Lee

Late last month, an underground hip-hop act called Slum Village broke the Billboard 200 with next to no traditional marketing. But Atomic Pop, the label that had helped promote the group online and through legions of street teams, lay on its deathbed.

Launched in February 1999 by music-industry icon Al Teller, Atomic Pop billed itself as "the 21st century music company." With an emphasis on digital distribution and an unheard of 50-50 royalties ratio, the online record label set out to revolutionize the music industry. But the revolution didn't pan out. Last week, Atomic Pop quietly shut its doors.

On the surface, the digital-music startup simply went looking for money at the worst time. The legal war over copyrights has made online music a particularly vexing business to be in. Consider the case of Scour, a multimedia search engine that is being sued by a battalion of copyright owners: It recently laid off three-quarters of its staff, citing an inability to attract funding because of projected legal costs.

But that's only part of the story. Despite its grand ambitions, Atomic Pop never managed to gain momentum with consumers, failing to register on either Media Metrix or Nielsen NetRatings traffic measurements since it launched. And Atomic Pop insiders, many of whom spoke on condition of anonymity, reveal that confusion surrounding the company's business model and direction, as well as management deficiencies, contributed as much to its demise as the market's general disillusionment with online content plays.

Teller, the Internet-savvy recording-industry veteran who aimed to put control back into artists' hands and build virtual communities of fans on the Web, has stumbled before. After being ousted from his chief executive post at MCA Music Entertainment in 1995, Teller started up a small independent label, Red Ant, which he later merged with Alliance Entertainment. As co-chair and CEO, Teller hoped to turn Alliance from a wholesale record distributor into a major music force alongside the majors. But the company wound up in Chapter 11. Teller did not respond to repeated requests for an interview.

Like Alliance's ill-fated attempt to expand, some say Atomic Pop spread itself too thin. Chuck D, the first big-name artist to sign on with Atomic Pop in April 1999, says the company lost its focus along the way. "It got convoluted," he says.

Two years ago, Chuck D rocked the music industry when he posted MP3 remixes of the Public Enemy anthem "Bring the Noise" on the rap group's Web site. Under threat of a lawsuit by the rappers' longtime label Def Jam, Public Enemy removed the MP3 files, but severed ties with Def Jam soon after. After signing with Atomic Pop, Public Enemy became the first band to offer a full album as an online digital download prior to a record-store release. (Earlier ventures like N2K's Digital Artists label, which was dismantled after the company merged with CDnow in early '99, experimented with digital downloads that coincided with release dates.) "We made history together," notes Chuck D.

But Atomic Pop was overly ambitions, Chuck D says, and though shifting business models is not unusual in the Internet Economy, it can become a problem. "The 'dot-bomb' climate made it difficult to support all those ancillary areas (the company) was dealing with," he says.

To be fair, Atomic Pop never intended to be just a Web record company. "People targeted the label when Chuck D became a spokesperson," says one former employee. "But it always meant to be much more than that."

With original editorial content, videogames, streaming video, online radio and a store that sold not just music but nail polish and comic books, Atomic Pop aimed to be "a one-stop jump-off point for a music-centric pop culture convergence," according to its Web site, which at press time was still up. Last fall, investors bit. Web services shop Rare Medium and New Valley— which owns investment-banking firm Ladenburg Thalmann & Co.—sank $10 million into the startup. (Rare Medium executives didn't return calls, and New Valley officials declined to comment.)

Despite other offerings, sources within the company say that the Atomic Pop label generated the bulk of the company's revenues—"a few million bucks," according to one former employee. But the company did little to develop other reliable sources of income, he says; e-commerce revenues were negligible, and there is no advertising whatsoever on the site.

Furthermore, projects like Web site development for bands not signed to Teller's label, such as a site created for the Smashing Pumpkins, diverted resources away from Atomic Pop's own bands like Flashpoint, which signed with the label just prior to embarking on Ozzy Osborne's Ozzfest tour last summer. At the time, Teller hoped Flashpoint would be the first band to break online. "The Web offers an avenue to begin the process of awareness for an artist, so that when we take it to the marketplace, there's a story to tell," he said in an interview last year.

The story didn't end happily. "I must have heard about four different marketing plans," says Flashpoint frontman Ollie Luttgenau of his album.

"Each time it came down to, 'The funds aren't there.'" He adds that the record release got pushed back three or four times.

Compounding Atomic Pop's lack of financial commitment to its core product, notes Luttgenau, was poor communication.

Others echo that sentiment. "There were mixed messages from one week to the next," says a former staffer. "The management was dreadful."

In the end, Atomic Pop's upper-level managers were honest about the company's difficulties in raising money. "They let us know we could look for other jobs, but that hanging around could be fruitful in the end," says one ex-employee. "They did everything they could to keep our confidence up."

On top of the record industry's legal war against some of the Web's best-known music sites, the demise of Atomic Pop seems just the latest sign that the balance of power still rests decidedly with the Big Five record labels. "People underestimated how difficult it is to market and promote music," says one music-industry insider who requested anonymity. "Selling records is a hard job, and just because you're doing it via the Internet doesn't mean you don't have the same challenges."

Others in the industry agree. "A lot of people in this space are scrambling, trying to retrofit their business in this new economy," says Andy Schuon, president of Farmclub.com, the online music company started by Interscope co-chairman Jimmy Iovine and Universal's chairman and CEO Doug Morris (who replaced Teller at MCA). "I wouldn't want to just do an online label," says Schuon. "I don't think that would be a smart business." Though Farmclub touts a "convergence play" with its cable TV show, the site's biggest advantage over a company like Atomic Pop is the fact that it's fully funded by heavy-hitter label Universal Music Group.

It's unclear what will happen to Atomic Pop's contracts with Flashpoint and with other bands, including the Gas Giants and Slum Village, or to its distribution deals with labels Goodvibe, RuffLife, 4AD and others. In a tersely worded statement, the company said it "has undertaken a major restructuring of Atomic Pop's business. Atomic Pop presently plans to continue operations with a significantly reduced overhead." No further comment was offered.

Looking to the future, Chuck D hopes to merge his Atomic Pop properties, including online hip-hop radio station Bringthenoise.com, which he says Atomic Pop never finished purchasing, into his Rapstation.com site. He also plans to launch his own online record label in the next month.

"Pioneers always get kicked in the ass," the rapper says. "Atomic Pop as a music label is still a fine blueprint to copy after some the kinks are worked out."

Pop.com Goes Poof

By Laura Rich, Los Angeles

Pop.com arrived on the online entertainment scene with the kind of buzz that only accompanies the mention of Hollywood's highest-voltage names, in this case Steven Spielberg, David Geffen and Ron Howard. Since they unveiled their joint venture last fall, everyone has been waiting to see how these giants of the big screen would bring their magic to the Internet.

The wait is over. And as it turns out, the moguls better hang on to their day jobs. They proved to be as clueless about what works in the digital entertainment realm as everybody else—or maybe a little more so.

Pop.com fizzled out for good last week, after never even launching the site. After a late-hour effort to merge with iFilm fell through, most of the staff was let go. This despite springing to life last fall with great fanfare and, seemingly, with every advantage needed to make a successful play where others have fallen short. As a melding of DreamWorks SKG (Spielberg, Geffen and Jeffrey Katzenberg) and Imagine Entertainment (Howard and director Brian Grazer), Pop.com looked certain to enjoy access to talent and ideas, and to benefit from the clout of its principal partners in cutting content deals.

Instead, with Pop's failure to launch—and coincidental layoffs at Shock-wave.com and Scour—the question of how to survive as a viable online entertainment site looms larger and more unanswered than ever.

Pop's big idea sounded an awful lot like ordinary TV or film shrink-fitted for Net audiences. Its broad mission was to offer online shorts, episodic programming, interactive games and video on demand. And the parent companies picked a management team with no Internet experience. Led by CEO Ken Wong, former head of Disney Imagineering, Pop's leadership never nailed down a specific business model for making money with content.

Sources say Pop was aggressive in trying to cut deals but drove away potential content providers by pushing for total ownership of content created. Most entertainment dot-coms tend to share ownership, if not let creators have it outright, as Shockwave did with *South Park* makers Matt Stone and Trey Parker. "Their failure to cut people in led to their demise," says one entertainment lawyer.

Other sources also report that working with Pop was not the collaborative process that many on the content side of online entertainment prefer. Too many meetings were required for decisions, and decisions were often made unilaterally. "They would submit concepts to us that were exactly what we'd told them we didn't want to do," says one content producer. "And the scripts were really bad."

Pop's explanation for what went wrong is that, after months of gearing up, they decided that Net users just aren't ready to support an original entertainment site. "We believe this space is not yet a business," says Wong. "We're not clairvoyants, but we think it's going to take years." They were looking to sell the company rather than fold it; the iFilm deal fell apart over Pop's valuation.

A core staff of about a dozen will remain to determine the next stage, if any, for Pop's content library and other assets.

Although Pop made mistakes, the reality may be that there aren't enough consumers of online entertainment to support all the purveyors. Small audiences mean small ad revenues. But it's still early, says Frank Biondi, the former head of HBO who runs the venture firm Waterview Partners in Los Angeles. In the big picture, he says, the loss of Pop may be "a nonevent."

He recalls the launch of HBO. "Does the *Pennsylvania Polka Festival* mean anything to you? It was the first original HBO program, 27 years ago," he says. Online entertainment probably won't take 27 years to become a booming business, "But it probably won't take seven months, either."

Broken Wing

By Megan Barnett

When WingspanBank.com launched last June, it had all the ingredients for success. It was an Internet-only bank but it had access to the deep pockets of its parent, First USA, the large credit card company owned by financial conglomerate Bank One. It had an aggressive champion in First USA's president, Richard Vague, who acted more like an Internet entrepreneur than a traditional banking executive. It had access to scores of banking and technical professionals from Bank One and First USA. And it had an estimated $35 million advertising campaign, designed to establish Wingspan as a leader in a market that had no clear leader.

Less than a year later, the prospects for Wingspan's success look significantly more dubious. Shortly after Wingspan's launch, Bank One announced that First USA was losing customers (it lost 8 million in the first quarter of this year), a revelation that led to a $500 million shortfall in Bank One's earnings for 1999.

Vague left in October, followed by Wingspan CEO James Stewart in November and Bank One CEO John McCoy in December. All three resigned amid internal strife and finger-pointing after First USA's astonishing shortfall. Two of the five other First USA executives who were handpicked to spearhead the launch of Wingspan departed to join independent dot-coms.

Advertising for Wingspan decelerated to a crawl, though the bank insists the slowdown was planned and unrelated to its parent's financial troubles. But then in March came the news that Bank One had hired Morgan Stanley to explore the possibility of selling Wingspan. And last month Bank One announced that its first-quarter earnings fell 67 percent. Losses in First USA's credit card business were primarily to blame, but officials fingered Wingspan as a contributor.

The story of Wingspan is a wake-up call, not only for the banking industry but also for any corporation that thinks it can fashion a nimble Internet presence from the cloth of legacy systems and bureaucratic red tape. Wingspan did a lot of things right. It was aggressive and fast to market, launching exactly 123 days after the concept was formed. It also had plenty of capital: Bank One said it would spend as much as $150 million on the venture in its first 12 months.

Now it looks as if all the cash and flash have been for naught. Bank One may have broken the mold in launching Wingspan, but it has learned that perhaps not all molds are meant to be broken.

Bill Wallace had led First USA's systems development for five years when he got a call from Vague in January 1999. Vague told Wallace that he needed a project manager with development expertise who could put together a team and launch an online bank in 60 days.

Wallace remembers that Vague and McCoy had spent time examining potential competitive threats to their financial-services business. They visited executives from Internet firms including Yahoo and Amazon.com to learn the intricacies of Internet businesses and to try to understand the new strategies driving them.

"They realized that the biggest competitive threat to the existing Bank One business could well be a startup capable of creating better customer service," says Wallace, now executive VP and CIO for Wingspan. "The majority of people in the U.S. are disenfranchised with the banking industry. They decided that maybe the time was right to create a new brand."

Wallace decided to take on the challenge, and Project Bluehen, as Wingspan was called back then, was born. Wallace and four of his First USA colleagues set up shop on the top floor of the train station next to First USA's office tower in Wilmington, Del. The office layout was meant to resemble that of a typical Net startup, complete with purple furniture and a Foosball table.

The goal was to create an Internet-based financial-services store featuring levels of customer service far higher than traditional banks could offer. The online bank would have traditional checking and money-market accounts, credit cards and brokerage services. It would partner with other companies to offer loans, insurance and bill-payment services. Customers would be able to apply online for accounts and loans with a single applications and access all areas of the financial supermarket with a single logon name and password.

By mid-February 1999 the launch team was in place. At an "immersion meeting" on Feb. 11, the group—which had now grown to 100—met for the first time. Participants included employees of First USA, Bank One and the iBank, as Wingspan was then being called internally, as well as representatives from content partners like E-Loan and InsWeb, and technology partners including Sanchez, Edify and USWeb/CKS. Wallace explained the site's product strategy and architectural outline. He then told the group they needed to make it happen in 90 days, tacking an extra month onto Vague's original time line of 60 days. Wallace knew 90 days would be a challenge, 60 days flat-out impossible.

"It was really an electrically charged environment," remembers Chip Weldon, senior VP of interface engineering and a member of the founding team. "We really made sure the vendors had a sense of urgency."

By April 8, iBank went into test. In early May the team shared the password-protected URL with friends, family and 500 people across Bank One. The advertising agency prepared to shoot television commercials before the company had a name; the actors rehearsed using the name iBank.

Executives didn't settle on the WingspanBank name until just before the launch—and not without some disagreement. The name is meant to sound new and different, and independent of a traditional bank. The shortened version, Wingspan, was what the executives had hoped for, but focus groups revealed customers would place more trust in it if the name included the word "bank." As the brand gained momentum, management decided, the word "bank" would gradually be phased out.

On June 24 the company's high-profile launch featured actor Jason Alexander, *Seinfeld*'s George, handing out $100 bills to people named Bill on the streets of New York. WingspanBank was born.

The Wingspan launch sent ripples through the banking industry. While nearly everyone agreed that the masses would eventually accept online banking, Bank One's aggressive move sparked a debate about the delivery of those services. Would consumers leave trusted brand names for better rates at online startups? Or would the offline behemoths retain their customers with online services at traditional rates? Chicago-based Bank One, which kept its original BankOne.com site even as it helped launch Wingspan, was clearly hedging its bets.

"Wingspan is a value proposition that appeals to the Netizen, the person for whom the Net is a way of life," says Bruce Luecke, executive VP of Bank One's retail group. "It has given Bank One a good opportunity to find out customers' willingness to accept that model."

It seemed a wise strategy. Most of the 9 million Americans banking online today do so through online outposts of brick-and-mortar. Internet startups such as Telebank (now E-Trade Bank), NetBank, Compubank and Wingspan have, in aggregate, attracted under a million customers.

Competitors took notice of Bank One's aggressive move, nevertheless. "I was impressed with the splash that Wingspan made," says Jim Jones, president of direct banking for Bank of America. "I think there is some population of customers that will want that niche solution, but we don't think that's the bulk of the marketplace." Jones says Bank of America never considered setting up a separate enterprise with a different brand like Wingspan.

Last summer some analysts speculated that BankOne.com could eventually be rolled into Wingspan. Now it appears the opposite is more likely. Wingspan had attracted 144,000 customer accounts as of March 31. BankOne.com has 500,000 active customers and Luecke says it's adding 35,000 per month.

"Bank One is finding that the market is not ready for a Net Bank that can capture the primary share of the market," says Gary Craft, a research analyst covering e-finance for Deutsche Banc Alex. Brown. "It's hard to make a buck on a purely Internet-based model."

Not all of Wingspan's struggle to attract customers can be attributed to external factors. While it markets itself as a one-stop shop, Wingspan actually outsources most of the services it offers. If a customer wants a car loan, for instance, Wingspan sends him to E-Loan instead of originating the loan itself.

"Wingspan's problems are in its strategy," say Rory Brown, CEO of online upstart Virtual Bank, which plans to attract customers through partnerships with high-tech companies that will cobrand the bank and offer it to employees. "By outsourcing everything they're actually paying money (in advertising) to attract customers and then they're sending them to someone else."

Wingspan gets referral fees from its content partners such as InsWeb and E-Loan for the customers it sends to them. While officials won't disclose the fees they receive, they no doubt amount to less than what the company would make from the customer if Wingspan originated the loan or insurance policy.

The bank has fought internal battles as well. While it succeeded in creating a startup atmosphere, it didn't offer employees lucrative startup stock options. As a wholly owned subsidiary of Bank One, Wingspan granted its employees Bank One stock options.

"The one fundamental, strategic flaw within the company was that it couldn't offer the equity opportunity that most dot-coms do," says one former employee of Wingspan who left to join a Net company and, like several other sources, asked to remain anonymous. "They tried to placate us, but when we asked about the possibility of Wingspan being spun out from Bank One in the future, we got very vague answers."

Wingspan executives insist that the lack of equity opportunities hasn't been an issue. "We've created a separate, unique culture here," says Wingspan President Michael Cleary, who joined shortly after the bank's launch last summer. "People love working here. There is a steep learning curve and people really enjoy it."

During the bank's development days, a lot of Bank One and First USA employees were interested in joining the Wingspan project. But the defections, and the attention paid to the new Net-only bank by the parent bank, left some

Bank One employees bitter. Now there's a certain animosity between the two groups. "Before launch Dick (Vague) was very aggressive about us having a good interaction with BankOne.com," says one former Wingspan employee. "We all played the game; we tried to look like team players."

Executives from Wingspan and from Bank One's Columbus, Ohio-based Internet team insist the relationship between the two groups is one of "competitive friendliness." The groups hold a conference call every other week to discuss progress. They share marketing experiences and exchange results from successful and disastrous campaigns. But they explicitly avoid discussing pricing strategies and new product developments.

Talk with executives on both sides, however, and it's clear which team they're on. Bank One's Luecke says Wingspan is a great test case, but "we've learned that having some level of physical distribution is still important to most customers."

Wingspan executives see things a little differently. In most of the rankings of online banks conducted by market-research firms, Wingspan consistently ranks higher than Bank One. Gomez Advisors recently ranked Wingspan second overall and Bank One 11th. The rankings are pasted to the office door of Kevin Watters, Wingspan's senior VP of marketing, and it's one of the first things he points out to visitors.

For now, Wingspan is plugging away. It has moved its operations from the train station to First USA's headquarters. The company has developed three new television spots, which it began rolling out in March. The campaign is more targeted than the earlier broad effort; it is aimed at women between the ages of 25 and 49.

Beneath the surface, however, there's still turmoil. Since the departure of Stewart in November, Wingspan has been operating under the direction of Cleary, its president, and First USA CEO William Boardman, who is leading First USA through a turnaround period. The heroes behind the aggressive launch of Wingspan last year are no longer there to lobby for the bank.

McCoy left Bank One amid intense internal politicking. He led the acquisition of First USA in 1997 with the promise that it would not interfere with Bank One's operations.

Vague and Stewart were longtime compatriots and, according to employees of Wingspan, they were regarded as a team at the helm of the Wingspan ship. One former Wingspan employee said there was widespread speculation that Vague and Stewart saw the First USA troubles coming before Bank One did, but some workers hoped Wingspan's success would negate First USA's problems. "If we're going down, we're going down swinging," Vague said to the troops, according to the employee.

Vague and Stewart are together again, this time for the launch of a financial-services startup called DryRock. They declined to comment for this story.

Wingspan may soon have leaders to replace them. In March, James
Dimon, former president of Citigroup, was named CEO of Bank One. In an
interview just after he started, Dimon said Wingspan "is a pretty high-quality
effort. In its own marketplace it's been quite successful."

Interestingly, Citibank, which is part of Citigroup's financial-services
empire, just launched its own version of Wingspan. Citi f/i, as it's called, is an
Internet-only bank with competitive rates that does not entitle its customers to
access Citibank's physical branches. The company quietly opened the site last
November and has done only one targeted advertising campaign for it, in Austin, Texas. Citibank spokesman Mark Rodgers says the company hasn't planned
mass marketing around the site, but he denies that the site is merely a test.

It's not clear who would make a likely suitor for the struggling Wingspan, if it is indeed on the block. One insider says there have been rumors of
interest from buyout firms and from financial-services firms that don't already
have a banking business. Another source says Stewart and Vague made several
attempts but Bank One would not entertain their offers.

One former employee who remains close to members of the Wingspan
executive team says many insiders are hoping for a sale. The employee says
First USA granted attractive retention packages to a handful of executives at
Wingspan, packages they will reap in the event of a sale. Some employees who
haven't been given packages hope Wingspan's savior will be a company with
more attractive equity options. A Wingspan spokeswoman declined to comment on whether the packages had been granted.

"There has been a lot of holding out for that opportunity," the former
employee says. "If they don't get it, I think you'll see a mass flood of people
(leaving)."

It would be a bittersweet end to the dream. When Bill Wallace headed up
systems development at First USA, he grew his team from eight to 500. He
says he saw Wingspan as an opportunity for him to return to technology
development. "I wanted that feeling like I was in a startup."

What he may not have taken into consideration is that not all startups
survive.

Apocryphal note regarding Wingspan—

A useful motto to remember in the computing failure world is "where there's smoke, there's fire." Translated into more specific words, what that means, I have found, is that if a company is floundering and flirting with bankruptcy or some other form of failure, the odds are it's not going to make it.

In our immediately preceding story, Wingspan was facing an "uncertain future." That was then (May 15, 2000), this is now. In the September 25, 2000, issue of *Computerworld*, an article resolved that uncertainty, announcing that "Bank One Corp.'s WingspanBank.com . . . will be downgraded to a test lab because it didn't attract enough customers." What does "test lab" mean? The article goes on to say that it will be "a pilot program in which Wingspan customers can open their accounts at Bank One branches." Ouch. That's about as close to total failure for an online bank as you can get.

The article concludes by quoting an analyst who said "The failure of Wingspan was [the result of] the expectations of the parent company . . . [they] weren't realistic."

Why Pandesic Didn't Pan Out

By Eric Young

Pandesic was a company that should have succeeded.

Consider where it came from. Launched in 1997, Pandesic was a joint venture of microchip king Intel and German software giant SAP. The two parents put in an initial investment of $50 million total, a nice start for Pandesic as it set out to develop its business helping other companies build and run their e-commerce operations.

Pandesic's target market, moreover, appeared vast. Hundreds of companies were clamoring for e-commerce services to establish virtual storefronts.

At Pandesic's launch, its corporate parents crowed about how their own prowess would aid their new creation.

"Intel and SAP excel at business process expertise, global presence and logistical know-how," and Intel President Craig Barrett, a Pandesic board member. "The combination of these capabilities gives Pandesic the potential to make a significant impact on electronic commerce."

But Pandesic never fulfilled its promise. On July 28 the company announced in a statement it was shutting down because it couldn't find "a timely road to profitability due to slower than anticipated market acceptance of business-to-consumer e-commerce solutions."

Nearly all of Pandesic's 400 employees have been fired, and the company is closing its Sunnyvale, Calif., headquarters and its offices in the U.K. and Japan. A handful of staffers will stick around to help customers find new e-commerce service providers.

Pandesic executives, as well as board members from Intel and SAP, declined to comment for this story.

Analysts and Pandesic sources suggest that the company's failure was due in part to the parent companies' remote management styles. Although executives from Intel and SAP occupied all six Pandesic board seats, the founding companies did not actively steer potential clients to Pandesic.

"Intel and SAP were very hands off. In fact, we were trying to figure out how to leverage those partnerships," says Aaron Ross, a Pandesic product manager for two years before quitting to become CEO of LeaseExchange, an equipment-leasing marketplace. "I know they had board meetings but they (Intel and SAP) did not help us get customers."

Meanwhile, despite a pile of cash from its creators, Pandesic lacked the agility required to adapt to the constantly changing Internet commerce landscape. The company had trouble nailing down its target market. It started by looking at SAP's customer base, hoping to sell to them. But Pandesic found that SAPs customers—mostly large corporations such as German chemical conglomerate BASF and French consumer-goods giant Danone—weren't interested in the consumer-oriented services that Pandesic offered.

Pandesic then came around to targeting small retail companies and startups, as well as Fortune 500 companies.

"We had this tremendous amount of money," says John Vincze, who left SAP to become director of sales channels at Pandesic and is now with software firm Vignette. "When you have that much money . . . if you're a little off track you don't worry about it."

Compounding Pandesic's woes was its revenue model. Unlike most of its competitors, Pandesic kept between 1 percent and 6 percent of sales flowing through its customers' sites. (That percentage later was set at 2 percent.) This fee structure turned off some large potential customers who failed to see why they should give up any revenue.

"I don't know if they anticipated that," says Dan Frank, VP of marketing and business development for BigTray, a restaurant-equipment seller and current Pandesic customer. For weeks before Pandesic's closure announcement, BigTray was looking for alternatives to the e-commerce service provider because of the transaction fee. "Maybe they thought people would be hooked and would not migrate off" the Pandesic service, Frank suggests. "As soon as anyone gets to be of reasonable size, they are not going to pay that."

Pandesic has about 100 customers—including athletic-wear maker Adidas, the San Francisco Giants, beauty-supply retailer Beautyjungle.com, clothier OshKosh B'Gosh, Net wineseller eVineyard and Children's Place, which sells kids clothes and toys. But none of those firms is considered a marquee e-commerce name.

Pandesic was launched at a heady time in the short history of e-commerce. Hundreds of companies began looking to the Net as a way to increase revenue. Intel and SAP saw Pandesic as a way to cash in on the phenomenon.

Some of the earliest plans for the company came in 1996 from Ed Harley, an Intel consultant, and Harold Hughes, Intel's VP of planning and logistics. They approached SAP, which had recently rolled out its business process software within Intel. SAP saw Pandesic as an avenue to get its software package, R3, installed in more businesses. Intel saw the venture as a way to expand sales of servers running on Intel-made chips.

Harley became Pandesic's COO and Hughes its chairman. Bryan Plug, executive VP of SAP America was named president and CEO.

Pandesic began slowly. By April 1998, its biggest customers—the names trotted out to attract new business—included the San Jose Symphony Orchestra and Koshergrocer.com. During that month, Plug quit, reportedly in a dispute over strategy. Hughes stepped in as CEO. Pete Wolcott, another Intel veteran, was named president.

In the two years since then, the company was able to attract more business. But although Pandesic never released financial information, it's clear that its customer base couldn't support the business.

While it was widely known that Pandesic was not profitable, the company gave no outward sign that it was on the verge of folding. On July 12, about two weeks before the news that it was shutting its doors, Pandesic announced a deal with PricewaterhouseCoopers that both companies said would generate $1 billion in sales over three years.

That wasn't enough, however, to save the company.

Pandesic's customers were caught off guard with news of the company's shutdown, leaving many scrambling to find a new way to power their e-commerce sales in time for the all-important holiday season. "I was totally surprised by the news because Pandesic has been instrumental in our growth," says Victoria Piper, CIO of Express.com, a seller of DVDs and a Pandesic customer since 1998. "There were no clues whatsoever."" Express.com is now looking at a variety of e-commerce service providers, including IBM.

Piper says Express.com was originally drawn to Pandesic because of the company's pedigree. "We went with them because of the strength of Intel and SAP," she says.

Pandesic says it will keep customers' sites running until January.

For Intel and SAP, the failed venture won't hit them hard on the bottom line. Consistent with their behavior, the companies have already begun to distance themselves from the venture.

"Pandesic's problems were their own. It was their business plan," says SAP spokesman Tom Holub.

But the venture is a reality check about the difficulties of making e-commerce pay off. Pandesic's service let businesses execute many complex tasks, including real-time inventory management, transactions, shipping and returns.

But well-known parents and plenty of cash aren't the only keys to success.

After a Life at Warp Speed, Netscape Logs Off

By Kara Swisher
Staff Reporter of The Wall Street Journal

In the end, the company that pioneered the concept of operating at the dizzying speed of Internet time rose and sold out in Internet time too.

Netscape Communications Corp. had been the fastest growing software company of all time, shooting from a start-up in 1994 to more than a half billion dollars in revenues three years later. But within a year after that, Netscape was forced into America Online Inc.'s arms by a withering assault from Microsoft Corp., which battered Netscape's profits, and the growing need for heft in the expanding world of the Web.

"It's probably the fastest learning experience I have ever had," says James Barksdale, who became Netscape's chief executive after a career in cellular phones and overnight mail. "It's absolutely been the wildest ride."

He added, "The real point is that we have built one hell of a company, with $4 billion in value in 39 months, and you can't say that about a lot of others."

But he says the end of an independent Netscape may have been ordained by the evolution of the Internet. "I think all industries, as they mature, consolidate," he says. "AOL has done an amazing job in building something nobody thought they could. Over time, we've become bigger and bigger fans of them."

Mr. Barksdale goes out on a high note. Netscape yesterday reported a gain in revenue for its fourth quarter ended Oct. 31 to $162 million from $152 million in the quarter ended Sept. 30 a year earlier. (Netscape changed from a calendar year to a fiscal year in 1998.) Although net income fell to $2.7 million, or three cents a diluted share, from $10.2 million, or 10 cents a share, he had managed to recover from disastrous losses earlier in the year.

He is also a wealthy new AOL shareholder. He opted during Netscape's hard times this year to give back a block of stock options and took just $1 in salary, but still holds 5.1 million Netscape shares now valued at $209.7 million in AOL shares.

Netscape co-founder James Clark is the biggest winner in the transaction. He holds 14.4 million Netscape shares, which would be converted into AOL stock worth $592.1 million at yesterday's close. Marc Andreessen, another early pioneer who has 745,000 shares of stock and 1.5 million options, would hold AOL stock worth $92.3 million.

In the early days, it looked as if Netscape, not AOL, would be the reigning king of the Internet. The company was founded in 1994 by Mr. Clark, the canny computer mogul who had previously started Silcon Graphics Inc., the big workstation maker. He persuaded Mr. Andreessen, then a graduate student at the University of Illinois, to turn some early work on graphical ways to navigate the Internet into the first commercial browser.

At the time, two notable students at Stanford University, David Filo and Jerry Yang, were starting a company called Yahoo! Inc. They held on to huge chunks of equity that eventually made them billionaires. But Mr. Andreessen agreed to join Mr. Clark for a stake that amounted to a mere one million shares, or 2.7% of the stock, at the initial public offering in August 1995.

It was a fair amount, Mr. Andreessen said yesterday in an interview, because Mr. Clark was providing all of the funding. "He put it together," Mr. Andreessen said. "He bet his own money on a motley crew of college students."

Netscape's tactic of giving the initial browser away for free, and then charging for it later, resulted in stunning growth.

Within six months, millions of copies of the browser were downloaded by Internet users, many of them new to the medium. For that feat alone, Netscape will always remain an icon of the digital age. It is to the Internet what Apple Computer Inc. is to the personal computer—a start-up that through innovation turned a hobby into a major global industry.

That early success turned Netscape's unruly bunch of young hackers into something of a religious cult, with some related hubris. A position at Netscape become the most desired job in the software world, "cooler" even than a job at Microsoft. The company was besieged with 5,000 to 7,000 resumes a month. A personnel manager, Margie Mader, printed up business cards identifying her as "Director of Bringing in Really Cool People."

Mr. Barksdale, then 51, was brought in to provide some adult supervision. As a chief operating officer, he had helped build both McCaw Cellular and Federal Express Corp. into multibillion-dollar companies. He was able to disarm the programmers with his folksy toughness. ("If I tell people chickens can pull trains," he once told McCaw staffers, "it's their job to hook 'em up!"). At the same time, he led the effort to sell increasingly complicated Internet software to major corporations such as Citicorp and Ford Motor Corp.

His pitch combined a detailed analysis of how Netscape's software was cheaper than Microsoft's "free" browser (because it didn't require Microsoft's other expensive products) with a cunning appeal to customers to keep Microsoft under control by supporting an alternative.

But it didn't work. By the end of 1997, Mr. Barksdale had a new job, keeping Netscape alive as Microsoft's tactics of giving away its browser, bundling it with its dominant operating system and cutting exclusive deals with big Internet service providers cut Netscape's browser share by nearly half. Just after New Year's Day, the company announced $82.3 million in losses, and plans to cut 500 of its staff.

Microsoft's tactics would lead to an antitrust complaint by the Department of Justice, currently being tried in Washington, D.C. Mr. Barksdale responded strategically by giving away his browser as well, moving Netscape into two new businesses. He developed the home page for its browser into a major "portal," or destination point for the Internet. And he focused on building electronic-commerce software for corporations.

He also kept his humor. When he was asked what he planned to dress up as at the company's Halloween party, he replied, "A witness for the U.S. Department of Justice" against Microsoft. With a whoop of laughter, he asked "How do you think I'd do?"

Mr. Barksdale doesn't really consider Microsoft a laughing matter. The government's first witness at the trial, he said yesterday "I certainly found out what it was like to compete with a monopoly with its predatory ways." But he doesn't solely blame Microsoft for Netscape's struggles.

"This Internet is the fastest moving medium of all time and it has been a challenge to change with it," he concedes. Indeed, he has been criticized for waiting too long to give away Netscape's browser, turning down help from AOL and forging an ill-timed shift to networking software for messaging and workplace collaboration rather than moving more quickly to electronic-commerce.

Mr. Barksdale says he will join the AOL board, overseeing the integration of the two companies and helping them deal with corporate customers.

CEO: Partnership Hurt Toysmart

By Julia King
Palm Desert, Calif.

Bad timing and a poor choice of partners are what ultimately killed Toys-mart.com Inc., not so long ago a darling in the crowded and highly competitive online toy market.

"It seemed like we had it all," said Toysmart CEO David Lord, ticking off a list of once-shining assets during a highly emotional keynote presentation at last week's *Computerworld* Premier 100 IT Leaders conference here.

Those assets included an enviable partnership with The Walt Disney Co., the indisputable king of the U.S. family consumer market; a spanking-new 126,000-square-foot fulfillment center; and a top-notch Internet development team that built from scratch a state-of-the-art Web site that was ranked in the top 40 by both Nielsen Corp. and MediaMetrix.

But it still wasn't enough.

On Friday, May 19, Disney, which last August invested more than $50 million and took a 60% stake in the Waltham, Mass-based toy retailer, pulled the plug on it all, leaving 200 employees out of jobs. The company's inventory and physical assets, including a fully integrated Web site infrastructure, is on the auction block, and both Lord and CIO John Puckett are visibly and abjectly heartsick.

"Everything we poured out hearts into for the past three and one-half years is gone," Lord said.

The biggest lessons learned, according to both executives, are first that you must choose your partners wisely, and second, that it's all about timing.

"I think timing killed us," Lord said. "We could have gotten an IPO and have been secure [financially] if timing hadn't killed us." For example, Lord said, Disney and Toysmart—which went online in 1997, after spinning off from the Holt Co., a maker of educational products whose CIO was Lord—agreed to their partnership in May 1999. But is wasn't until August that Disney announced the deal and Toysmart saw any money.

"We couldn't get product because we didn't have the cash yet, and we had to delay our marketing spending, which meant losing our chance to convert customers in the pre-Christmas buying season," Lord said.

Disney officials didn't return calls by press time.

Culture Clash

There also was a major culture clash with Disney, which languished far longer over business decisions and operated much more bureaucratically than its faster and nimbler dot-com partner.

Case in point: It took Disney until January 2000—after the end of the crucial holiday retail season—to approve the sale of Disney books on Toysmart.com, which was supposed to be its official online bookseller. Disney baby items didn't make it to the Toysmart.com Web site until February, again too late to cash in on the Christmas shopping rush.

"We were on very different timetables. We wanted to make decisions the next day vs. the next month," Lord said.

In late 1999, Disney decided to switch its Internet focus away from toys to leisure and entertainment. That, coupled with Wall Street's steady souring on dot-coms, particularly electronic retailers, made an early 2000 initial public offering (IPO) out of the question.

"Any one of these things might have been easy to overcome, but combine them all and no one can overcome them," Lord said.

Carol Ferrara, an analyst at Gartner Group Inc. in Stamford, Conn., said she expects to see more failed ventures between traditional companies like Disney and their quicker dot-com partners.

Smaller Internet companies "need to carefully consider who they're going to be with," Ferrara said. Big retail companies think a lot differently than pure-play electronic retailers, she noted.

"Traditional retailers are very focused on the bottom line and inventory turns, and we don't see as much of that in the virtual retail space," she said. "A lot of these virtual companies are technologists rather than merchants and lack the understanding of what it takes to succeed in the toy market and in retail generally." Other examples she cited include Boo.com, Violet.com, and some of the recently shuttered online pet stores.

Still, Puckett, who came to Toysmart from GTE Internet working last August, said he wouldn't change a minute.

"It was painful, with incredible highs and lows. But I learned more in the last year than I learned in 10 years in corporate America." Puckett said.

Five weeks after Disney pulled the plug, more than 90% of Toysmart's 200 employees have new jobs, many at other dot-coms.

"The first day [after the shutdown announcement], we had 250 companies call and try to hire our employees," Lord said. "We've had calls from companies wanting our entire systems department."

In fact, Lord said, about 75% of Toysmart's Web team went to Core Change Inc., a Boston-based Internet services firm.

Lord and Puckett have also had hundreds of telephone calls from potential employers. Neither has decided what to do.

But there's one place you probably won't find Lord.

"I don't think I'll stay in the toy business," he said. "I don't think I'm that much of a glutton for punishment."

Interval: The Think Tank That Tanked

(How Paul Allen's Dream of Inventing the Future Fizzled Out)

By Tia O'Brien

It was supposed to be Shangri-La, Silicon Valley style.

Imagine: The world's second-richest man pledges $100 million and a 10-year commitment to build what he hopes will be the most ambitious research venture in valley history. He hires some of the greatest minds on Earth and charges them with inventing the future.

Shrouded in secrecy, cloistered away from competitors, they will innovate Paul Allen's vision of the next great revolution after the personal computer, his futuristic Wired World in which consumers will receive information anytime, any place on demand.

The billionaire co-founder of Microsoft wants his elite research troop—unlike the corporate labs of IBM, Xerox and Microsoft—to be free from commercial pressures so they can pursue that valley rarity, pure research. Only after four or five years will they have to start spinning ideas into profitable start-ups.

This was 1992; the Internet and the World Wide Web as mass communication tools were in their infancy. Allen felt the personal computing revolution was stagnating. So his idealistic Palo Alto-based lab, Interval Research Corp., would leverage this "interval" between PCs and the next great wave, looking over the horizon and designing technology that would have an impact in five to 10 years and drive the computer industry for as long as 20 years.

That was the dream.

Eight years and a staggering $250 million later, Shangri-La is a Silicon Valley ghost town. On April 21, 2000, Paul Allen prematurely—and with little fanfare—killed his grand experiment. Once touted as a bold incubator of innovation, Interval is now reduced to a handful of researchers working on commercial applications for Allen's portfolio of cable and broadband ventures.

The story of Interval's demise is a cautionary tale not just for researchers, but for all entrepreneurs and Silicon Valley dreamers, revealing how the best brains, wads of money and abundant creative freedom can implode, leaving behind a stack of unexploited patents, accusations of betrayal, damaged careers and failed start-ups.

"They were plopped down in the middle of the greatest technology minds on the planet, in the middle of the biggest revolution of the century, and they never came out from behind their sand bags," scoffs Paul Saffo, director of the Institute for the Future. "They hermetically sealed the place from Day One, and it meant they lost touch with the intellectual life of the valley—potential collaborators and business partners."

Over the years, such critics had been skeptical that Interval would ever produce groundbreaking work. The few projects that Interval publicized heavily included a traveling exhibition of computer games, two interactive toy start-ups and another one focused on computer games for girls. After its death, the criticism intensified:

- Was Interval just the whimsy of a billionaire eager to gain credibility among high tech's titans?
- Why did Allen's lab miss out on the Internet while the rest of Silicon Valley was getting rich off just the kind of innovation Interval set out to find?
- Did Interval researchers lack the speed, business savvy and risk-taking bravado needed to launch successful start-ups?

Or is it so simple? While Interval is being dismissed as a waste of eight years and the work of great minds, there lingers this very tantalizing thought: Maybe Allen has the keys to groundbreaking technology tucked away inside the 140 patents that now are being scrutinized by technologists at the Seattle headquarters of Allen's investment firm, Vulcan Ventures, Inc.

Interval's collapse remains a valley mystery for this reason: Even in death, the defunct lab is embalmed in secrecy. A Vulcan spokesperson confirms that, in order to receive service-based severance pay, employees had to sign what they refer to as gag orders. Says one former staffer with a sarcastic laugh, "The joke is, 'We're so secret that no one even knows we've died.' "

Let a thousand flowers bloom

Everyone agrees that, for the first few years, Interval was an incredible place to work, a rare "let a thousand flowers bloom" approach to research.

"I went to Interval because of the really interesting people. Some of the ideas were out there, not the typical stuff floating around in the computer science world," says Interval alum Sean White, former vice president of technology for Lycos. White signed on to Interval in 1992, fresh out of Stanford, where he'd been a star computer science student. He'd never seen such a wild mix of talents in a tech lab.

Inside a series of low, nondescript industrial park buildings at 1801 Page Mill Road, mechanical engineers, programmers and signal computation experts collaborated with videographers, behavior scientists, psychologists and visual artists, a group totaling about 150 full-time staffers and contractors at the lab's peak.

It was all part of the effort by David Liddle, Allen's hand-picked CEO, to pioneer a new kind of research in which the focus was on what consumers—not businesses or technologists—would want in the year 2002 and beyond. He and Allen were betting that computers would be woven into the fabric of people's lives—TVs, stereos, bedrooms, kitchens, cars and clothing.

"We were exploring new media, devices and services that individuals would choose to buy in a discretionary way," says Liddle, 55, an imposing professorial figure with gray hair and a beard. "So it was important to understand early in the game aesthetics and preferences. Technologists just aren't great at that."

Liddle should know. At the legendary Xerox Palo Alto Research Center (PARC), during the '70s, Liddle led the team working on the Xerox Star, the first PC to use a graphical user interface—easy-to-use words and icons—instead of text commands. But Xerox, worried that PCs would undermine its copier business, did not commercialize the Star; Apple and Microsoft seized the opportunity and launched the PC industry. Liddle quit in frustration, moving on to found Metaphor Computer Systems, a business software start-up that made him a millionaire when IBM acquired it.

Allen and Liddle viewed Interval as the next PARC but with a twist: It would be part think tank, part venture capitalist, part business incubator. (The lab's location smacks of symbolism: Perched on a knoll on Page Mill Road, Intervalites could almost look down on PARC half a mile away.)

Instead of the typical scenario in which technologists engineer products, then test them on consumers, Interval folks spent weeks in the field videotaping and interviewing people about their use of high technology. To get out of their "skins," Liddle urged his crew to don masks and role-play during "informances" (information performances) so they could imagine what kind of products a grandmother, a punk rocker, or a sports fan would want.

It was this novel approach that led Liddle and computer user interface expert Brenda Laurel, one of his first hires, to ask this question: "What would it take to get little girls to put their hands on computers?"

For 22 years, Laurel had been researching, designing and producing video games, primarily for boys, at Atari, Apple and Activision. She'd earned a rep not only as an expert in how people interact with computers but also as an independent, opinionated iconoclast.

Laurel's employers had nixed several game products she'd proposed for girls, claiming that girls considered computers too geeky. But Liddle agreed with Laurel that the subject could produce groundbreaking research—and open a potential $6 billion market. With Liddle's blessing, she undertook an 18-month, multimillion-dollar study to look at gender inequities, play patterns and why there were no successful computer games for girls.

After interviewing experts and 1,100 kids, Laurel's team concluded that girls found he-man superheroes boring. They wanted complex, relationship-driven games.

Laurel's team developed prototype games for the 8-to-12-year-old-girl market, and by 1994 the games were getting a thumbs up.

The idea for Purple Moon, Interval's boldest start-up bet, was born.

Pointing fingers

Deconstructing the life and death of Interval is difficult because so many employees do not want to talk. Take Liddle, now a general partner with U.S. Venture Partners in Menlo Park. He initially bristled at the idea of an interview about Interval. Friends describe Liddle as having a protective big brother-like relationship with Paul Allen. Three weeks later Liddle agreed to discuss Interval, but certain topics—including Allen—were off-limits.

Allen himself refuses to discuss what skeptics are billing as his $250 million escapade, a mere drop in the bucket for his $20 billion dollar investment empire. Allen, whose personal net worth totals $28 billion according to the latest Forbes magazine survey, has a portfolio that reflects the convergence of his passions: high tech, telecommunications, entertainment, sports and the latest—extraterrestrial life.

As for Interval, once the crown jewel of Vulcan, spokeswoman Susan Pierson Brown explains that the media-shy mogul declines an interview because he's "said all he has to say" on the topic. Which is about zip. Weeks later, we finally were hooked up with Allen's business czar, Vulcan president Bill Savoy.

In that intervening period, several former Interval employees, frustrated that they have nothing to show publicly after years of work, agreed to talk (both on and off the record) about what happened. What they described sounds more like a Greek drama than the goings on at a cutting-edge tech lab.

There is plenty of finger-pointing over who's ultimately to blame for Interval's flame-out. One camp heaps criticism on Allen and his Vulcanites, claiming they were too impatient to let Interval play out its bets, aborting start-ups and changing the lab's mission seven years into the experiment.

Another group sees David Liddle as a brilliant research leader but a flawed manager whose preoccupation with secrecy and control, and loyalty to Allen, slowed decision-making, leaving the staff without the business alliances needed to launch winning start-ups.

Savoy questions the tight control Liddle exercised over the spinoffs. "We probably should have brought in more outsiders earlier so we weren't breathing our own air," he tells me. "But David felt like they were his kids, and felt personally responsible for them."

One former Intervalite, who spoke off the record, compares his time at the lab to being shanghaied on an island: "The owner and manager of the island had absolute power so we always were in the position of subjects."

Apartment cats

By 1995, as Laurel geared up to launch Purple Moon, Interval was buzzing with dozens of projects, from wearable computers to Webcam-like devices. A visit to Buildings C and D at 1801 Page Mill Road was a walk into science fiction.

Video cameras hooked up to computers tested information-age video encounters, and the resulting problem of protecting individual privacy.

Interval was a snug cocoon, flush with money and creative freedom, leading Liddle to warn against the danger that projects, especially potential commercial spinouts, would become "apartment cats": pretty, plump creatures incapable of surviving on their own.

"We did a personal video recorder in 1994, a replay TiVo-like machine," recalls Glenn Edens, inventor of the first laptop, who is now president of AT&T Strategic Ventures. Edens led Interval's wired Homeworks project. TiVo, a set-top device produced by TiVo Inc. of San Jose, allows viewers to watch what they want on TV whenever they want it. But Interval didn't develop the device—someone else had a similar idea and built a company around it.

Why? For the same reasons that researchers didn't spin out Internet-related technology. Says one frustrated researcher, "We never could take our big ideas and launch them into little devices that perhaps could seed future industries."

Every commercial proposal had to meet the test of Interval's original mission: Would it grow an entire new industry of products?

And even though Interval's goal was ultimately to commercialize its discoveries, there was no formal structure for quickly recasting researchers and their innovations into entrepreneurs and start-ups. A full-time business development person wasn't hired until 1998, a year and a half before Interval's death.

Consider the story of Sean White, who as early as 1993 was proposing work on several Internet-related technologies. Before graduating from Stanford, he'd been researching how people would use information on the Internet. This was a couple of years before the Netscape browser helped to transform the Internet from a government-backed network, largely for academics, into an information tool for the masses.

With Liddle's approval, White continued exploring how people would interact online through text, video and audio. But White and Roger Meike, another Internet proponent, failed to convince Liddle and others that the public was about to log on and that Interval should make the Net and the Web a prime focus of research. "They saw it [the Net] as a rarefied experience of academics that wouldn't make it to the public," White says.

Liddle insists he never dismissed the Net as a "fad," although that's the word several staffers recall him using in the early '90s. They also recall him swearing that he'd never launch a dot-com. "God no," Liddle retorts, explaining his reasoning for rejecting many proposed Net spinoffs. The former lab chief says many ideas were just too early for the marketplace. Others failed to meet the lab's tough financial test, or if they did, Interval wasn't built to compete on Internet time. Says Liddle, "Had we started a different firm in 1992, it would have been different story."

In 1994, White and another researcher thought they had a potentially winning business idea: a company that would provide technology and services such as setting up Web sites for those unfamiliar with the Net—which at the time was just about everybody.

As the youngest staffer, he couldn't do much when his idea was shot down, ultimately by Liddle. "I think Paul and David still wanted to figure out some sort of Next Big Thing. So this was going to be too mundane," recounts White. Mundane maybe, but a similar idea made the founders of USWeb multimillionaires. Says fellow Internet crusader Meike, "Some of our friends got incredibly rich and we didn't. It's OK, I'll get over it." Pause. Laugh. "I'm lying. I'll never get over it."

In retrospect, White shakes his head at the whole process. "We took six months to put together a business plan. An entrepreneur would have taken six days. We had researchers running marketing spreadsheets." He chuckles at the memory. "Everybody there was creative and smart, but were they marketers? Absolutely not."

Frustrated staffers began to wonder if Interval itself wasn't evolving into a monster apartment cat or, as Edens puts it, "an industrial park cougar." After more rejected Internet proposals, White finally left to join WhoWhere, an Internet search engine startup; its acquisition by Lycos made his fortune.

Girls go bust

In fairness, some of high tech's best minds missed the Internet in the early days. But once they realized it wasn't going away, they rebooted. Interval didn't.

After his experience at PARC, Liddle kept Interval's work sealed under a strict secrecy policy. Talking with the news media without clearance was grounds for dismissal. Employees protested, especially academics who argued that their reputations hinged on publishing their research. Outsiders as well were hesitant to collaborate with Intervalites.

Liddle contends that every major industrial research lab had the same policy. But Xerox PARC's chief scientist, John Seely Brown, who ran PARC for years, says that wasn't the policy at PARC. He believes that Interval's secrecy policy backfired. "If you run too secretive a shop, you lose connection to the outside world," says Brown.

If failing to leverage the Internet sounds bad, Intervalites say there was an even more fundamental problem: an inability to successfully launch start-ups.

In November 1996, Interval launched its first three start-ups amid a blaze of publicity: Purple Moon; Carnelian Inc., an Internet software maker; and ePlanet, an interactive toy company. The media loved the politically correct Purple Moon and its attempt to fill the gap between action heroes and Mattel's Barbie games. Purple Moon's CD-ROMs revolved around the friendship adventures of Rockett, a spunky pre-teen.

"I considered Barbie a 'culture crime,' " says Laurel, who viewed Barbie's empire as a pink ghetto, catering to the stereotypical beauty and fashion dreams of young girls.

But behind the glowing headlines, Purple Moon was piling up debt as it battled to grab sales away from arch-rival Barbie's fashion design CD-ROMs. It was an unexpected fight because, according to Laurel, no one at Interval or Vulcan knew that Mattel was entering the girls' software market. "We didn't have the intelligence," concedes Purple Moon's founder, who now works as a technology design and research consultant with the Nielsen Norman Group of Mountain View.

Purple Moon had been kept secret from the valley, which meant Laurel and others weren't picking up information about the competition from the normal sources. "David knew it was a land mine not having VCs involved, because a healthy company needs venture investments to make it tough, but we had nothing legally protectable," says Laurel, referring to their fear that someone would steal their idea for a girl computer game company.

When Purple Moon finally did reach out, it was rebuffed. No investors bit at what Laurel describes as the high valuation set by the Interval- and Vulcan-dominated Purple Moon board. Instead of weaning itself from Allen's seed money, Purple Moon remained almost entirely dependent on Vulcan and Interval for its funding.

By the summer of 1998, the Internet was eating into the CD-ROM market. Purple Moon CEO Nancy Deyo and Laurel needed an infusion of cash to reposition the company as an Internet-based business. (Purple Moon's Web site was going gangbusters, sometimes getting more hits than Disney's site.)

The Purple Moon team was thrilled when Nickelodeon, the popular kids' TV network, pitched a partnership deal—equity and an opportunity to collaborate on TV and online projects. It was just what Deyo and Laurel believed was needed to turn Rockett and the company into a national brand.

But when Nick came in with a low valuation of Purple Moon, the board rejected the offer—even though Interval's star spinoff was rapidly burning through its cash. Vulcan's Bill Savoy, one of the votes, never took the Nick offer seriously. "They wanted to be a partner, build some TV stuff while we kept footing the bill," Savoy says.

What happened next still baffles Laurel. In the fall of 1998, just months after rejecting the Nickelodeon offer, CEO Deyo was ordered to sell the company for the best deal she could get. Savoy, who admits he'd always been "a little dubious" about Purple Moon, couldn't imagine how it would ever make money. "Even today, if you said you're building an entertainment site for 8-to-13-year-old girls, there aren't enough of them online to justify it," explains Allen's business czar.

It's no coincidence that the order to unload Purple Moon coincided with a Vulcan-ordered audit of Interval: Vulcan clearly was losing its patience with the lab's slow pace, fast cash burn rate and floundering spinouts.

Arch enemy Mattel was the only company that nibbled. Sources familiar with the negotiations say Mattel made a verbal offer to acquire Purple Moon pending a review of the company.

But before a deal could be finalized, Savoy announced in February 1999 that Allen was killing his prize start-up. The board voted to put Purple Moon in Chapter 7 bankruptcy, which meant creditors would be paid only pennies on the dollar.

"Web hits were at an all-time high and we'd just implemented e-commerce," says a still bitter Laurel, who can't understand why Allen killed Purple Moon when there was an active deal on the table. Liddle is mum about what happened; however, insiders say he pushed to win more time for Purple Moon but couldn't budge Allen or Savoy. Savoy has no regrets: "My recollection is that Mattel wanted to buy certain assets but not the whole company."

Deyo and Laurel were furious that creditors wouldn't get paid. According to Laurel, Purple Moon's CEO went back to Mattel and within days sealed a deal for the toy maker to buy Purple Moon in a Chapter 11 bankruptcy fire sale. Rockett now would be Mattel's property and creditors would get their money. Savoy suggests that this deal never would have happened without the imminent threat of Chapter 7 bankruptcy.

Even though Mattel has not done much with the Purple Moon property, the irony that Barbie's maker saved the day, allowing creditors to be paid, isn't lost on Laurel. "Pink money saved my ass," says the woman who celebrated her 40th birthday by feeding Barbies into her trash compactor.

An empty rat hole?

"The very public debacle of Purple Moon was the point at which I wrote off Interval as a lost cause," admits Institute for the Future director Saffo. "It looked like it had a chance and, at the very least, they could have gotten it to a safe harbor."

By the fall of '99, Purple Moon, Carnelian and ePlanet all were dead. Like Laurel, Adi Gamon, the non-Intervalite CEO of Carnelian, questions why Vulcan killed the start-up when it did: Carnelian was one month away from its first beta testing, with such prominent customers as Charles Schwab and Dell Computer lined up. "A venture capitalist never would have shut it down at that point," he says.

Gamon is candid about his inability to recruit non-Vulcan investors, a problem echoed by other Interval spinoff executives and confirmed by venture capitalists. They were wary of partnering with one of richest guys on the planet, who could, in the words of one former exec of an Interval company, abruptly change his agenda and act "on whim, not hard business decisions."

Liddle grows angry at criticism that Vulcan was run like a family business, contending that the real problem wasn't Allen, but the Internet frenzy. "The venture community lost interest in consumer technology projects," he says.

In fact, Allen himself was shifting his investment focus. His fast-growing empire certainly involved collaborations with other investors. But the primary difference was that, unlike Interval, his newer investments generally involved existing businesses with proven track records. According to Savoy, a long-range research lab just didn't fit with Allen's cable/broadband portfolio.

Ironically, by the time it spun out its last venture, Fantasma, in February of this year, Interval seemed like it finally was getting the hang of birthing independent companies that could fly on their own. "Interval doesn't control the company or have anybody on the board," says Robert Aiello, CEO of Fantasma, the wireless home networking venture, pointing out that non-Vulcan investors hold the majority stake.

But it was too late for Shangri-La.

The beginning of the end started with a terse news release last September in which Allen announced that Interval's focus now would be on quick turnaround projects for his broadband communication companies, not long-range research.

And the release stated that CEO Liddle was stepping down, although he'd retain the title of chairman. Was Liddle elbowed out by the man who'd hired him?

"Absolutely not," he says, denying reports of a rift. While he fully supported the lab's new direction, Liddle says he left because he wanted to pursue his own interests.

Over the next seven months, a steady succession of brains headed out the door, with the staff dwindling to about 50 by April 21, the Friday when Savoy unexpectedly flew in from Seattle and called an employees' meeting.

"He said it had become clear that the Internet was moving too fast for a lab like Interval to keep up. It was the last day of Interval's operation," recalls a former staffer. Savoy says the lab simply wasn't pulling its weight in Allen's investment portfolio: "We tried to do big things, to have the right vision but the world changed around us."

Since its closing in April, only about 10 employees have accepted Vulcan's offer to help launch a new broadband research venture.

The irony is that Interval's innovations are just starting to make sense in our increasingly wired world. One example is technology developed by Sean White and others, nicknamed the Web Phone, which anticipated the issue of privacy in homes where the Net is always on (think DSL). An electronic screen allows you to be seen or heard—only to the degree you want. The Web Phone is among that stack of patents now being reviewed by Allen's staff.

Meanwhile, Interval's biggest legacy may be the void it has left. Silicon Valley's leading researchers worry about who now will chase the seemingly wild ideas, who will pay geeks to dream up the stuff that will drive the next New Economy. Valley lab chiefs have started meeting informally. "We are discussing how to make sure that all the efforts to commercialize technology doesn't suck away the brightest researchers," explains Bob Iannucci, vice president of corporate research for Compaq.

Researchers aren't the only ones worrying. Asks venture capitalist Stewart Alsop, "If one of the world's richest guys has given up, then who's going to throw money down the rat hole?"

The betting money is on a stepped-up alliance of private industry, university and government funding—not another billionaire. Meanwhile, Alsop, a partner with New Enterprise Associates, has a more immediate problem. He'd love to recruit some Intervalites for his companies. "My CEOs are trying to find people. But Interval was so secret," he says with a laugh, "it's hard to know who was there."

The Foreclosure at Mortgage.com

By Megan Barnett, New York

Six miles west of Ft. Lauderdale, Fla., the small town of Sunrise felt the tremors of the dot-com shakeout last week. Sunrise-based Mortgage.com laid off 518 of its 618 employees—in Sunrise as well as in its California, Nevada and New Jersey offices—and announced it would sell its remaining assets.

Mortgage.com was riding the wave of the Internet frenzy when it raised $60 million in an IPO in August 1999. The company's lead underwriter was Credit Suisse First Boston, a top-tier investment bank with a formidable reputation in the online financial services industry. The stock priced at $8 per share and hit a high last fall of $16.81 before heading downward. Last week the shares traded at 3 cents, giving the company a market capitalization of just $1.4 million. Cash levels at Mortgage.com fell below the levels necessary for it to continue to fund loans. While the company's bank agreed to let Mortgage.com finish processing its outstanding loans, it ordered the company to cease making new loans.

While many struggling Internet companies have scaled back operations or restructured their business models in an attempt to survive the market's broad retreat, Mortgage.com's move was drastic. The news, delivered to employees on Oct. 31, came as a surprise to everyone, says Debbie Franklin, the firm's investor relations manager.

While its employees may have been shocked, the management of Mortage.com should not have been surprised that its cash reserves were falling to critical levels. Franklin would not say why no one had planned for this day, or whether the executives were aware of the severity of the situation.

Perhaps realizing it had helped fund a company with only a short time to live, CS First Boston distanced itself from Mortgage.com months ago. Jake Peters, CS First Boston's banker on the deal last year, did not return calls seeking comment. Mortgage.com retained Lehman Brothers for advisory services in January.

Jim Marks, CS First Boston's online-finance research analyst, was not with the bank at the time of Mortgage.com's IPO, but he admits the company probably went public prematurely. "When you take a company public, you do so on the basis of their projections and the company's ability to meet and sustain those projections," Marks says. "It turns out that they weren't able to do that. In a sense, it wasn't entirely their fault. There was a shift in interest rates that made it difficult for them to achieve those projections."

Indeed, rising interest rates have swept aside the business plans of many online mortgage firms. Most were established during a period of low interest rates, when many homeowners looked to refinance their mortgages. The Internet enabled them to easily compare rates and refinance online. When rates rose, the refinancing business dried up—and with it the lifeblood of these companies.

Mortgage.com's failure doesn't bode well for the rest of the online mortgage industry. Still, other companies are forging ahead. E-Loan is adding auto loans, credit cards, and other loans to its roster of products. And LendingTree, which is a marketplace for loans instead of a mortgage processor like Mortgage.com, says it has about six months of cash left.

Dot-Com Liquidator

New Breed of Vulture Gets Fat on Remains of Expired 'E-Tailers'

By Nick Wingfield
Staff Reporter of The Wall Street Journal

San Bruno, Calif.—Inside an office park on the outskirts of Silicon Valley, not far from the local cemetery, an increasingly common death ritual is under way: A dot-com liquidator is poking through the remains of a start-up.

In one room, dozens of computers sit idle in rows of deserted cubicles. Through a back door that leads past a metal detector to a high-security warehouse, two women hunch over a table, tallying up what's left of Miadora Inc., an online jewelry retailer that folded several weeks earlier. Patrick Byrne grins as he watches them pull trays of glittering merchandise from the refrigerator-size safes that line the walls.

Another woman plucks a necklace out of one the safes. It's a strand of champagne Tahitian pearls with 18-karat-gold settings studded with diamonds. Mr. Byrne is buying the piece from Miadora's creditors for approximately $10,000, or about half what he estimates Miadora paid for it.

"We'll sell it to the customer at $19,000 so we can say, 'You're getting a better deal for it than the jeweler.'" Mr. Byrne says.

The vultures of e-commerce have arrived. After burning through one of the most concentrated waves of investment in retailing history, many online merchants are in critical condition. Of the growing number that have gone belly up, little remains except for computer equipment, customer lists and warehouses filled with unsold goods. But that's just what the 37-year-old Mr. Byrne and the small band of businessmen like him are looking for.

Mr. Byrne's company, Overstock.com Inc., employs about 70 people and buys goods from distressed Web start-ups, manufacturers and other sources for anywhere between 30% and 50% of their wholesale cost. Then, it uses—what else?—the Internet to sell the very same stock, offering the goods to consumers at less than the original retailer's cost. Overstock might, for example, pay $25 for an item that wholesales for $50 and retails for $100. The closely held Salt Lake City company can then sell the item online for $45 and still pocket a tidy sum on the transaction.

So far, the formula hasn't added up to an overall profit. Overstock, which started out using faxes, rather than the Web, as its primary marketing tool, has incurred losses of $22 million since its inception in 1998. Mr. Byrne, its chief executive officer, expects the company to be profitable by January when the company's sales will be enough to offset the cost of running and marketing the business.

Since he acquired a majority stake in Overstock in May 1999, Mr. Byrne has invested $15 million of his own money in the business, and it has been growing rapidly. Overstock now is the 25th most-visited shopping site among those who surf the Web from work, according to Internet traffic-tracking service Nielsen/Netratings. The company sells about $1 million a week of merchandise ranging from stereo speakers to Fendi handbags. And Mr. Byrne says sales should approach $50 million this year.

A Long Tradition

Liquidators have been around as long as retailers have been going out of business. Bricks-and-mortar stores often turn to specialists such as Gordon Brothers Group LLC, a 97-year-old liquidator based in Boston that manages closeout sales. Manufacturers also depend on liquidators to help dispose of excess or out-of-season inventory without polluting traditional sales channels with low-priced goods.

Distressed dot-coms are a potentially huge new source of goods for the industry. Venture capitalists have invested $4.6 billion in Internet retailers since 1997, according to the PricewaterhouseCoopers MoneyTree Survey. Now the high-profile failures of furniture site Living.com Inc., toy merchant Toysmart.com Inc., and others, as well as a sharp pullback in venture-capital investment in Internet retailers, have created widespread pessimism about the sector's prospects. A May Doonesbury comic strip aptly captured the mood, featuring a character who plans to start a company called MyVulture.com to recycle the inventory of failed Web firms. The MyVulture.com theme made a Doonesbury reappearance yesterday. (Mr. Byrne says he taped a copy of the strip on the wall in his company's kitchen.)

Even some old-line liquidators are getting in on the action. In August, Tuesday Morning Corp., a discounter based in Dallas, bought Toysmart.com's $10 million inventory, which included everything from Thomas the Tank Engine train sets to Winnie the Pooh collectibles.

Gordon Brothers, meanwhile, is backing a new Internet venture, called SmartBargains.com, in an alliance with America Online Inc., Boston venture-capital firm Highland Capital Partners and others. John Kerney, SmartBargains' president, says the venture is counting on inventory from failed dot-coms and is currently in talks with a home-furnishings Web site, an online toy merchant and two apparel e-tailers, which he declines to identify.

Mr. Byrne is pursuing failed Internet retailers more eagerly than most. In September, his company paid $3.7 million for the inventory of ToyTime.com Inc., a Torrance, Calif., operation that went under earlier this year. He says the goods in its warehouses had an estimated retail value of about $11.5 million. Last month, Overstock bought another Internet liquidator, Gear.com Inc., which specialized in sporting goods, and Mr. Byrne says he recently bid 30 cents on the wholesale dollar for 25,000 Stetsons, baseball caps and other headgear being sold by the creditors of eHats Inc., an Internet retailer that filed for bankruptcy protection earlier this year. That deal is still pending.

Mr. Byrne learned some of his first business lessons as a teenager from value investor Warren Buffett. Mr. Byrne knew the legendary investor through his father, John Byrne, who once ran Gelco Corp., an insurer now owned by Mr. Buffett's Berkshire Hathaway Corp. Among the principles Mr. Buffett imparted in the younger Mr. Byrne: The essence of value investing is trying to buy dollar bills for 30 cents.

Mr. Byrne took that advice to heart, applying it to a string of deals. In the mid-1990s, he bought an old shoe factory in downtown Manchester, N.H., that had been converted to office space. The building's previous owners had stopped making payments on the mortgage on the property, and Mr. Byrne was able to pick it up for $3.5 million. Earlier this year, he sold it for $10 million. With one of his brothers, Mr. Byrne acquired the ailing Inn at Jackson Hole, in Wyoming, in 1987. He also has acquired distressed strip malls and apartment buildings across the West. Then there's the Grease Monkey oil change outlet in Florida Mr. Byrne bought from an airline piolot who needed money to settle a divorce.

"I realized in the last couple of months that there's a certain theme to my life—bottom feeding," Mr. Byrne says.

'Like Buying That Bank'

One of his biggest successes came in the early 1990s, when Mr. Byrne and a group of investors that included his father and two brothers, purchased New Dartmouth Bank, a collection of five failed New Hampshire savings banks. On its investment of $7 million, Mr. Byrne's family reaped a $20 million profit when the banks were later sold to another institution.

Buying Internet retailers is "like buying that bank in New Hampshire," says Mr. Byrne. "It's the same principle."

Between his forays into business, Mr. Byrne earned a Ph.D. in philosophy from Stanford University over the course of nine years, two of which he spent battling testicular cancer. He also says he is fluent in Mandarin and holds a black belt in tae kwon do. For a time, he says, he trained to become a professional boxer but quit because chemotherapy had so weakened his lungs. Nonetheless, Mr. Byrne, who is a muscular 6-foot-5, has a pugilist's profile—his nose was broken during a bout.

Mr. Byrne has little sympathy for failing Internet retailers. "I think a sophomore economics student could have told you why these business models were garbage," he says. As for venture capitalists, they "have no understanding of what will make a good business," he adds, they just "try to pick what's going to be hot in six months."

On a recent day, a substantial amount of venture capital is sitting in Miadora's safes here in San Bruno in the form of diamond-encrusted Cartier chronometers, Rolex Oyster watches and gold earrings. Mr. Byrne is paying Miadora's creditors $2.5 million for the jewelry, which has a retail value of about $11 million, and he says he hopes it will fetch $5.5 million on Overstock.com.

Founded in April 1999, Miadora managed to raise a total of $46 million from sources that included Sequoia Capital in Menlo Park, Calif., which backed such high-tech successes as Yahoo! Inc. and Oracle Corp. It sunk much of the money into a costly marketing campaign, including a sweepstakes in which the top prize was a $100,000 diamond necklace. It also embarked on a hiring binge that helped drain its cash. In the end, it couldn't persuade its investors to pony up more capital.

'I Have Cash'

Mr. Byrne found out about Miadora's problems through Joanne Dalebout, Overstock's jewelry buyer. On the day the company closed in September, Mr. Byrne drove to its headquarters in San Mateo, where employees, some in tears, were still boxing up their belongings. He says he scribbled "I have cash" on the back of his business card and asked an employee to deliver it to Miadora's CEO. About 10 days later, Miadora accepted his offer.

Mr. Byrne is always on the alert for signs of weakness at other-dot-coms. That becomes clear as he and Ms. Dalebout talk shop with Richard Caniglia, Miadora's vice president of operations. Mr. Caniglia mentions that the Web site of Adornis.com, an Irish jewelry retailer with offices in Greenwich, Conn., is no longer accessible.

Mr. Byrne and Ms. Dalebout exchange glances. "Interesting," Ms. Dalebout says.

"Oh, you gonna get a plane ticket?" Mr. Caniglia asks Mr. Byrne with a chuckle. "This is like the Grim Reaper here." Mr. Byrne says he has since bid less than 40 cents on the dollar for Adornis's inventory. An Adornis executive confirms that a deal to sell its inventory to Overstock is pending.

Mr. Caniglia says he bears no grudge against Mr. Byrne, saying the liquidator is paying a fair price and helping out Miadora's creditors. Still, Mr. Caniglia adds: "No one wants to see his car pulling up in the parking lot."

Some of Miadora's suppliers are concerned. Last month, Ms. Dalebout got calls from jewelry designers seeking to buy back pieces they had sold Miadora. They are worried Overstock's discounts will hurt their relationship with full-price retailers, but Mr. Byrne says he isn't going to sell the items back. One of the designers, Jordan Schlanger, who is based in New York, confirms that an employee at his company contacted Overstock about purchasing pieces it had sold to Miadora.

Mr. Byrne routinely scours F-dcompany.com, a Web site that keeps track of dot.com deaths. He recently posted an appeal there for failing companies to contact him. His user name on the site is Hannibal, after both the Carthaginian general and Hannibal Lecter, the infamous cannibal in Thomas Harris's novels.

After hearing that a gourmet foods e-tailer was interested in selling its inventory, Mr. Byrne recently drove to the company's address in Oakland, Calif., to see whether he could make a deal. The address turned out to be a residence; when no one answered, Mr. Byrne stuck his business card on a nail on the front door. And when Mr. Bryne heard last week that Pets.com Inc., an Internet pet-supply retailer, and MotherNature.com Inc., a vitamin and natural-products seller, were shutting down, he quickly sought to contact executives from the companies.

Mr. Byrne says he hopes Overstock's discounts make things harder on rival dot-coms. He thinks the deals he plans to offer on Miadora's jewelry will be especially painful for Ashford.com Inc., one of the best known Internet jewelry stores. "The people at Ashford are bringing a knife to a gunfight," Mr. Byrne says. "If we can use this to put a big dent in their Christmas, I'll be knocking on their door."

Kenny Kurtzman, Ashford's CEO, says he isn't afraid of Overstock, however. "We're very confident that we'll be around next holiday season as a profitable company," he says, adding that Ashford considered buying Miadora's inventory but passed, because it was mostly old merchandise "that won't sell this holiday season."

There are few things overstock won't scavenge. At the company's 175,000-square-foot warehouse near the Salt Lake City airport, conversation is difficult because of the racket made by workers pounding shelves into steel racks that extend several stories high. The shelves belonged to ToyTime. Mr. Byrne bought them along with the company's toy inventory. Digital photos and copy describing the inventory are usually parts of the package. In Toy-Time's case, Overstock even bought the maintenance staff's brooms and screwdrivers.

Overstock does much of its bargaining on the spur of the moment, scribbling out offers for packing material, label machines and other items on scraps of paper.

At Miadora's headquarters, for instance, Mr. Byrne hears that the company's creditors are entertaining a $4,000 offer for several safes he thinks are probably worth more than $27,000, "Offer $7,500." Mr. Byrne says to Miadora's Mr. Caniglia as a representative of Miadora's creditors drifts out of earshot.

Ms. Dalebout, the Overstock jewelry buyer, whispers back: "Why not offer six?"

"OK, offer six," Mr. Byrne responds. Miadora's creditors later accept the bid.

The rapid pace of Mr. Byrne's acquisitions has created some recent challenges for Overstock's operations team. On one side of the Overstock warehouse, the company is scrambling to build high-security cages to store the incoming Miadora jewelry. Next to the half-finished shelves, pallets full of Barbie Deluxe Dreamhouses, Intel Computer Microscopes and other ToyTime items occupy a football-field-size section of floor space.

"This has been a juggling act," says Scott Stuart, vice president of logistics.

Mr. Byrne thinks most e-tailers will fail eventually, with the exception of standouts such as Amazon.com, Inc. Executives within Overstock acknowledge that the supply of wounded dot-coms won't last forever, but Overstock has other sources of inventory, including manufacturers and traditional retailers. While the trend lasts, Overstock plans to exploit it.

Ms. Dalebout says she sometimes feels guilty about preying on falling dot-coms. Mr. Bryne says scavenging isn't a moral issue to him. "I say, 'Fella, you're in this position because you're in this position—I didn't put you there,'" he says. "I'm cleaning up the mess."

REPORT TO YOUR MASTER!

SOON, A NEW CAREER...

AN INFUSION IS NEEDED!

BUT... WHERE'S THE MONEY?

LATER...

CHAPTER 4

Don't Forget the
Dot-People in Dot-Com

This chapter is about some of the people in the dot-com revolution. And a stranger cast of characters would be hard to find.

In the stories that follow, there are con men and saints, naive youngsters and high-stakes players. You will intensely dislike some of the people, and find considerable sympathy and respect for some of the others. Prepare for a roller-coaster ride.

These are in-depth stories. You will learn in astonishing detail about the lives of some of these dot-commers. Sometimes in more detail than you would wish—not all of these stories are pretty ones.

In fact, the first two stories of the chapter are about the darkest side of the dark business of failure. They are also amazingly similar, given that the two stories have absolutely nothing to do with each other.

The key player in each of these stories was on the lam from one or more criminal convictions, and had changed his name before getting into the dot-com business, as their stories in this book begin. Both were "golden tongued salesmen." Both had tempers. Both were tyrannical managers. Both were excessively heavy, weighing over 300 pounds. Both were suspiciously secretive. One, in fact, somewhat ironically renamed himself Hoquim (pronounced "hokum," which the dictionary defines as "nonsense, material chosen to appeal to the uncritical"). The other masqueraded as a religious figure, holding prayer meetings in his office and—according to some—behaving as if he thought he were Christ's reincarnation.

These are not the kind of people you'd want to know, let alone do business with. And yet, in our first story, Michael Fenne (previously known as David Stanley) aggregated a group of sometimes-fanatical loyalists. It was apparently easy to believe in him. Even his father, whom he eventually forced into bankruptcy, according to the story, continued to laud him after the fact. And there was something else. Fenne, who apparently continues to believe that he has done nothing wrong, didn't put his gains into fast cars or summer cottages or fancy yachts. It was his company, Pixelon, that seemed to be the focus of his energy, not personal gain. But his fearful coexecutives, once they began to understand what kind of person he was, forced him out of the company. (They were fearful because, among other things, Fenne behaved increasingly strangely and was accompanied by apparently armed bodyguards.) As of the writing of this story, Fenne is in jail for his previous crimes, which included fleecing neighbors in the mountain counties of Kentucky, Tennessee, and West Virginia out of $1.25M (that's no mean feat in an area better known for its poverty). Pixelon, meanwhile, teeters on the edge of bankruptcy.

In the second story, the main character's new name, as previously mentioned, is Hoquim—Robert Hoquim. He was born John Paul Aleshe, and was on the lam for stealing the gun of a police officer who had arrested him, and trying to kill him with it (the gun didn't fire). He got into the computing business, as did Fenne, because he was "utterly brilliant." But he was also "a prodigious and prolific liar," who had engaged in "computer scams" before opening his latest company, IQuest (ironically, there is no evidence that IQuest was a scam. The company survives after he sold it, and the present owners are careful to dissociate the company from Hoquim the man).

It is perhaps in the deceptions that the two men practiced that these stories reach their most absurd heights. Hoquim's company had no identification on its building, "customers were not allowed in the building," and Hoquim's "bunker mentality" was reflected in the fact that both his corporate office and his personal apartment in his home were in the basement of the building. Fenne had no driver's license or Social Security number, and demanded that he be paid out of the company's expense account. If one were reading these stories in order to learn how to avoid being sucked in by "golden-tongued salesmen," then perhaps paying attention to personal weirdnesses is one way to accomplish that.

Far from the con men of the first two stories, we have the sad story of Drkoop.com and its namesake, former Surgeon General C. Everett Koop. Koop was a man with a "sterling reputation," "the best-known surgeon general of the 20th century," a man whose motives appear to be as high-minded as any leader of any enterprise. And yet, as our story tells us, his involvement with this and a previous business have "tarnished" that sterling reputation, leaving him looking at the very least like a man who "wasn't a savvy businessman." And there are hints of something worse. Koop sold a million dollars worth of stock in Drkoop just before the company released some particularly bad news and its stock plummeted. There are laws against knowingly doing that sort of thing.

As our story is told, Drkoop the company is struggling on its death bed, achieving a transfusion of venture capital periodically, hoping to stave off its demise. Dr. Koop himself, now 84 years old, continues to be optimistic about both his company and the key players running it (some of whom have been involved in "questionable deals"), while also continuing to "know next-to-nothing" about the running of the company. It all began with such high hopes—the company was to provide accurate health information to the public. This is a case where all of us can hope, I think, that Drkoop the company survives.

Yet another completely different story is the one about strangely named Boo.com. Boo was to be a high-priced spread Web clothing store where buyers could enter a "virtual changing room," use the 3D graphics to examine clothing choices from any angle, and solicit the advice of animated consultant "Miss Boo."

The founders of Boo were a couple of hip Swedes—one a "dreamy" and "shy" visionary, the other a "brainy" and "focused" childhood friend of the first and a former model. Both were 29 as our story begins, and yet both were referred to by financiers who threw money at the company as the opposite of the "adults" the financiers hoped to put in charge to replace them.

Were they less than adult in their behavior? The story mentions corporate discussions, "which would rage for days," about how Miss Boo (who was animated, remember) should behave. Miss Boo was the icon, the "mascot," for the company, of course. But she was also a piece of corporate fiction.

In the end, Boo was a case of technology gone wild. The web site, when it finally went on the air nearly six months late, was "complex," "very slow" (the founders bet that people interested in high-priced clothing would also have high-priced, fast computers), and "hard to navigate." Yet the brashness of the ideas, and the innovativeness of the underlying technology, fairly took the breath away from those who truly understood the concept.

But Boo lived all too fast, and died all too young. There were the six "trophy" offices opened in major cities around the world. There was the "throwing money at problems," especially into ever-more tricky technical solutions. The good news was that the site, at its peak, was drawing in a fabulous $1 million a month. But the bad news is that expenses were "ten times" that.

Boo the original concept is gone. The financiers eventually pulled the plug and called in the liquidators. The name Boo, on the other hand, momentarily lives on, bought by a competitor that wants to ride the tail end of the

Boo wave for whatever it is worth. But the founders of Boo, those shy and brainy Swedes, are apparently getting lots of calls from other dot-commers. We may hear from them again, some day. Adults or not.

Earlier we spoke of the dark side of failure, in the context of the dot-com con men. The next story is about a "gentle and special human being" who explored another dark side, descending into the depths of alcoholism, eventually drinking himself to death ("acute pancreatic bleeding caused by chronic alcoholism"). As the founder of a company that developed a file compression software scheme, he was "beneficent" and brilliant. As a human being who increasingly failed to cope, he led a "strange, underground life."

As things began to go bad, Phillip W. Katz of PCWare "would go straight to his desk among the programmers—rarely using his president's office—and write code late into the night." As drunken driving convictions piled up and he sought to evade the law, he later stayed away from work entirely (communicating only by fax and email) and also stayed away from his home ("knee deep in trash and garbage.") His eventual death, in a hotel room, was inevitable—and the sad waste of a capable human being.

Most of the stories of this chapter are in-depth, full of fascinating detail. In the last few stories, however, we return for some quickies. The first is a kind of neat mystery story, in fact. Is the key player in this story a bad guy who has stepped away from four bankruptcies and has left customers who "paid for goods that were never delivered"? Or is he a good guy, one who has had megamillion dollar successes, from which he has earned a yacht and a $14 million mansion? The story we include here is about his "ugliest" failure, a sort of general store for the Web that intended to sell just about anything. The bottom line to date is this: the company itself is bankrupt. No charges have been filed against the principle. But the case is still open. This is one of those stories that is simply not yet over. Stay tuned.

The remaining quickies study the stories of dot-com defectors—people who decided enough is enough, and bailed out for saner/greener/calmer/less-lucrative pastures. In each story, there is a description of the dot-com workplace, the epiphany that caused the subject to strap on a parachute, and a description of the person's current occupation. They are fascinating tales.

And what about the dot-com executives who don't bail out, who ride the rollercoaster all the way to the bottom? There's a steep price to be paid, the final story in this chapter tells us. From tens/hundreds of millions of paper profit dollars, they fall into what some call "the 90 percent club," where the members have lost 90 percent or more of their assets! Should we feel sorry for such dot-com derelicts? To be honest, it's a little hard to. The expression "easy come, easy go" leaps to mind. Or is it "he (or she) made his bed, now let him (or her) lie in it." (Our old homely expressions have a cruel streak to them, don't they?!)

The Great Internet CON

By Dan Goodin

Late in the afternoon of Nov. 12, several squad cars from the Orange County Sheriff's Department converged on the San Juan Capistrano, Calif., corporate headquarters of Pixelon, a high profile Internet company selling a new way of broadcasting television-quality video over the Internet. A hastily formed coalition of company officers and directors were planning to oust Pixelon's founder and chairman, Michael Fenne, a formidable 350-pound man. They called the deputies because they worried that Fenne might turn violent.

The day's trouble had begun much earlier. At a morning meeting with investors, Fenne pounded his fists on a conference table and vowed, in a two-minute tirade laced with profanities, that he would never willingly leave the company he had worked so hard to build. An irate founder bent on sabotage was something Pixelon's leaders openly worried about, especially considering the company's millions of dollars worth of computer equipment. But what most concerned this coalition were the two large bodyguards who stood outside Fenne's office that afternoon. The pair wore large pouches strapped around their waists, leading some—including Pixelon interim CEO Paul Ward, according to a lawsuit—to believe they were armed.

From the start, Fenne, who was partial to signing his e-mail messages as the "Big Giant Head of Pixelon," had proven to be an unusual founder and board chairman. He had no driver's license or Social Security card, and demanded that he be paid solely out of the company's expense accounts. He also displayed a tyrannical management style, requiring some employees to work 36-hour shifts. He launched into tirades over the public address system and held a mandatory prayer meeting in his office.

Later, in the weeks before his ouster, Fenne's behavior grew worse. Without the board's consent, he had promoted the company's public relations director to CEO only to fire her two weeks later, and went on a stock-granting spree, handing out millions of shares to employees and partners.

The company's investors had also just learned that Pixelon had spent no less than $16 million—out of $20 million in financing closed just one month earlier—for a star-studded launch party that included performances by the Who and the Dixie Chicks.

Pixelon director Lee Wiskowski was chairman of Advanced Equities, the Chicago investment bank that had handled the financing. When he heard about Pixelon's party tab, he and his two lieutenants left for Orange County for an emergency board meeting.

They arrived at company headquarters on the morning of Nov. 12. The first thing Wiskowski and his two cohorts heard was the sound of Fenne's voice over the Pixelon public address system. "This is the master speaking," at least a half dozen people present remember Fenne barking. "George better respond to me immediately, and if he doesn't have all the answers I might have to take him out behind the barn for a whooping!" Then, another message rang out, "Frank, report to the woodshed, your uncle is going to give you a whooping." The repeated messages, which appeared to be randomly directed at various employees, might have been funny were it not for the air of fear they created.

Later that morning, a Pixelon executive briefed Wiskowski's group. A week or two earlier, the executive told them, he had walked into Fenne's office for a scheduled meeting to find another executive on his hands and knees with his head bowed before Fenne, who was sitting in a chair with his hands on the back of the kneeling executive's head "I've never been around a cult leader," the executive told the team, "but that's the way it felt."

The Wiskowski team had arrived at Pixelon headquarters thinking they might ask the interim CEO, Ward, who was also an early investor and director of the company, to take the fall. But the trio decided on the spot that it made more sense to oust Fenne, even though only several months earlier he had been given an employment agreement guaranteeing him the position of chairman for at least seven years. The three investment bankers retired to a nearby parking lot with Ward, a second Pixelon director, and several Pixelon officers, to hatch a plan. They needed at least one more board vote to take Fenne out, however, and frantically tried to reach two other board members. In the meantime, they agreed, they needed to keep Fenne from discovering their plans and be ready to call the sheriff's office.

"This feels weird," one member confided to another after they hatched the scheme. "This feels like someone could die tonight."

Only later, after Fenne was given the boot and the company was struggling to regain its footing, would the full truth emerge: Michael Fenne, the charismatic man who raised $30 million claiming he had invented a new way to broadcast video on the Internet, was in fact David Kim Stanley, a convicted con artist and fugitive on the lam since 1996.

Stanley was born in the rural south, the son and grandson of Appalachian preachers. In his 20s, he used his status and a near-hypnotic speaking style to fleece many of him impoverished neighbors, including parishioners of his father's church, out of over a million dollars. In 1989 Stanley pleaded guilty to more than 50 fraud-related charges. A judge sentenced him to 36 years in prison and agreed to suspend all but eight if Stanley wold repay his victims. In early 1996, while working as a traveling salesman and having paid only a fraction of the money he had promised his victims, according to court records, Stanley vanished.

He turned up in the sleepy town of San Juan Capistrano in late 1996, just as the Internet was transforming the most unlikely people into overnight multimillionaires. The setting would provide the perfect environment for the then 35-year old con man.

With little more than a made-up name, a dilapidated Hyundai and his wits, Stanley wold convince an unsuspecting group of locals that he had found the Holy Grail of Internet broadcasting: a unique means for stuffing television-quality video into ultra-thin files that could download in a matter of seconds. It was only later that Stanley would learn rudimentary programming in languages such as C++ and Visual Basic, but his polished sales pitches convinced just about everyone at the time that he was an accomplished programmer whose skills were sought after by the CIA and the Saudi royal family. He was also emerging as a pillar of the community, teaching Bible studies at a local church and playing piano during services.

By mid 1999, Stanley had convinced Advanced Equities, a fledgling investment firm in Chicago, that his technological breakthrough was about to transform the way video would be delivered over the Internet. The investors were so smitten by Stanley's claims that they coughed up $28 million. They were hardly the only ones to fall for Stanley's scheme: Pixelon was also cutting high-profile deals with the likes of VH1, Paramount Pictures, the Republican National Committee and actor and singer Will Smith.

Now, just one year later, Pixelon is nearly a goner, and Stanley sits in a Virginia county jailhouse. During a rare jailhouse interview in Wise County, Va., Stanley comes off as a humble man, bright and gifted with words. Though this blue-eyed, cherubic-faced man seems large enough to wrestle a bear, the soft-spoken Stanley can make just about anyone feel warm in his presence. Many who have known Stanley for only a short time are quick to call him a genius, a deeply gentle soul and one of the most gifted piano players and singers they've ever heard. Even after it was revealed that he was a convicted con artist living under a fake name, his supporters remain steadfast, as convinced as ever that Stanley has a special blessing from God.

From his sweaty jail cell and in the many accounts passed along to friends and acquaintances, Stanley claims over and over that he's the real victim, horribly abused by family members and fellow parishioners, conned by double-dealing business associates and betrayed by a legal system that won't let go a minor transgression he made 10 years ago.

It's no coincidence the judge hearing Stanley's case branded him the golden-tongued salesman. Many who met him were so hungry to strike it rich that they were ready to believe just about anything he said. They lost their fortunes and personal reputations, and tolerated the indignities of a man inclined to humiliate them publicly and deceive them privately. The Pixelon story reminds us of the old adage: Deals too good to be true usually are.

Wise County, Stanley's home through much of his early life, is in the Appalachian Mountains near the Kentucky, Tennessee and West Virginia state lines. Unemployment is in the double digits, and a great many of its residents try to adhere to the Ten Commandments. Even during the coal boom in generations past, only a handful of residents ever got rich, and times have only gotten tougher since then. It was here, in a country where even $40,000 can be considered a nest egg, that Stanley worked his first cons.

Fred Pack had every reason to think the world of Stanley. A highway construction manager, Pack was a parishioner in the Beverly Hills Tabernacle, the church where Stanley's father preached, and it was upon the Rev. Robert Stanley's enthusiastic recommendation that he believed the junior Stanley's promise to double Pack's investment inside of three years. Shortly after giving Stanley $133,000 to invest for his retirement, Pack's wife was diagnosed with liver cancer and required costly treatment.

Pack says he asked Stanley for his money back, but instead got a runaround. At first Stanley said he couldn't pay him because of a bounced check, then it was a long story about his life being in danger because of dealings with some questionable people living in Florida. Pack eventually had what he called a "gentlemen's discussion" with Stanley; essentially, Pack says, he demanded that Stanley "pay up or else." He finally got most of his money back, but the episode left him with a strong impression.

"He was the most convincing liar you ever met in your life," recalls Pack, one of the few victims to be repaid. "He was so convincing when he told you something that I don't think it registered with him what he was saying."

Tiny Baker, still trying to recover her investment in the scheme, was a more typical victim. Baker says she invested just over $129,000 after J.C. Osgood, Stanley's grandfather and the founder of the Beverly Hills Tabernacle, recommended his grandson's investment services. As a preacher, the owner of a land-surveying business, and the holder of valuable mineral rights in the area, Osgood was widely regarded as a town elder. His seal of approval was all Baker needed to convince her of the wisdom of investing money with Stanley, a fellow parishioner who played piano during Sunday services.

But later, when Baker needed some money for heart surgery, Baker couldn't even get a call through to Stanley. According to her attorney, Baker hasn't received a dime from Stanley. "David Stanley ruined my life and he ruined my children's lives," Baker says. In all, prosecutors allege, residents from Wise County and nearby Sullivan County in Tennessee lost more than $1.25 million in Stanley's investment scheme.

In 1989, when Stanley pleaded guilty, he knew, he says now, that the insurance company for the securities firm where he had been working would repay his victims the more than $1 million they had lost. Stanley failed to take into account, however, that one-third of the payout would go to an attorney representing Stanley's victims, and Stanley would be left to repay the remainder.

The prospect of living in poverty while paying hundreds of thousands of dollars in restitution—only to then spend eight years in prison—was unappealing. In 1996, with only a fraction of his restitution paid, Stanley fled.

Among the victims he left behind were members of his own family. Besides conning a relative in his investment scheme, Stanley left his parents with thousands of dollars in debt and restitution payments when he vanished. Last year the couple filed for bankruptcy, and they face legal problems after co-signing some of the loans he never repaid.

The Rev. Stanley can hardly show his face in town without the locals pointing him out as the preacher whose son bilked his following out of a million dollars. Yet the elder Stanley, who says he had no idea whether his son was dead or alive during his four-year absence, steadfastly defends the honor of his son.

During a recent Sunday service at the Beverly Hills Tabernacle, the elder Stanley referred to his son, incarcerated in the county lockup less than a mile down the road, in mellifluous tones no fewer than three times. "He's still in jail, but we have faith that what has been spoken through prophecy is going to come to pass," the Rev. Stanley said. Like Stanley and so many of his supporters, the preacher seems to believe his son occupies a special place with the Almighty.

Between 1989, the year of his sentencing, and 1996, when he skipped town, Stanley traveled the country as a salesman for an earplug manufacturer and lived in nearby Tennessee. He existed on the edge of poverty as a goodly portion of his paycheck went toward restitution. As Stanley tells it, he lived without electricity for more than six weeks, was evicted seven times and twice had his car repossessed, all because of the restitution requirements. While the authorities at the Tennessee halfway house where he lived a few days per week for three years dubbed him a "model resident," he repeatedly raised the suspicions of the special prosecutor assigned to his case.

There was the year that Stanley paid more in restitution than was reported in his earnings statements, prompting special prosecutor Gerald Gray to accuse Stanley of misleading the court. Citing numerous violations of probation, Gray repeatedly filed court motions for Stanley to serve his prison sentence. Then, in 1995, Stanley faced new charges, including writing a bad check. When he left Tennessee in February 1996 with just $3,300 to his name, his third wife chose to remain in the state with the couple's first child, due in a few months, rather than live on the lam with her fugitive husband.

The teary-eyed departure, he says, was the beginning of a sad and soul-searching journey westward as he tried to rebuild his life. Using a laptop computer and portable printer, he forged a temporary driver's license. In St. Louis he painted his 1993 Hyundai gold, and bleached his dark curly hair bright blond. While on the road one of his molars became abscessed, but he says he so feared being identified that he anesthetized himself with Jack Daniels and yanked out the tooth with a pair of pliers. He says he was stabbed at a truck stop in Kansas City, Kansas during a robbery attempt, receiving a six-inch gash in his torso, but was forced to suffer in silence. "You can't call 911 or the police when you yourself are living underground," Stanley says from jail. Fear and heartache, he adds, dogged his every waking moment.

But in a five-page, single-spaced letter Stanley sent to his wife shortly after he fled, he paints a starkly different account of his life on the run, lashing out at the mother of his child for not leaving with him. "Every single time you look at our child, I want you to remember exactly what YOU and YOU alone did to its biological father," Stanley wrote. "Every day of your life. You deserve that." (Within a few months of sending the letter, Stanley would marry his fourth wife, who would soon be pregnant.)

Beside revealing his gift for manipulation and a tendency to become enraged, the letter shows the tentative but grandiose self-image Stanley worked so hard to construct. "In the new life I have here, (the one I so desperately wanted to share with you) EVERYONE loves me," Stanley's letter continues. "In my home, my female roommate and my new friends all flock around me just to 'touch the flame.'" He goes on to compare himself to biblical figures and promises to throw authorities off his trail by having plastic surgery. "It has always been, and always will be, a mistake to lose faith and underestimate me," Stanley wrote. "God has blessed me with a unique ability to defy reality."

Stanley and his new wife Sheila stumbled upon San Juan Capistrano in November 1996, and decided to stay because she liked the sunny days and mild winters. His weight, once a fit 220 pounds, had ballooned to more than 350 pounds. He had no bank account, no driver's license, no Social Security card, and he could only accept cash for the few odd jobs he took on. They lived out of their Hyundai and showered at a nearby beach.

But the city, roughly an hour's drive southeast from Los Angeles, had an added benefit: Its residents tended to be as trusting as they were affluent. They didn't seem to suspect a thing about the man now calling himself Michael Fenne. He explained away his unusual circumstances with a series of tales, including that he had done covert work for the CIA, had appeared in numerous major movies, and had written songs for and performed with some of the most notable country and western and rock acts of the 1970s. He also said he was keeping a low profile because his wife had recently escaped a Mormon cult that was bent on getting her back. Remarkably, many people believed them.

Looking for work, Stanley responded to an ad placed in the local newspaper by Chuck Hauswirth, now 68, the owner of a "tele-business center" that leased furnished office space to people so they wouldn't have to commute to Los Angeles. Hauswirth wanted someone who could teach tenants how to use Microsoft Word and other computer applications. Stanley arranged a barter: In exchange for a modest-size work cubicle, Stanley offered a cut of his fledgling computer repair business, which he called Restec, an anagram of the word "secret." He claimed his clients included the Saudi royal family.

Hauswith wasn't the only one being taken in by Stanley's charm, good manners and Christian piety. Shortly after his arrival in San Juan Capistrano, Stanley and his wife began attending church at the South Coast Christian Assembly. In only a few weeks, he was playing piano during services and teaching Bible studies.

Some of his Restec customers who had ties to the church eventually asked Stanley if there was a way to replay races at the local horse track over a computer so that people in other locations could place bets. Stanley told them their inquiry had caused him to stumble on a totally new way of playing high-quality video over everyday computers. Excited by the news, Hauswirth and two customers give Stanley money to help him move into a modest hotel. By the middle of 1997, Stanley, Hauswirth and two associates founded Digital Motion Video.

Pulling video off a television and turning it into a file that can be played over a computer is no small feat, and this was even more true in 1997. The amount of information carried in the typical video is so vast that it would take a day or more to download a 30-minute sitcom, even with a super-fast broadband Internet connection. Computer scientists have learned to work around this problem by mathematically "compressing" the video in order to produce significantly smaller file sizes. The compression, however, comes at a price:

The smaller the file, the smaller the picture, and the more jerky the movement and grainy the picture.

But in less than a year's time, Digital Motion had come up with video that seemed on the cutting edge. Unlike software that Apple Computer and Microsoft were marketing at the time, Digital Motion's software produced images that took up a computer's entire monitor and could be refreshed 30 times every second, giving the video the same size and fluidity it would have on television.

The magician who performed this feat was Digital Motion cofounder and president Robert Dunning, a former marketing manager at high-end computer manufacturer GST-Micro City in Southern California. Dunning used highly specialized hardware and software, much of it still in the testing phase, designed by Sunnyvale, Calif.-based FutureTel and other niche companies in the graphics and publishing industries. Dunning's achievement, according to Dunning, Hauswirth and the third Digital Motion partner, was in assembling off-the-shelf components in a way no one else had done before to produce high-quality video. Soon enough, Stanley would hijack Dunning's work, wrongly calling it proprietary technology that Stanley himself had developed.

Digital Motion would soon dissolve, and to this day the four business partners disagree over who is to blame for the failure. Stanley's three business partners, however, all remain adamant that he used his easygoing charm to talk them out of their money and time. They say he also deliberately sabotaged deals that could have gotten the company off the ground. "He's slick," says Hauswirth, who claims that Stanley still owes him more than $60,000. "All of these transactions were based on friendship and a handshake. I just fell under his spell."

Stanley, however, denies that he wronged anyone at Digital Motion, and pins the blame for the company's woes on others. Stanley was able to assuage Hauswirth's anger over the collapse of Digital Motion, he says, by going out of his way to later secure a job at Pixelon for Hauswirth. Hauswirth was laid off once Pixelon hit hard times.

Within weeks of Digital Motion's breakup, Stanley was showing off Dunning's technology to a fresh crop of unsuspecting associates. This time, according to the former Digital Motion partners, he claimed he was a mathematician and computer programmer who had developed the device using a series of technologies he had designed himself. Stanley remains adamant that he was the one who discovered the technology while living out of his car. "I knew I was on the frontier of a totally new area and I got real, real excited," he says.

Soon Stanley was pitching his plan to launch a 1,000-channel Internet broadcasting empire that would rival anything that CBS or Disney could ever build. San Juan Capistrano proved the perfect base. Populated by an ample supply of affluent people who recognized the tremendous investment opportunities offered by the Internet, it was close enough to Los Angeles and Silicon Valley to attract talented employees and business partners—but far enough to escape any careful scrutiny.

Fenne's first crop of takers included a psychologist, the owner of a tile company, a local insurance agent and a marketing manager from Procter & Gamble. Each of them invested between $50,000 and $125,000 in the business. Paul Ward, a lawyer who owned a local insurance company, donated legal services in exchange for a small piece of the company. And thus was born Future Link Communications, later renamed Pixelon.

By the spring of 1999, Pixelon was giving every impression it was well on its way to a hot IPO within the next year. The company struck an exclusive deal with Paramount Pictures to make Web versions of its trailer for the upcoming movie, *Star Trek: Insurrection*, and forged a similar pact with Will Smith to make his *Wild Wild West* video available over the Web in Pixelon's format. In May, the company announced that eCommercial, an Aliso Viejo, Calif.-based startup that adds thin video attachments to e-mail, was purchasing a 10 percent stake in Pixelon for $4 million.

"We are using our patented media-compression technology to deliver true TV-quality video and stereo-quality audio over the Internet rather than the moving slide show available from other technologies," Stanley claimed in a widely distributed press release.

As it turns out, about the only true claim in the entire press release was eCommercial's intention to make the investment. Neither Pixelon nor Stanley have a single patent registered with the U.S. government, though he now insists from jail that he has several pending applications for patents. Nor was Pixelon's technology proprietary. To make matters worse, its playback software actually borrowed heavily from Microsoft's Windows Media Player, according to two former Pixelon executives familiar with the technology.

Touting its deals and cutting-edge tools, this year-old company with just over $1.2 million in its coffers hoped to follow in the footsteps of Broadcast.com, which Yahoo had recently purchased for $5 billion. It was against this backdrop that Advanced Equities, an investment boutique looking for its first hot deal, met Pixelon. What would clinch the firm's interest, however, was the eCommercial announcement, which not only suggested Pixelon's founder and technology were real, but that they were likely to be snapped up by some other investor if Advanced Equities didn't get them first.

On a Saturday morning in May 1999, Advanced Equities principals Lee Wiskowski and Dwight Badger visited San Juan Capistrano to learn more about Pixelon's technology. Having recently founded Advanced Equities, Wiskowski and Badger saw Pixelon as the perfect way to hit a home run.

Already, their friend Rich Callaghan had made a bundle off Pixelon. Callaghan received a salary of $75,000 per year and stock valued at $1.75 million at the time in exchange for arranging funding. Evan Callaghan's previous baggage didn't prevent him from being listed in a Pixelon prospectus as an officer and head of investor relations. A real estate wheeler-dealer, Callaghan and some business associates were fined by a court in Dallas for $70 million over loans made by a savings and loan in Texas, according to court documents. Callaghan declined to comment.

The May meeting with Advanced Equities included Stanley, Steve Curtis, an early investor who eventually became a Pixelon director, and Callaghan. As he did with most of Pixelon's potential business partners, Stanley rattled off the usual litany of his former employers, which in addition to the CIA now included Walt Disney and Sony. He showed them the eCommercial press release and the Will Smith Video. The financiers were impressed.

Though Advanced Equities had yet to receive its general securities dealer license, Pixelon was now agreeing to make the firm its agent for a $20 million private placement, a method of raising money from individuals with a high net worth. (Ultimately, the placement would come to $28 million.) In return, Advanced Equities charged a stunning 12 percent commission and warrants to purchase more than 1 million shares of Pixelon stock, according to internal Pixelon documents.

Most of Pixelon's inexperienced executives didn't know it, but they were being taken for a ride. Standard commissions on private placements of that size were in the neighborhood of 5 percent, with no warrants. Additionally, because Advanced Equities' general securities license was still pending, the firm wouldn't be able to solicit investors for at least a few months, forcing Pixelon to postpone its first major infusion of cash.

Speaking from jail, Stanley says the deal was a classic case of the former con getting conned. "They signed us up and had us by the short hairs, and they knew it, months before they had the legal right to solicit funds."

Advanced Equities says it disclosed to Pixelon that its license was pending and defends the fees it charged, saying they were in line with the amount of work it took to solicit funds. The firm adds that it has since returned the warrants, the value of which are now in question.

Advanced Equities was so eager to fund Pixelon that its due diligence checks into the company's executives and technology was superficial at best. A simple credit check of Fenne, who throughout his tenure at Pixelon had unlimited authority to cut checks and hire employees, would have revealed that the man didn't exist. Yet, the only background check the financiers did into Stanley was to ask him to fill out a questionnaire, in which Stanley represented he had no convictions, Wiskowski said in an interview. Advanced Equities never bothered to call relatives, former business associates and employers, as is routine when handing a company millions of dollars in financing.

The firm also never bothered to speak with anyone at eCommercial, which dropped its plan to invest in Pixelon shortly after issuing the press release. Technicians at eCommercial, which recently changed its name to MindArrow, say they had put Stanley's claims to the test shortly after agreeing to the deal in principle and found the technology lacking. "It was the pursuit of the Holy Grail that sucked everybody in," says MindArrow's CEO Tom Blakeley, referring to Pixelon's claims to have a proprietary method for producing high-quality video that could be compressed into small packets. "That's what got us, until we did a little due diligence. And then we realized that their technology was paper-thin."

Had Advanced Equities paired up with an interested industry leader—as is typical in many private placements—the financiers would have had a well-informed partner to help them assess the authenticity of Pixelon's claims to a proprietary technology. The firm, however, wanted the deal all to itself.

So Wiskowski says that he sent a friend with expertise in video compression and telecommunications to check out Pixelon's technology. The expert, whom Wiskowski declines to name, was so impressed that he invested in Pixelon prior to the private placement. Wiskowski decided Pixelon was too hot to pass up. "We were seeing them come up on MTV and VH1 [Web sites], bumping multimillion-dollar companies like Real-Networks," Wiskowski says.

Others were duped too. At a press conference that summer, Republican National Committee Chairman Jim Nicholson lavished praise on Stanley: "I want to express my personal thanks on behalf of the Republican National Committee and to Michael Fenne, the founder and chief technical officer of Pixelon, for making this revolutionary and exciting technology exclusively available to the RNC," he said.

While Pixelon's backers were gloating, employees inside the company were among the first to grow suspicious. Gary Devore, a video-encoding engineer in charge of training new employees, was among them. Lured to Pixelon by promises that the company's proprietary compression scheme was going to turn the startup into an overnight success, Devore quickly went from being a contract employee to a manager in charge of encoding baseball games and other content so that highlights could be downloaded from Pixelon's Web site. Devore was ultimately fired after Fenne complained he was not performing his job properly.

Devore says he had suspicions about the technology, but he didn't fully appreciate the deception until the middle of August, when Pixelon claimed it was using its proprietary platform to broadcast highlights of the Iowa Straw Poll live over the Internet. When Devore reported to work that day, he discovered Pixelon was using Microsoft's Windows Media Player—the very technology Pixelon so often cast as inferior—to broadcast the event. Three other former employees—including Russ Reeder, Pixelon's VP of product development—confirmed the account. A shortcoming in Pixelon's platform, Reeder says, was that it couldn't compress video into small enough pieces to send out live over the Internet. To disguise the ruse, Devore says, Stanley used a customization feature in Windows Media Player to remove all Microsoft branding.

There were other signs of trouble. Stanley demanded that he be paid out of an expense account. For another, nepotism at Pixelon was rampant. According to Reeder, Paul Ward had at least three relatives working at the company, while Reeder had two. Dave Snyder, a board member, had recently taken a paying job at Pixelon, as had Snyder's daughter.

Stanley's management style was also becoming increasingly erratic. Not only was he requiring some employees to work 36-hour shifts, but he was also becoming increasingly abusive.

Perhaps most alarming was a mandatory prayer gathering. One Sunday in August, Stanley instructed all employees to meet in his office for what was described as a worship service to bless a new space Pixelon had just taken over. Among those attending was Robert Feldman, who, although he was Jewish, says he had received an e-mail saying he was expected to attend. Dave Snyder was there with a book of religious scripture in hand. Reeder, who carried a Bible, was also there.

Some say Snyder began the meeting by reading a New Testament passage in which Jesus miraculously feeds 5,000 people with just five loaves of bread and two fish. As was always the case, the air-conditioning in Stanley's office was turned up high, and it was so dark that the light from a nearby computer monitor cast an eerie glow on Stanley. Stanley's chair sat on a small platform so that he was elevated above everyone else sitting in the room. After the readings, Stanley played a piano and sang a hymn he said he had written. His wife sat close by, wiping tears from her eyes.

Snyder says he remembers reading scriptures with some employees at Pixelon once, but is sure he didn't read the story about the loaves of bread and fish. He also strenuously denies there was anything out of the ordinary about the meeting. "I certainly wasn't trying to equate Michael Fenne with Jesus Christ," says Snyder.

Devore says he was offended by the meeting, but he went along to keep from rocking the boat and because he still had hopes of becoming rich in March, when Pixelon was supposed to go public. "Michael would say in meetings that everybody in this company is going to be a millionaire in a short period of time," says Devore. "The mania [was] the glue that kept the dysfunctional family together."

Up until the fall of 1999, the drama and deception unfolding inside Pixelon was a carefully kept secret, touching perhaps only a few dozen people at most. It likely would have remained that way were it not for iBash '99, Pixelon's extravagant launch party.

Held at the MGM Grand in Las Vegas on October 29, the day-long extravaganza included a reunion by the Who and performances by the Dixie Chicks, Chely Wright, Faith Hill, Tony Bennett, the Brian Setzer orchestra and Kiss. Originally intended to cost Pixelon only $1 million and take place at Anaheim Stadium, not far from San Juan Capistrano, those modest plans quickly vanished with the hiring of music veteran Danny Socolof as Pixelon's chief marketing officer, according to at least four people familiar with iBash discussions.

The idea behind the event was to get Pixelon's name in front of all kinds of people, from stock brokers addicted to classic rock to truck drivers hooked on country music to senior citizens who liked lounge crooning. The event, the thinking went, would provide the perfect opportunity for Pixelon to showcase its unique ability to broadcast high-quality video live over the Internet. Exclusive rights to the archives of iBash would keep the masses coming back to Pixelon's Web site for months after the event.

But it never happened that way. Despite some spectacular performances, Pixelon was unable to broadcast the event live using the very proprietary platform the event was designed to hype. Even worse, the vast majority of footage from the event never made its way online. If Pixelon meant to become an instant success among a public hungry for unique content on the Web, it became only the object of scorn. "This has got to be the most incompetent, pathetic Internet company I've seen to date," one person wrote in an Internet discussion group after unsuccessfully trying to access iBash footage for days. "Pixelon is a perfect example of how new technology should NOT be used," another frustrated viewer wrote.

Worse than being a public relations disaster, iBash turned into a financial black hole that largely sank Pixelon's chances of ever getting off the ground. Socolof, who was fired two months before iBash, received a severance package of $150,000 in cash and stock conservatively valued at $870,000, Paul Ward says. The music veteran, his secretary confirms, went on to take the coveted position of road manager for the Who's North American tour.

For their efforts the Who received $2 million in cash and a generous offering of stock; LeAnn Rimes made $1 million; and the Dixie Chicks got $875,000 and at least $230,000 in stock. All told, iBash cost more than $16.2

million, more than 75 percent of the capital Pixelon had taken in during its year and a half existence. As if it made any difference, the company continued to tell the press the event's price tag was $12 million.

Fuming over the launch debacle, the principals from Advanced Equities were in no mood for negotiations when they arrived at Pixelon on Nov. 12. They had received enough reconnaissance information to know that the situation was dire. The trio's message as they stopped at each executive's office was the same. "It's not a negotiation. It's not a debate. It's not a discussion," one person remembers one of the principals saying. "If we don't have an agreement by the time we leave, you will have a class-action lawsuit on your desk within 48 hours."

Interim CEO Ward called Michael Kelley, a director living in Northern California, and told him to take the next available flight to San Juan Capistrano. He also began tracking down Bart Moore, another board member who was on a horseback riding trip for the day.

It was 10:30 that morning when the investors had their first contract with Stanley, who was clearly unhappy about their visit. Badger, who had been instrumental in sealing the deal with Pixelon, stood up and offered to shake his hand, but Stanley, who appeared out of breath and badly in need of sleep, just walked past the man. Stanley, according to some in attendance, then launched into a long and sometimes vulgar rant about how he would never give up control of the company. He seemed on the edge of violence.

The investors, however, were digging in. "We sold this deal as a $57 million market cap and we're not taking a percentage point less," one of them responded. "If you don't rectify this, you'll never raise money again."

The investors ticked off a plethora of concerns. There was the firing earlier that week of Pixelon's newly appointed CEO, Judy Smith, a former deputy press secretary during the Bush Administration and communications exec at MSNBC. She was probably best known for being Monica Lewinsky's spokeswoman after the intern's affair with President Clinton became public. For months, Stanley had been pushing Smith as a candidate for the CEO spot, but Advanced Equities had resisted. Finally, at a shareholders meeting just two weeks earlier, Stanley had stunned the investors when he stood and with great fanfare introduced Smith as Pixelon's next CEO. Now, just as they were getting used to the idea, they had learned she had been fired. Advanced Equities was also upset about the massive and unauthorized grants of Pixelon stock that grossly diluted current shareholders' holdings.

As the day wore on, Wiskowski and others who wanted to oust Stanley were concerned about whether they had the votes. Of course, Stanley was sure to vote against the measure, as was Snyder. That meant the plan would need the support of either Moore, who was unreachable on his riding trip, or Kelley, who was still in flight from Northern California. In the meantime, they continued to worry that Stanley might get violent if he learned of the plan. They decided to get Stanley into the conference room and that Feldman, the recent Pixelon hire, would keep an eye on the room from outside through a window. If the plotters thought Stanley was about to go ballistic, one of them would gesture to Feldman with a thumbs down, the agreed-upon signal for him to call the police.

As the group attempted to meet again with Stanley, they encountered a new problem: Posted outside Stanley's office were two large bodyguards, and word around the office was that they were armed. Wiskowski and Badger walked past the guards and entered the office. Sensing he was close to being ousted, Stanley suddenly was in a mood to bargain, according to people present at the meeting.

"Give me 90 days and I'll turn the company around," he told them. Cam Fraser, another recently hired executive, approached the office door and asked the bodyguards to leave, but they refused. As nonchalantly as he could, Wiskowski feigned a yawn and a stretch, clasping his fingers together and turning his hands so that his two thumbs were clearly pointing downward – the prearranged signal to call the cops.

Within a half-hour, squad cars arrived and removed the bodyguards peaceably. Although Stanley steadfastly denies bodyguards were ever on the premises that day, the two men, Lindsey Largess and Anthony Vaughan, would file suit three months later accusing Pixelon of false imprisonment and slander in connection with the incident.

The bodyguards gone, the three Advanced Equities principals remained in Stanley's office trying to coax him into the conference room. Meanwhile, board member Kelley was arriving by cab. The driver, panicked by the cop cars, refused to stop, and Kelley says he jumped out of the car while it was still moving.

By nightfall, the board meeting finally got into gear. In addition to Stanley, five board members—Wiskowski, Curtis, Ward, Kelley and Snyder—were there. People were still trying to track down Moore, the seventh director.

Fenne, ever a master at deception, opened the meeting with a cryptic remark: "I've reached an interesting agreement with the gentlemen from Advanced Equities, but we'll leave that action for last in our meeting," at least four people remember him saying.

His remark spooked the group and Ward now worried that the plan to remove Stanley had been derailed. He silently counted votes, wondering if the needed four members would turn against Stanley. Just a few hours ago, three members—Ward, Wiskowski and Curtis—had vowed to vote in favor; it was unclear how Kelley and Moore would vote. Any splintering of this fragile coalition would surely sink the plan. Stanley's unique ability to defy reality was showing itself again.

"I kept thinking, 'This son of a bitch is going to survive this meeting with his chairmanship intact,'" one board member recalls. "'This 350-pound guy is going to squeeze through the crack!'"

The meeting moved on to other matters. Finally, Wiskowski smacked his palm on the table and made a motion that Stanley be suspended as chairman and CTO for 30 days. "You betrayed me," one meeting participant remembers a clearly stunned-looking Stanley saying. Ward seconded the motion before Wiskowski had a chance to respond. Stanley was now even more shocked. "Now I know who my Judas is," Stanley replied.

A clearly irate Snyder called the move illegal in light of the employment agreement Stanley had executed only a few months earlier. As the sparks continued to fly, Bart Moore finally appeared, dressed in cowboy boots and jeans that were caked in mud. When Wiskowski's measure finally came up for vote only Stanley and Snyder failed to vote in favor. Stanley's reign at Pixelon was over.

Almost immediately, however, it was clear that the drama would not be over. Soon after the board meeting, word circulated in Pixelon's inner circles that someone had found a document on Stanley's computer suggesting he had been harboring a profound secret. Addressed "Hi guys," the undated letter laid out a detailed plan in the event an unidentified "they" ever discovered his con. "The fact remains that someday they might get lucky . . . and I need to be ready to depart the country altogether in that event," he wrote. "If that is God's will for our lives, then so be it." The letter discusses using hair dye and colored contact lenses to create a new identity, and eventually reentering the country as a naturalized citizen. "I would only do this after a face change through plastic surgery," the letter says. Snyder says Stanley wrote the letter but never sent it out. He declines to discuss the letter further, saying it is likely to be the subject of a lawsuit he plans to file against Pixelon.

Despite the rumors that flew about the document, a December severance agreement shows Pixelon agreed to pay Stanley $660,000 over 30 months to purchase 2 million shares of his stock. (Stanley had owned 3 million shares and had options to own another 9 million. He says he has since sold yet more shares but still owns a small amount of Pixelon stock.)

Besides facing the extreme legal exposure of paying off an officer whose integrity there was good reason to doubt, Pixelon's management faced other problems. It was only after Stanley signed his severance agreement preventing

Pixelon from making any future legal claims against him that executives learned they had failed to secure the rights to future versions of the Pixelon Player, the software used to play video over a computer. In their haste to execute the agreement, they had failed to notice that the player had been developed for Digital Motion by an outside consultant who still owned rights to the source code.

By February, Pixelon's troubles just seemed to get worse. The CEO brought in to reorganize the company suddenly resigned, creditors began demanding payment for hundreds of thousands of dollars in unpaid bills, and jilted partners began taking legal swipes at the faltering company.

More serious still for Pixelon are lingering doubts about the value of Pixelon's intellectual property. Several investors and potential partners who had considered forging deals with Pixelon say their initial inquiries into Pixelon's technology gave them pause. The Pixelon Player, they say, appears to borrow so heavily from Microsoft technologies that its worth is questionable.

Meanwhile, the encoder, or compression technology, attracts slightly higher investor interest. A prospectus and at least two Pixelon executives say the company's current version of its technology has at least as much to do with work done by LocoLabs—a San Jose, Calif.-based company that bills itself as having "magnetically attracted a staff of mad-scientist types,"—than it ever did with anyone at Pixelon. (Brad Hoffert, LocoLabs' president, didn't respond to numerous requests for an interview.) The arrangement means that LocoLabs has joint ownership of the technology. Also, the technology is generally regarded as comparable to products already being manufactured by companies such as Ligos and Digital Bitcasting.

That might explain why a $70 million offer in January by New York-based Internet broadcaster On2.com quickly fell by the wayside. Pixelon entertained the suitors, according to two sources familiar with the negotiations, but ultimately refused to let On2 engineers inspect Pixelon's technology. In May, Pixelon laid off its remaining employees.

Acting CEO Ward and Pixelon's remaining executives were fired last week. Ward was not available for comment. Peter Foley, executive vice president at Unified Financial Services in New York, was named president. Wiskowski says the new management plans to assess the true worth of the company's assets in an attempt to either sell Pixelon or attract new investors. An initial audit conducted Wednesday indicated Pixelon has proprietary rights to an advanced encryption scheme and technologies for inserting personalized ads that collect user feedback in real time, which might be considered a core asset. One executive still believes Pixelon's assets could be worth as much as $25 million.

Stanley, meanwhile, wasted no time rising from the ashes of his failed company. A week after receiving a down payment of nearly $200,000 from Pixelon, public records indicate he paid nearly $181,000 in cash for a house in Big Bear City, Calif., and put it in the name of a company he had set up called Landragon Development. Through Landragon, he had several other properties in escrow, according to real estate and law-enforcement sources in San Bernardino County. Working with Snyder and several other close friends, Stanley established several other businesses, including Lazaron Ventures, Axitar and Ailos. Snyder, who is president of Lazaron, says the company's initial focus will be on using satellites to access the Internet.

Then, in early April, Stanley got the call he had dreaded for four years. A disgruntled associate from one of Stanley's earlier San Juan Capistrano ventures had spotted a picture of David Kim Stanley, one of Virginia's 12 most-wanted fugitives, and thought it looked a lot like the man called Michael Fenne. A few days later, as San Bernardino sheriff's deputies moved to take custody of Stanley, they found only his empty house, which had clearly been vacated in a hurry. Stanley says he turned himself in after Snyder, who had heard about the imminent capture through the grapevine, convinced him there was no other way to respond.

He now sits in Wise County jail, where he is being held pending a hearing in which a prosecutors will ask that Stanley finally serve the prison sentence he received more than a decade ago.

From coast to coast, over a span of 15 years, wherever Stanley has gone, he left behind a chorus of associates, acquaintances and former friends who call him the biggest scam artist they've ever met. What is less clear, however, is what drove him to deceive. There seem to be no fast cars, no summer cottages in the Hamptons, and no fancy yachts that suggest Stanley ever pocketed any money from his scams.

For now, no one knows for sure if Stanley was simply good at concealing a fortune in ill-gotten gains or if the con artist simply lied and cheated out of sport and revenge. What is clear is that he believes he has done nothing wrong, sees great things in his future and, when he gets out of jail, plans to finish what he started at Pixelon.

"In running for my life, I found my life in technology," says Stanley, who likes to remind people of all he was able to accomplish at Pixelon without so such as a Social Security number. "When I'm operational again, whenever that will be, without the chains and limitations of being underground, I am going to build that network."

Hidden Past Sheds Light on Ex-IQuest Chief's Odd Ways

By John Masson and John Flora
Staff Writers

Sometimes a name really does say it all.

Hokum.

As in Robert Hoquim—pronounced like the old-fashioned term for hog-wash—founder and former owner of IQuest Internet in Indianapolis. Hoquim, whose real name was John Paul Aleshe, was found dead in his Noblesville home May 23.

His assumed identity began unraveling a few days later as police looked into his death. Investigators soon determined that the death was natural, but they also learned that Aleshe, whose prosperous Internet service provider boasted tens of thousands of clients in four states, had been a fugitive since 1986. That's when authorities say he tried to kill a Texas police officer during a struggle for the officer's gun.

Between then and the founding of IQuest in 1992, Aleshe, who died at 42, left a trail of computer scams that racked up thousands of dollars, according to police, the FBI, and people who say they were his victims.

In the wake of his death, some of his associates have painted a sunny portrait of a brilliant, friendly, self-made Internet entrepreneur. But another picture of the reputed millionaire began emerging, as well.

Several former employees said he was a gruff, distant boss with a hot temper and a broad streak of paranoia. Many commented on the unique and pervasive security at the company's unmarked offices on Indianapolis' Northeastside, security so forbidding that customers usually weren't allowed in the building.

They talked about the two classes of people in the little cyberworld of the man they knew as Bob Hoquim. There were Friends of Bob, who could park inside the 10-foot-high, razor wire-topped security fence in the company's back parking lot. And there were non-Friends of Bob, who parked outside the fence.

David Cook, who did business with IQuest, said Aleshe was approachable and charming early in their relationship but became more distant and security-conscious as time went on. And he wasn't completely surprised when he heard that Aleshe had assumed his new, playfully ironic surname.

"He was utterly brilliant," Cook said. "But this has been nothing but a gigantic mind game, which he seemed to enjoy thoroughly."

Almost everybody could agree on one point: Aleshe was a prodigious and prolific liar.

Hokum.

Twist of fate

In an odd way, Officer Ned Thurmond of Texas' Irving Police Department is responsible for the creation of what became Indiana's largest Internet service provider.

If he hadn't linked Aleshe to a stolen car at a cheap motel, Aleshe's fugitive path might never have brought him here.

But Thurmond did make that link, eventually tracing the expensive stolen car in the parking lot to the motel room alongside an Irving freeway.

Just before midnight on June 3, 1986, Thurmond arrested Aleshe and put the handcuffed man in the front seat of his police car. At the time, according to Irving Police public information officer David Tull, the department's patrol cars didn't have a screen separating the front and back seats, so the safest way for a lone officer such as Thurmond to transport a prisoner was in the front.

So far, everything was routine.

"But four blocks from the city jail, the guy got one hand free and grabbed Thurmond's gun." Tull said.

The two struggled over the weapon, a standard police revolver. At one point, Tull said, Aleshe aimed the gun at Thurmond's head and pulled the trigger. The officer saved himself by jamming the web of skin between his thumb and forefinger between the revolver's hammer and the cartridge.

The gun didn't go off.

Moments later, Tull said, Thurmond wrestled away the weapon and fired a shot that blew off one finger on Aleshe's left hand. The fight was over.

But not the story. Aleshe faced a string of preliminary felony charges, including attempted capital murder, car theft and possession of less than 28 grams of cocaine. He also was held on a fugitive warrant for theft.

But he was allowed to bail out of jail. His brother, who lives in Florida, dutifully posted Aleshe's bond. And never saw him again.

Hokum.

Cultivating victims

By June, 1987, Aleshe was living near Minneapolis after spending some time in Portland, Ore. He followed a pattern in Minnesota that became familiar to his victims nationwide.

"He basically was the type of guy that would ingratiate himself with people for the exclusive purpose of worming his way into their souls, so they would become susceptible to possible fraud," said Steve Sherwick, who knew Aleshe in Minneapolis-St. Paul and now runs the Internet service provider Minnetonka Micro.

At the time, Sherwick was active in establishing a Minneapolis-area BBS, or computer bulleting board system—a computer network service similar to a crude Internet. Aleshe, who now was going by the name John Richard, came on the scene and set up a BBS system called PC Info Exchange. Then he offered to take over moving huge amounts of electronic mail for others in the computer community.

But Sherwick says that by lightening others' loads, Aleshe really was working on building trust—trust he later wold betray.

"He could massage the moment," Sherwick said. "He was the most talented liar I've ever met. After he skipped town, I couldn't believe that I accepted a lot of the stuff he was telling me as plausible."

Among those claims by Aleshe was that he was a "full-bird colonel" in the Air Force and an F-14 pilot. He told Sherwick he'd been transferred from Portland to Minneapolis and assigned to a local electronics manufacturer as an inspector.

Before long, Aleshe was doing what he'd always done: wheeling and dealing with computer people, swapping parts and offering equipment at ultra-low prices until people had enough confidence in him that he really could set the hook.

"He was a bad man," Sherwick said. "He caused a huge amount of damage."

For Sherwick, who never lost any money to Aleshe, that damage was limited to cleaning up the mess he said was left among Aleshe's 300 paying network subscribers after he abandoned them and abruptly skipped town in April 1988.

Not so lucky was David Garner, who owned Cascade Electronics and who said he lost more than $68,000 through bogus business deals with Aleshe.

An Internet posting that Garner wrote warned other computer brokers about the convoluted scam Aleshe ran on him, a scam that put him out of business.

So outraged were the Minnesota computer users, Sherwick said, that they posted Garner's warning, and others, on computer bulletin boards throughout the country. They dutifully updated the warnings for more than a decade whenever new information about Aleshe came up.

"It's one of those things that we haven't let die, because he ruined the lives of some people we really liked," Sherwick said.

Some of Aleshe's Minnesota victims already are contacting Gordon Wishard, the attorney for Aleshe's estate, seeking reimbursement for their losses, Garner said. But he's not getting his hopes up.

"If everybody he defrauded goes after their money . . . there won't be anything left," he said. "If I'm able to recover anything it'll be a miracle."

Wishard said he couldn't discuss whether any of the victims contacted him.

No similar tales of bogus dealings have surfaced in Indianapolis. Sherwick speculates that Aleshe set up IQuest at just the right moment, as the Internet was taking off among the general public. Perhaps, he said, Aleshe made enough money from his legitimate business that he didn't need to resort to more crime to raise capital.

"You guys [in Indianapolis] are lucky," Sherwick said. "When financial straits got to the point where he could not support his lifestyle, he'd get a bunch of money together and blow town."

And move onto the next burg, shoveling hokum all the way.

Tough to work for

Aleshe might have given up the criminal life after he founded IQuest, which he sold earlier this year to retire and pursue an interest in racing. But that didn't make working for him particularly easy—especially for his lower-level employees.

Despite Aleshe's apparent preference for basements—his office and apartment were in the basement of IQuest's building, and he lived in a basement apartment at his luxurious Noblesville home—some said he had an "ivory tower" leadership style

Others say Aleshe had a bunker mentality. Most watched in amazement as security at the building grew ever tighter.

"It was basically a paranoid organization," said Nathan Harris of Greenfield, who worked at IQuest for 2 and a half years. "Nobody was trusted. I worked there a year before I even had a key to get in the building. It was kind of spooky, to tell you the truth."

One ironic twist, according to several former employees, was Aleshe's fondness for a cap with the embroidered letters "FBI" on the front. Considering his place on the organization's Most Wanted List, it was an odd talisman.

As Aleshe's business grew, so did he. His penchant for Ruth's Chris steaks, pizzas, and a variety of other foods helped pack pounds on his frame, Cook said. The 300-pound man who died of a heart attack bore little resemblance to the younger man peering out from old police photos.

And through it all, according to many of the people who worked for him, the lies—Hoquim's hokum—were continuous.

"We'd always assumed the man was a compulsive liar," Harris said. "But at this point, I know he was lying to cover up."

For Harris, the puzzling routine at the state's largest Internet provider all became clear as news of Aleshe's secret past burst forth in newspapers, on television and on the Internet.

"You have something that perplexes you and then one day it's all explained," he said. "He was just a criminal on the lam."

The Life and Near Death of Drkoop.com

By Todd Woody
Austin, Texas

On the eve of his 83rd birthday last October, former Surgeon General C. Everett Koop sat glumly in his suite at the Waldorf-Astoria in Manhattan. As an attorney grilled him about fraud charges leveled against executives at Drkoop.com, he must have wondered what had gone wrong at the Web site that bore his good name.

Just four months earlier, Drkoop had gone public, making Koop an instant Internet icon, a multimillionaire on paper and an elder statesman in an industry of young turks. Drkoop quickly had become one of the most popular health-information sites on both the Web and Wall Street. It seemed that Koop's high-minded objective—to get important health information to the public by exploiting the gold-rush mentality of the Internet—was paying off.

But as Koop was beginning to discover, success can be fleeting in the Internet Economy. First came a startling front-page story in the *New York Times* questioning Koop's online ethics, of all things. Now, just weeks later, he faced serious questions from an attorney about whether his chief executive and vice chairman had cheated a consultant out of stock options worth millions of dollars.

As surgeon general, Koop stared down senators and took on Big Tobacco. But as chairman of Drkoop, he had trouble answering the most basic questions about his own company. He conceded to the consultant's lawyer that he knew next to nothing about the allegations of wrongdoing. Nor was he aware that CEO Donald Hackett had handed out stock options worth $1 million to a lawyer friend. Nor did he know what services Drkoop's biggest investor had provided the company. As the deposition dragged on, it was apparent that Koop was almost completely out of the loop about the goings-on at Drkoop headquarters in Austin, Texas. "I don't micromanage problems that I delegate to people that I trust," said Koop, parrying with the attorney.

Perhaps he should have. Today Drkoop is struggling to survive as its cash runs out, its stock price hovers near $1, and senior managers and staff head for the door. While Koop remained in his Hanover, N.H., home, Drkoop executives were cutting questionable deals and handing out lavish salaries that drained the company's coffers in a matter of months. Now, some angry investors, feeling swindled after Koop and three other directors sold stock at a handsome profit before releasing damaging information about the company, are suing Drkoop and its executives for fraud. Koop, who made nearly $1 million in his stock sale, won't escape shareholders' ire—as chairman he has a legal duty to safeguard their interests.

Koop isn't talking, but the reversal of his fortune has left his old friends and supporters bewildered. Koop, the best-known surgeon general of the 20th century, stepped down from public office in 1989. His principled stands on divisive issues like AIDS and his proselytizing on behalf of public health made "Koop" a symbol of integrity. A pop culture fixture, "Koop" continues to carry weight years after he returned to private life. Now, in the twilight of his career, Koop's reputation is in jeopardy.

Koop may have been a good doctor, but events would show he wasn't a savvy businessman. It was only three years ago that his first venture into the private sector—a health videotape series backed by Time Life—collapsed in bankruptcy. Then, like now, Koop trusted business associates bent on making a profit to carry out his public health mission. "I have been quite saddened at the turn of events affecting my good friend since the summer of 1999," says George Lundberg, the former longtime editor of the *Journal of the American Medical Association* and now editor of MedicaLogic/Medscape, an online health company.

In an industry that has attracted its share of dreamers, schemers and oddballs, no dot-commer has ever been quite like C. Everett Koop. A pioneering pediatric surgeon in Philadelphia, Koop was 64 years old when President Ronald Reagan appointed him surgeon general in 1981, when many of today's Net executives were barely out of elementary school.

Koop's knack for doing the unexpected—who would have guessed he would become chairman of an Internet firm—was apparent soon after he took office. His anti-abortion views and ties to the religious right made him a natural choice for the Reagan administration. Once installed as surgeon general, however, Koop surprised his liberal critics and infuriated the White House by crusading against tobacco companies and making AIDS a priority. Koop's white beard and bearing gave him the air of an Old Testament patriarch delivering the Word from on high. Koop gripped the public's imagination, and after eight years of service had earned the title of "America's doctor."

"As I came to the end of my surgeon general years, I felt that I had gained the public's trust and that I should do something with it," Koop wrote in his 1991 autobiography. "First, I wanted to make sure that I did not use that trust only for private gain. Like many Americans, I was disgusted with the way retired politicians—even presidents—cashed in on their celebrity status."

Koop's celebrity was built on doing just the opposite, on standing up for the public good. After having his post in Washington, he continued to work on problems patients had with managed health care organizations obsessed with controlling costs. To help patients learn more about medicine and take more control of their health, in 1992 he established the C. Everett Koop Institute, a nonprofit at Dartmouth College.

So Koop was receptive when former advertising executive J. Keith Green pitched him a proposal in 1994 to market a series of health information videotapes that would take Koop's message to the masses. Green had lined up Time Life to license its venerable name and provide financial muscle. But he needed Koop as the company's public face. As an incentive, Green reportedly promised Koop a salary of $750,000. Koop signed on as chairman of the company, Patient Education Media, but his chief responsibilities were to appear in the Time Life Medical videos. "These videos are designed to help newly diagnosed patients get their feet on the ground and communicate more productively with their physicians," Koop said at the time.

The venture's fate would foreshadow Drkoop's later troubles: it had an unproven business model—selling $19.95 videotapes in pharmacies—spent extravagantly, and ultimately failed to meet sales projections. "We didn't spend too much, we just didn't raise enough," Green told the *Wall Street Journal* in 1997 before the company filed for bankruptcy with liabilities of $39 million. Green would later resurface at Drkoop.com.

By most accounts, the Time Life debacle left Koop bewildered and embarrassed. But the experience didn't inoculate him against the charms of smooth-talking Internet entrepreneurs who could spin a vision of using Koop's name to promote his public health mission while making a buck for themselves.

One of those entrepreneurs was John Zaccaro, who would play a key role in the formation of Drkoop.com. Zaccaro has not been shy when it comes to selling himself to others. "Actor, stunt man, adventurer, million-dollar-a-year salesman and master consultant John F. Zaccaro reveals the secret forces that bring riches and help you change your life and fortune," reads a publisher's blurb for a 1986 motivational book Zaccaro wrote titled *Climb your Own Mountain: The Ultimate Success Guide.*

The reality of his career is somewhat more prosaic. Zaccaro, now 65, made his fortune in carpet padding and pool covers. Even when selling pool covers, Zaccaro infused the job with a sense of grandeur. "I did indeed personally help install the solar pool cover on the White House pool while President Gerald Ford was in office," he writes in an e-mail. "He's a super salesman, a promoter, a media-type guy, but a man of integrity," says T.J. Dermot Dunphy, chairman of Sealed Air, which sold the pool blanket Zaccaro marketed. "It's absolutely natural he would end up promoting an e-commerce company."

In the early 1980s, Zaccaro joined a startup founded by the ex-wife of health-and-beauty mogul Vidal Sassoon. The relationship ended badly, and Zaccaro sued the company for nearly $20 million, claiming Beverly Sassoon and her partners reneged on an agreement to make him president and COO "at an annual salary of $120,000, plus luxury automobile and 20 percent equity," according to Los Angeles County court records. Zaccaro later dropped the case. He then jumped back into the pool industry. By the end of the decade he switched gears again, joining Physician Computer Network, a New Jersey company that sold software to doctors.

While at PCN, Zaccaro hired a then-thirtysomething former computer salesman named Donald Hackett. Like Zaccaro, Hackett was ambitious, entrepreneurial and a natural salesman. But if Zaccaro could strike associates as arrogant, Hackett displayed a charisma and a sincerity that inspired loyalty among his colleagues. (Even after suing him for fraud, a former consultant fondly recalled his friendship with Hackett.) Hackett left PCN in 1996 and began a short-lived stint as COO and later CEO of TradeWave, an Austin company that made Internet security software. But he had bigger plans.

Hackett wanted to start a company that would market an electronic medical record to enable patients to share information with their doctors and health plans. The Internet would provide a way to widely distribute such a document. But Hackett needed a trusted name to persuade consumers to put their sensitive health information online.

Zaccaro had just the person. By this time Zaccaro and Koop had become good friends, having met in the early 1990s when Zaccaro was producing the International Health and Medical Film Festival. Koop had attended the festival, and soon afterward Zacarro wooed the former surgeon general to join his board by telling him the event needed an "icon." "Since 1991, we have become very good friends. There's a great trust and a bond between us," Zacarro says in a deposition.

That Zaccaro would be attracted to Koop's star power was not surprising. "I'm well connected . . . I know how to bring people in from both the entertainment community and the [medical] community," Zaccaro brags in the deposition, dropping the name of heart-transplant pioneer Michael DeBakey as someone he knows.

Hackett also began attending the festivals, and in 1996 met Koop at one of the events. To Hackett, it was a no-brainer: Who better to endorse an online medical record than "America's doctor"? And who better to broker Koop's participation than their mutual friend, Zaccaro?

"Don viewed getting a commitment from Dr. Koop through John as really the key element," testified consultant Andy Agrawal, who helped write the company's early business plans, in his fraud lawsuit against Drkoop. "That without Dr. Koop's participation, he had serious reservations about whether the company focusing on a personal medical record that would be accessible through the Internet would ever fly without Dr. Koop's credibility."

Hacket approached Zaccaro with his pitch for a company called Personal Medical Records. Zaccaro liked the proposal from the start. Then Hackett talked about the need to associate the company with a trusted name. "I knew what he was getting at," recalled Zaccaro. "He wanted an introduction to Dr. Koop. I was very guarded about that because of the many years of good relationships with him."

Zaccaro decided to visit Koop alone. It was a delicate time. By early 1997, Koop's Time Life video venture was sliding toward bankruptcy and Koop was wary. "It was one thing for me to say to Dr. Koop, 'This is a great idea, Dr. Koop. This is going to help you, you know, realize your mission,'" says Zaccaro. "A man who has given 52 years to the public-service sector is not used to this kind of approach."

Koop did not dismiss the idea out of hand, and on Zacarro's next trip to Koop's home Hackett came along. Over the next two months, Zaccaro and Hackett visited Koop twice to discuss his participation in the company. The lobbying paid off. On Oct. 1, 1997, Koop officially signed on as chairman and director of the company that would become Drkoop.com. At age 80, Koop became America's most-senior Internet entrepreneur.

At the time, the idea that Koop would risk his reputation again in the private sector—and with something as new as an Internet startup—did not seem so foolhardy. After all, he had known Zaccaro for six years and Zaccaro was personally vouching for the integrity and skills of Hackett and his team. And the Internet offered Koop a new medium to deliver his message. "I have tried to deliver those messages to patients all of my life. The Internet is invaluable in this. It has the potential to help people take charge of their own health by providing a wealth of knowledge," Koop told *Yahoo Internet Life* magazine. Still, he acknowledged it was not an easy decision to lend his name to an untried Net company. "As surgeon general, I had developed a following. I became a sort of folk hero because of my work with tobacco and AIDS. It took a lot of persuasion in my own mind to decide to do it."

Koop's earlier video venture at least carried the prestige of the Time Life name and a Sixth Avenue address; his foray onto the Internet came with no such flash. When Zacarro and Hackett were courting Koop, the company was run out of Hackett's home in the Austin hill country. Hackett paid the bills from his own pocket.

The company, still called Personal Medical Records, was developing technology for an electronic personal medical record, or PMR. An April 1997 business plan that Hackett showed to potential investors described how consumers could use a PMR stored online or on their computers to share information with physicians and health plans.

It seemed a questionable premise, especially in 1997. At the time, consumers were still leery of entering their credit card numbers online, let along sensitive medical information, and Hackett was gambling that the Koop name would overcome such resistance. There were plenty of other hurdles. To succeed, the company had to persuade consumers to track down their health records from their physicians and enter the information into an online database. Doctors also had to cooperate. The medical-software industry had spent decades unsuccessfully trying to create an electronic medical record for physicians, and whether doctors would now accept the legitimacy of medical records created by patients was anyone's guess.

The company's plan to make money was hazy at best. The 1997 business plan discussed how the health care industry would use the company's software, but Personal Medical Records had no product to offer at the time. All company executives had was the Koop "brand" and an almost mystical belief in the power of a brand to overcome all obstacles.

Hackett moved the company out of his home and eventually into modest offices with used desks and chairs that, as one former staffer recalled, "made your butt hurt at the end of the day." Hackett sat in a cubicle like everyone else and installed a Web camera so colleagues could check on his whereabouts.

The surroundings were modest, but not the executive perks. The company paid chairman Koop $8,333 a month as a consulting fee—that would rise to $12,500 a month in 1999—and awarded him an initial 11 percent ownership stake in the startup. His duties, as outlined in his contract, were few, though. He was charged with helping to organize a medical advisory board and, at his discretion, speaking with clients and at conferences on the company's behalf.

Zacarro, who was vice chairman and a board member, originally received a 7 percent stake in the company. He signed a three-year consulting contract that also paid him $8,333 a month, topping out at $12,500 a month in 1999. Drkooop also paid for Zacarro's office near his home in the upscale Los Angeles suburb of Rancho Palos Verdes. The contract called on him to serve as a strategic adviser to the company and to act as the "primary liaison" with Koop and fellow board member Nancy Snyderman, the television doctor and medical correspondent at ABC.

Celebrity-wrangler was Zacarro's most visible role to some employees, who saw him squire Koop around company headquarters on the chairman's rare visits to Austin. "He was like the protective right arm of Dr. Koop. If he didn't want someone to talk to Koop, he would step in between them," says one former staffer. Zaccaro calls that characterization untrue.

Hackett also signed lucrative, three-year compensation agreements with the founding executives in August 1997. The salaries were more appropriate for a well-funded company with revenues than a development-state venture with few assets other than a licensing agreement with its well-known chairman. In a move that would cause a rift in the company, Hackett installed his brother, Robert, a pharmaceutical industry veteran, as an executive vice president. Robert Hackett received a 5 percent ownership stake in the company, a salary of $165,000, guaranteed annual raises of 20 percent and a $600 monthly car allowance. The company's chief technologist received a similar package.

Hackett started off with a $195,000 salary, 20 percent annual raises and a $700 monthly car allowance. (When he loaned the company $216,043, he received 1.8 million shares of stock to cancel the debt. The shares were worth $30 million the day Drkoop went public. Even at Drkoop's depressed stock price, they're worth more than $2 million.)

Hackett recruited a number of colleagues from his days at PCN (which filed for bankruptcy last year) and TradeWave (which was sold for $350,000 a few months after Hackett left). He also tapped Koop's connections. Tom Ferguson, a well-known health care industry figure, joined as a consultant in the company's early days. "I'd been impressed by the passion and the vision and the enthusiasm of Don. I didn't know or ever maintained that one could make money doing this. But he seemed to think you could," Ferguson says. "It was a couple of guys and a bunch of computers in a big empty office. We were really making it up as we went along."

By the spring of 1998, the company changed its name from Personal Medical Records to Empower Health to reflect Koop's philosophy of empowering patients. The company also expanded its Internet focus with the goal of becoming a health portal. The move seemed less a result of a carefully constructed business plan than a desire to jump on the latest trend. "At that time it was, 'Jeez, everyone else is getting on the Internet. Why don't we actually go full force as an Internet company, launch a Web site, and then we can distribute the [personal medical record] through that,'" recalled Ian Bagnall, who was hired in 1998 to develop the Drkoop site, in a deposition.

The new idea was to create "Dr. Koop's Community," a collection of chat rooms, support groups and health information that would make money through advertising and e-commerce. While the company deployed marketing staff to drum up media interest in the upcoming July 1998 launch of Drkoop.com, it still was struggling to develop a solid business plan for how the site would make money.

Consultant Agrawal reviewed the company's business plan before meeting with potential investors. "Don wanted a business plan prepared basically as a marketing document," Agrawal testified in his fraud suit against Drkoop. "The version of the business plan that existed...wasn't well drafted. It was cut and pasted. A lot of things were wrong. So basically, [we] spent the entire weekend rewriting a major business plan, again, over our objections that it wasn't a very good way to do it." Zacarro also was not pleased with the document. "I felt [it] was too fragmented, not focused," he said in his deposition.

Meanwhile some senior executives began to grumble about the competence of Robert Hackett, the CEO's 48-year-old brother. Robert Hackett had been installed as executive VP for business development and worked from an office near his home in suburban Philadelphia. "We often complained that he was in the wrong position. He was in too instrumental of a position in an Internet company, specifically a Web-based company, and didn't understand the fundamentals of how Web companies operated," Bagnell testified. When pressed, Zaccaro testified that he was "not completely" happy with the job Robert Hackett was doing in negotiating content deals for Drkoop. Robert Hackett declined to comment on his colleague's characterization of him, as did Donald Hackett.

A deal Donald Hackett negotiated with a Michigan health care consulting firm, Superior Consultant Holdings, also caused some friction in the executive ranks. The company became Drkoop's biggest outside shareholder in April 1998 when it agreed to invest $6 million. But in return, Drkoop was bound to purchase $3 million in consulting services from the company and give Superior a seat on its board. Such quid pro quo deals often are the cost of doing business in the Internet Economy, but the arrangement rubbed some the wrong way. "In the beginning, I don't think we got as much as we should," Zaccaro said. "But, you know, that's what it is when you look for startup capital."

Drkoop's relationship with another consultant, brought in during the summer of 1998 to help get the company's house in order, would prove to be more problematic.

Andy Agrawal was a South Carolina attorney and health care executive who Donald Hackett had met in 1996 through mutual friends in the medical industry. The two hit it off and Hackett asked Agrawal to help develop the business plan for Personal Medical Records. In the company's April 1997 business plan, Agrawal is listed as director.

Agrawal never joined Personal Medical Records, and he went on to form a consulting firm. But in June 1998 Hackett brought him back to Austin to work on legal and business matters for the company's latest incarnation,

Empower Health. Hackett asked Agrawal to join the company as COO, offering him options on 31,000 shares of stock. In an August 1998 e-mail, Hackett offered Agrawal an additional 40,000 stock options as further incentive.

Hackett then withdrew the job. Instead, he signed another consulting agreement with Agrawal, giving him 30,000 stock options, court records show.

Hackett subsequently accused Agrawal's company of overbilling Drkooop and terminated the consulting agreement. Hackett's handling of the Agrawal dispute would soon come back to haunt him in a fraud lawsuit. But as the year came to a close, more pressing problems were on the horizon.

Not surprisingly, Drkoop was facing a cash crisis at the end of 1998. Only five months after the site's launch, the company counted a grand total of $303 in cash on hand.

Relief came in January from Adventist Health Systems, a Florida company that operates the Seventh-Day Adventist Church's hospitals in the U.S. The company invested $3.5 million in Drkoop in exchange for 1 million shares of stock. Adventist also gave Drkoop 10 percent ownership of HealthMagic, its medical software subsidiary.

As part of the deal, Drkoop turned over its electronic medical record technology to HealthMagic, which then assumed the task of developing the personal medical record. Yet only three weeks after Hackett closed the HealthMagic deal, and with a technology that was still a long way from being ready, the company trotted out Koop to make a big promise that would not be kept: Koop vowed to provide a free personal medical record "for all Americans" by the summer.

The next month the company filed for what became a $88.5 million initial public offering and changed its name from Empower Health to Drkoop.com, binding Koop even closer to the company. Never mind that the company sold only $15,470 worth of advertising the previous year and had accumulated a deficit of $15.2 million in 18 months. Never mind that such a cash flow prompted Drkoop's auditors to warn that there was "substantial doubt" about the company's viability. Net IPO fever was upon the land. Even the company's lengthy disclosure about the risky nature of investing in Drkoop was not about to deter Wall Street.

So confident of success were Drkoop executives that before one share was sold, they signed a three-year, $57.5 million portal deal with Disney to become the featured provider of health information on Disney's Go site. Portal deals were all the rage in the spring of 1999. After all, analysts applauded when equally unprofitable competitor WebMD signed a series of high-profile deals with the likes of CNN, creating a buzz that helped propel the startup into a multibillion-dollar merger with Healtheon.

And so no one paid much attention when three days after the Go deal hit the headlines, Agrawal filed his multimillion-dollar fraud suite against Drkoop, Hackett and Zaccaro. The company's former consultant claimed he had been cheated out of stock options, and his suit would open a window into the internal machinations at Drkoop.

On June 8, 1999, the former surgeon general saw his name literally transformed into a symbol of the new economy when KOOP appeared on Nasdaq trading screens. Drkoop ended its first day on the market 83 percent over its opening price of $9 a share. The company now had $88.5 million in the bank. Three weeks later it essentially turned over its IPO proceeds to America Online when it agreed to pay the online giant $89 million over four years to be its premier—but not exclusive—provider of health information. The agreements had been principally negotiated by Bagnall, a 27-year-old community college dropout and tech company veteran originally hired to oversee the Drkoop Web site. Three weeks after the AOL alliance was announced, Hackett promoted Bagnall to chief strategist.

Analysts and journalists would later fall over themselves in slamming the AOL and Go deals as reckless. But at the time Wall Street was not exactly punishing Drkoop for trashing the capitalist rulebook. On the contrary, news of the AOL deal pushed the company's stock to an all-time high of $45.75 on July 6.

Flush with success from its IPO and portal deals, Drkoop signed a lease for 81,000 square feet in a new trophy building in Austin's high-tech corridor with a skyline view of downtown. Drkoop's interior designer told a local business journal that the company spent $1 million on employee workstations and $250,000 on other furniture. Price was not an object. "You don't have that many opportunities of a startup company with an unlimited budget," the designer said.

But the bills quickly started piling up. The AOL and Go deals together would cost Drkoop $40 million their first year. The company had taken a huge gamble that the portals would drive enough visitors to Drkoop.com to bring in advertising and e-commerce revenues—from selling health products on the site—sufficient to pay the high cost of the agreement.

"Did anyone ever run the numbers to see how much traffic you have to generate to pay for $89 million?" asks a former Drkoop employee who was not involved in the deals. "I did the math—it does not wash." The company later revealed that only about 5 percent of its traffic came from Go, while the percentage of traffic routed through AOL was equally disappointing—in the teens.

But in the fall of 1999, even the Koop name, the company's most valuable asset and key to its success, was beginning to lose its luster. Success hinged on transferring the respect and trust consumers had for Dr. Koop the man, to Drkoop the brand. But on Sept. 4, five days before Drkoop's content began to appear on AOL, the *New York Times* published a front-page story questioning the ethics of Koop and his company. The article pointed out that Koop was receiving commissions on products sold on the site (he made $41,000). The company's filings to the Securities and Exchange Commission disclosed that Koop made a commission, but there was no such disclosure on its Web site. Moreover, the company also failed to tell visitors that hospitals paid for placement in a list of health care resources.

Although Koop's contract gave him the right to review and approve all information on the site, he denied he had compromised his integrity. "I cannot be bought. I am an icon," he told the *Times*. And in a message to DrKoop visitors that appeared on the site two days after the *Times* story broke, Koop wrote: "Providing consumers with credible, independent information is something I have worked toward all my life. I take great pride in my active participation in Drkoop.com."

To some longtime employees, however, the imbroglio only highlighted Koop's isolation from Drkoop.com. "The reality is we've only seen him about a total of four times," says one former employee, whose account was confirmed by three other ex-staffers. Even Koop in his deposition said he knew very little about the workings of the company. But Zaccaro tells a different story, saying Koop was actively involved in the company. "In fact, Dr. Koop was, and is, in daily contact with our company's CEO," Zaccaro says.

In the wake of the *Times* story, Koop took a leading role in Hi-Ethics, an industry group formed to issue ethical guidelines for Internet health care companies. But Koop's continuing less-than-watchful eye on his own site allowed some questionable practices to flourish. For instance, online mental health company Lifescape.com paid the company $11 million to sponsor Drkoop's mental health center. But unlike other sponsorship deals, Lifescape was also providing medical information for the mental health center.

To this day, the financial relationship between Lifescape and Drkoop is not disclosed on the mental health center part of the site, which describes Lifescape as an independent organization and content provider. In actuality, Lifescape is co-owned by FHC Health Systems, a managed care company that operates mental health and substance abuse programs for 22 million people. Drkoop also had reserved $10 million of its IPO stock for FHC at the offering price. "I didn't feel we were as forthright as we could have been," says John Grohol, a psychologist hired to create Drkoop's mental health center. Grohol estimates that at one time Lifescape provided 90 percent of the mental health center's content.

The ethics flap prompted Koop to dispatch a doctor friend to Austin to keep tabs on the site's medical content, according to Grohol and other staffers. The doctor later became the company's medical director.

More puzzling was the appearance in Austin of J. Keith Green, another old colleague of Koop's. Green was the CEO of Koop's failed Time Life Medical video company. Given the embarrassment the company's bankruptcy caused Koop, it seemed more than a little strange that Green would join Drkoop to advise the company on strategy. Green declined to discuss his work at Drkoop, referring a reporter to Hackett. Hackett also refused to talk about Green's role at the company.

If Koop was attempting to exert more oversight of Drkoop, it was too little, too late.

The company spent the summer of 1999 fighting attempts by former consultant Agrawal's lawyers to take testimony from Koop. But a Texas court ordered Koop to testify, and in October Agrawal's Austin attorney, Donald Taylor, flew to New York to depose the former surgeon general while he was there on business.

The disposition had barely begun when Koop betrayed his ignorance of the company that bears his name. While Zacarro looked on, Taylor asked Koop if he understood that Superior Consultant Holding, Drkoop's largest outside investor, had acted as a key consultant in the company's early days.

"I don't think I ever was aware of that, who they were," replied Koop. His answer seemed incomprehensible given that he sat on Superior Consultant's board between 1998 and 1999.

Although Agrawal's suit potentially could cost the company millions of dollars, Koop testified that he became aware of the dispute only after receiving a letter from Agrawal's parents, who were investors in Drkoop, asking him to investigate the alleged wrongdoing. Their son was claiming that Hackett and Zaccaro reneged on a promise to hire him as COO and cheated him out of stock options worth millions. Koop turned the letter over to Zaccaro and Hackett and asked them to investigate, even though they were named in Agrawal's suite.

"I realized it was something that I had nothing to do with, knew nothing about," Koop told Taylor. "Inasmuch as [Zaccaro and Hackett] were both involved in it, I asked [Zaccaro] to continue to act for me in this matter with Mr. Hackett, and that is all I have ever done about this thing until I heard that I had to appear to give a deposition." Koop admitted he was relying on legal advice from a company attorney who also was representing Zacarro and Hackett. (Hackett would later obtain his own attorney. Agrawal later dropped his suit against Zacarro.)

Koop seemed unfazed by the potential conflict of interest of having one attorney represent the company as well as the executives accused of wrongdoing. He conceded he had not sought independent legal advice for Drkoop.

Did the chairman know that his CEO had given stock options worth, at one time, at least $1 million to a lawyer friend who did legal work for the company at $200 to $250 an hour? Taylor asked.

"No," Koop answered.

"This is the first time you have learned about that, isn't it?" said Taylor.

"That's right."

Such admissions are the stuff that shareholder lawsuits are made of, and attorneys have been pouring over the Agrawal case. Even more damning was Hackett's testimony that he signed an employment contract with Agrawal and promised him stock options without the consent of the board of directors.

The board, however, was unlikely to act as much of a watchdog over Drkoop's executives. Three of the eight board members—Koop, Hackett and Zacarro—were company insiders. Two other board members—Superior's CEO and Adventist Health's president—were officers of companies with significant investments in Drkoop. That left just three independent board members – a retired Ziff-Davis executive, a Dell Computer VP and celebrity doctor Nancy Snyderman. The outside directors received stock options worth, in some cases, millions of dollars. (Superior's CEO and Adventist Health's president have since resigned, as have the ex-Ziff-Davis and Dell directors.)

By the end of 1999 it was becoming apparent that the company's business model wasn't working, despite that Drkoop.com had become one of the most popular health sites on the Web. The company took in $9.4 million in 1999. But Drkoop faced some big bills in 2000—$38 million in payments to AOL and Go combined.

Meanwhile, executives couldn't make up their mind about the company's direction as it drifted from an online medical record provider to a media outfit. At the time, the online medical industry was moving in the opposite direction, from providing medical information to consumers to connecting them to their doctors, hospitals, health plans and pharmacies.

"I think [Drkoop] management got enamored with the media play; they didn't stay focused on the medical record," says one former high-ranking Drkoop associate.

Hackett recognized that Drkoop was increasingly out of step with its industry. In January he told investment bankers at a closed-door meeting that the company was evolving into a disease-management company that would offer services like medical monitoring through its personal medical record.

"We've been very quiet about our plans in this area," Hackett said at the meeting.

For good reason. The personal medical record project, already months late, was foundering. Patients testing the record at a Florida hospital were reluctant to put their medical information online. There also were problems with the technology being developed for the company by HealthMagic. "The relationship never produced satisfactory results," Drkoop subsequently reported in an SEC filing. Under the terms of a settlement, Drkoop retained the technology it contributed to the project, but is barred from developing a similar product until next year.

While Hackett reassured the bankers that Drkoop had a plan to be profitable by 2001, the company's auditors were preparing a report with a starkly different projection. In a letter to the board of directors dated Feb. 15, the auditors at PricewaterhouseCoopers expressed "substantial doubt" about Drkoop's viability give that the company was hemorrhaging cash while racking up huge debts.

The settlement of Agrawal's case in February contributed to the cash drain. Hackett agreed to pay $600,000 as his share of the settlement. The company has not disclosed what it paid out, but the litigation surely contributed to Drkoop's $2.5 million in legal expenses in 1999. The company spent a quarter of its 1999 revenues on lawyers, almost as much as it spent on marketing.

By late February, two weeks after the date on the auditor's report, four directors—Koop, Zaccaro, Snyderman and Richard Helppie, representing Superior Consultant—sold chunks of their Drkoop stock—hardly a vote of confidence in the company's prospects. At the time, its stock was trading between $9.75 and $12 a share. Koop sold about 10 percent of his holdings for $914,850. Zaccaro took home $791.017 and Snyderman unloaded stock he had purchased for 12 cents to 16 cents a share for $2.6 million. Superior Consultant, the company's largest outside investor, sold about 16 percent of its stock for $6 million, recouping its initial investment in the company.

Hackett claims the company didn't receive the auditors' report till late March, after the directors' stock sale. "The board had no idea, management had no idea, that we would receive the ongoing concern opinion," he says. But given Drkoop's financial troubles, they should have expected it.

Nevertheless, the directors who sold stock escaped the subsequent plunge in the company's share price when the auditors' statement was released several weeks later as part of Drkoop's annual report. Things got only worse for investors. In April, the company revealed that it had enough cash to survive only another four months and had directed its investment bankers to explore "strategic alternatives"—or buyers—for the company. Shares would fall to an all-time low of $1. As the Drkoop's fortunes went into free-fall, the company loaned Hackett $966,000 at no interest. Hackett repaid the loan, made for "personal reasons," a week later.

The board members weren't the only ones to profit from the timely selling of stock. Donald Hackett's brother, Robert, left the company in November. In his last year at Drkoop he took home $243,940 in salary and bonuses. The value of Robert Hackett's stock when he exercised his options was $22.8 million, according to Drkoop's SEC filings. Drkoop's share price has fallen since then but Robert Hackett says he still was able to sell part of his portfolio in February before the wipeout.

Morale at Drkoop was sinking as fast as the stock price. Some employees fumed at the profits Koop and other insiders made while they were left with nearly worthless shares. "People were pissed," recalls a former Drkoop employee. "It was like, the end is obviously coming if they're bailing."

Koop, Snyderman and Helppie declined to discuss their stock sales. Zaccaro emphasizes that he sold less than 5 percent of his Drkoop holdings and hadn't seen the auditors' report. Koop told the *Wall Street Journal* that he sold the stock for money he had promised to charity.

By May the ranks began to thin. Thirty employees were laid off as part of a 35 percent reduction in staff that began at the end of March. No executives were fired. There was no need—they had begun to depart on their own in the wake of the auditors' report. Among those leaving were executives for content, marketing, operations, business development and the Web site's editor in chief. Also heading out of town was J. Keith Green, the former CEO of Koop's failed Time Life video venture.

Hackett, meanwhile, described by associates as ferociously loyal to the company, has not sold a single share of his extensive holdings in Drkoop.

The dawn was breaking over the Austin skyline in late June when Hackett walked confidently into a conference room at Drkoop headquarters wearing a white shirt emblazoned with the company logo. Drkoop was trading at $1.53 a share, but Hackett, tanned and fit, betrayed no hint of the turmoil that is afflicting the company, or himself.

In the cafes and restaurants frequented by Austin's high-tech crowd, however, there's been talk: "Did you hear? Don's lost his home." In fact, according to Texas property records, Hackett and his wife sold their $2.8 million mansion in May, just seven months after they bought it. Hackett would only say that he often buys and sells property. Ironically, a few weeks before Hackett sold his home, his brother Robert—who had cashed in some of his Drkoop stock before the shares crashed—bought a $2.9 million house on eight acres of land in Maryland.

But Don Hackett doesn't want to talk personal and business problems. He is determined to stay on-message. His diagnosis of Drkoop's predicament? "The whole capital market crumbled. It wasn't just Koop. Look at all of e-health, from Healtheon on down," he says evenly. True, as far as it goes. But Healtheon, for instance, has about $1 billion in cash. And although other health-information companies are suffering through rock-bottom stock prices, none so far faces Drkoop's dire circumstances.

What about the AOL and Go deals that bled Drkoop dry? "Had the capital markets not crumbled . . . they were great deals and they are great deals today." Hackett also maintains that the company has pursued a consistent strategy.

But will Drkoop survive, and how? "Great companies manage through tough times," he says. "Companies fail because they don't make tough decisions. When there's an inflection point you need to change, and we believe we have."

That inflection point, Hackett believes, is the end of easy money for Internet companies. Just as Hackett once preached the virtues of spending money he didn't have to build the Drkoop brand, he now has embraced the new Net austerity. "We'll publish numbers shortly showing where we went from burn rate of X to nothing," he promises. And the company did convert its $89 million in payments to AOL into equity in Drkoop and renegotiated its Go deal.

Hackett glanced at his beeper and fidgeted. The interview was over. Three days later Drkoop announced it had obtained a $1.5 million bridge loan from an unnamed merchant bank as a prelude to arrange permanent financing. The price is high, however. The merchant bank gets the right to name a director to the Drkoop board and warrants to purchase 4 million shares of stock at 75 cents a share. If a bailout comes through, the new investors will likely get control of the Drkoop board. The cash infusion hasn't stopped the exodus of Drkoop managers, though. The company's CFO, COO and longtime spokeswoman recently left, leaving Hackett to field press calls. He has extended his contract for one year and cut his pay by 15 percent.

Even if Drkoop survives in some form, the damage has been done to the company's namesake. Beyond the criticism in the press, shareholder lawsuits filed this month could make Koop look less than charitable in court. The new crack in his sterling reputation pains even some of the company's detractors, who tend to forgive the former surgeon general's trespasses in the business world. "How many 80-year-olds do you know who understand what the Internet is all about?" says the former employee, who remains highly critical of the company's management and who may join a shareholder suit against

Drkoop. "Here was a new venture to make some money, but he had an altruistic vision of truly empowering people to take control of their lives and not let the medical profession be the ones to make the decisions. I truly still believe that." Altruistic or not, Koop still stands to make a healthy profit from Drkoop.com. His holdings are still worth more than $1 million, even now.

Koop seems determined to press on with his mission. As he approaches his 84th birthday, he's apparently decided to take his chances with whomever takes control of the company. In a move of exceeding optimism, Koop last month agreed to let the company use his name until 2006. "I am pleased to see that Drkoop.com is leading the e-health market with the highest of ethical standards, while simultaneously taking action to separate its business more efficiently," Koop said in a statement.

The doctor is nothing if not trusting. "It takes years to build a reputation and just seconds to destroy it," says one old friend, disheartened by what's happened to Koop. The Koop name still carries credibility, but sadly for him, KOOP, the stock symbol, is leaving a less distinguished legacy.

Spooked:
Money Men Liked Boo and Boo Liked Money; Then It All Went Poof

Flashy Web Site for Clothes Had Lots of Cool Ideas,
Few Financial Controls

'MissBoo' and Her Makeovers

By Christopher Cooper
and Erik Portanger
Staff Reporters of the Wall Street Journal

London—On a gloomy afternoon last January, Ernst Malmsten confronted the limits of his expertise as an Internet mogul.

The shy Swede, who had sold his first Internet start-up for millions, was chief executive of Boo.com Group Ltd., the most hyped and hip of European e-commerce start-ups. He made the cover of Fortune magazine before age 30. But when it came time to lay off 130 staffers in a do-or-die cost-cutting drive, Mr. Malmsten wasn't sure how to proceed—"Do you break the news to them one at a time or do it all at once?" he recalls wondering. He finally decided the honorable thing was to call them in one by one.

Four months later, a bankruptcy liquidator finished the job for him. It summarily fired the rest of Boo's staff.

The demise of Boo, an ingenious way of selling clothes over the Web, was the flashiest failure of the dot-com shakeout so far. With its virtual changing room and 3D graphics that let customers examine clothes from any angle, plus prices calculated for 18 countries and given in seven languages, the Boo site was a wonder. "As an Internet business, Boo was like the moonshot," says Ben Narasin, whose U.S. company fashionmall.com picked up Boo's Web site at the liquidation auction.

Catching the Internet frenzy, prestigious investors ranging from Italy's Benetton family to France's Bernard Arnault eagerly poured money into the project.

All that was missing was a little adult supervision.

In the summer of 1998, Boo's business plan was five typed pages that Mr. Malmsten had pieced together in his Stockholm apartment, along with Kajsa Leander, a former model and his childhood friend. The two, both 29 years old, had just sold an Internet book retailer they started called Bokus for several million dollars and were game for something more ambitious.

They flew to New York and began cold-calling investment banks. Lacking contacts, they bluffed their way through corporate switchboards and won meetings with top financiers, armed with a packet of magazine clippings describing a New York poetry festival they had organized through Sweden's foreign office.

One Is Interested

Many of the banks, including Goldman Sachs Group and Morgan Stanley Dean Witter & Co., declined, explaining that they didn't cater to start-ups. J.P. Morgan & Co. didn't either, but it was intrigued by the boldness of the idea. Fashion suppliers, Morgan bankers thought, were likely to applaud the plan, because Boo wouldn't undercut traditional retailers with cut-rate pricing as many e-retailers do. The bankers also were impressed that the founders had Internet experience and complemented each other: The dreamy Mr. Malmsten saw the big picture, while Ms. Leander was brainy and focused on details, almost to the point of obsession.

If Boo succeeded, the rewards could be enormous: The company promised 55% gross margins and profitability within two years. "If branded retailing on the Internet is going to work, this is going to be the way it looks," says a former J.P. Morgan banker. If it made Boo a success and took the business public, J.P. Morgan could become a leading financier of hot European Internet properties, leapfrogging dominant underwriters such as Goldman and Morgan Stanley.

After refining his plan for a week in J.P. Morgan's London offices, Mr. Malmsten got thrilling news: J.P. Morgan was willing to fund early-stage investors for Boo, taking its fees in stock. Though unschooled in the ways of finance, he grasped the significance. "J.P. Morgan doesn't do start-ups. The last start-up they did was General Electric," he says.

Benetton and Arnault

With J.P. Morgan's involvement, investors weren't hard to find. Within weeks, the bank had recruited two of its best clients to the deal. European fashion titans both. The first was Luciano Benetton, patriarch of the family that controls the trendy Italian clothing chain.

Reminded that Ms. Leander had once been a Benetton model, Mr. Benetton invited the founders to supper at the family's Villa Minelli in Treviso, Italy, in the winter of 1998. There, as they ate a simple meal of pasta and red wine in the cavernous dining hall, Ms. Leander explained the finer points of the business. Mr. Benetton put up $5 million in seed money and volunteered his son, Alessandro, to take a seat on Boo's board.

At a later meeting in a Paris office, described by Ms. Leander as "all bullet-proof glass and bodyguards," the founders got a similar cash commitment from billionaire Bernard Arnault, head of luxury-goods empire LVMH Moet-Hennessy Louis Vuitton. He ultimately poured $12 million into Boo.

With the big-name investors roped, J.P. Morgan bankers decided in early 1999 to raise $12 million to start, $12 million about six weeks later and $40 million more by midsummer. There were plenty of takers. One latecomer says he was drawn to the deal after seeing the founders on the cover of Fortune magazine, which dubbed Boo a "cool company" a full six months before it launched. A British magazine ran a glowing spread on Mr. Malmsten's Notting Hill apartment, decorated in a minimalist Scandinavian style with pale walls and plenty of teak furnishings. Boo paid the rent.

Competitors of J.P. Morgan were suddenly bewitched as well. Fanning their interest was a third Boo principal, a 31-year-old Swede named Patrik Hedelin, who had spent six months as a junior investment banker at HSBC Holdings PLC and arranged the sale of the founders' Internet bookstore. He helped them find their way around Wall Street and the world of investors. "Patrik spoke their language," Mr. Malmsten says.

Mr. Hedelin became chief financial officer, although J.P. Morgan had doubts about his accounting skills. For his part, Mr. Hedelin doubted J.P. Morgan's ability to put a value on a hot Internet concept.

While J.P. Morgan preached prudence, Mr. Hedelin pushed for sharply higher prices with each slice of equity sold. By last fall, before the site had even launched, he was attempting to value the company at $390 million, although Morgan talked him into reducing that figure somewhat.

More disturbing to J.P. Morgan was that Mr. Hedelin appeared to be shopping for new financial advisers. He shuttled between Europe and New York to meet with Morgan Stanley, Credit Suisse First Boston and Goldman Sachs. Goldman in particular seemed keen to cultivate Boo's favors, and it eventually became a $3 million investor in the company. Its presence infuriated the J.P. Morgan bankers.

Mr. Heldelin says now that he never intended to let J.P. Morgan take Boo public. Yet the planned IPO was the chief motivator for J.P. Morgan. Mr. Hedelin acknowledges that his wooing of other banks "affected our whole relationship with J.P. Morgan. They were very upset."

Mr. Malmsten sometimes had to intercede. "I had no idea how much these banks all hated each other," he says.

Mr. Malmsten had more pressing concerns. The complexity of the Web site, featuring rich graphics, a virtual inventory system, multiple languages and currency conversions, delayed its launch from mid-summer to September 1999, and then to November. Investors grumbled but could do little: Management controlled most of the board seats.

Not that the outside directors were an activist bunch. Mr. Arnault's designated board member attended one meeting and didn't show up again for months. Mr. Benetton, instead of putting his son on the board, sent a lawyer who barely spoke English. J.P. Morgan abandoned its board seat, citing a potential conflict in case it was called on to take the company public. None of the four outside directors had much retail or Internet experience, and few attended meetings with any great regularity. A reason some give is that they had little control anyway.

Despite the launch trouble, Boo's spending continued apace. Employees say Ms. Leander was obsessed by the appearance of the Web-site mascot, Miss Boo, originally a blonde but then made a brunette and less wholesome-looking. Ms. Leander hired a noted hairdresser to redesign the animated character's hair, plus an ad copywriter to write dialogue for her. Debates about Miss Boo could rage for days, and employees complain they were sometimes called in on weekends to discuss her attributes. "Everyone in the company had strong feelings about Miss Boo," Ms. Leander says.

Anticipating a midsummer launch, Boo secured satellite office space in Munich, Paris, New York and Amsterdam, and hired hundreds of staffers to service orders. With the Web-site postponements, many sat idle.

The founders traveled with an entourage and stayed at hotels like New York's swanky Soho Grand. "With all those trophy offices, Boo looked more like a 1950s multinational than an Internet start-up," says Marina Galanti, who was marketing director.

But investors' initial eagerness to pour money into Boo fueled executives' free-spending ways, she adds, and "made them think they could solve any problem just by throwing more money at it." The biggest investor of all wasn't one of the first backers. The Hariri family of Lebanon, who made their fortune in construction, ultimately invested $41 million in Boo.

What Boo really poured money into was technology. Boo devised its Internet platform and customer-fulfillment system from scratch, in-house. "It was like they were trying to build a Mercedes-Benz by hand," says a prospective investor who took a pass.

In September, with its site still not up, Boo said it has burned through nearly $70 million and needed a fresh infusion. The news sparked recriminations. J.P. Morgan and investors complained about the company's lack of financial controls, and Mr. Hedelin specifically. "His figures changed from week to week," one investor says.

Mr. Hedelin says that he isn't an accountant, and that even though he passed financial figures along, "I wasn't in charge of the finance department." In general, he says, the investors are correct: The company did suffer from a profound lack of financial controls.

At a board meeting in October, the founders began what came to be a monthly request for more shareholder cash. The Benettons' board designate clamored to take the company public. J.P. Morgan said it couldn't do so until management agreed to quit tinkering with the Web site and simply launch, and to replace Mr. Hedelin with an experienced CFO. But the founders felt kindly toward him and were loath to let him go.

In November, Boo launched its site—to horrible reviews. Customers said that it was very slow for most computers and didn't work at all on Macs, and that it was complex and hard to navigate. The poor launch scared off one prospective new investor, Federated Department Stores, say people familiar with the matter. Federated declines to comment. Within six weeks, Boo was discounting its clothes 40% in a desperate attempt to move them.

The new year brought glimmers of better news. J.P. Morgan began working on an IPO plan after Boo stripped Mr. Hedelin of his executive rank. Boo hired Dean Hawlins, an experienced CFO from German sportswear maker Adidas Salomon AG. "The first adult," one investor later called him. Mr. Hedelin now was a nonexecutive chairman.

By April, monthly sales had grown to $1.1 million, although expenses were running 10 times that. But that month, the market for Internet start-ups abruptly soured, scotching Boo's plans. And then the brand-new CFO left for another Web company.

A few weeks later, J.P. Morgan jolted Boo executives and investors by abruptly bowing out of the deal. The bank's departure came as its client Benetton fired off a letter complaining about how its investment was faring, say people familiar with the matter. Benetton and Morgan decline to talk about the letter.

In April, lacking a banker and a CFO, Mr. Malmsten tried to devise a restructuring plan of his own. To raise another $50 million, Boo called in Texas Pacific Group, a U.S. private-equity firm. Its people arrived and went through all the numbers carefully. The verdict: Boo could have the money but only if it cut the equity of existing investors to zero.

Although Texas Pacific held out the promise to restore some equity if Boo ever went public, the response was harsh, Benetton vetoed the proposal in a sharply worded letter. One person involved says that Francois Tison, the Arnault board representative, was more blunt: "Tell them to go to hell." Mr. Tison says he can't recall his exact words. He adds that he was told that better offers were waiting in the wings.

Boo's lead investors then sought to raise $30 million among themselves for a stripped-down version of the restructuring, but fell $12 million short. After a series of intense meetings on May 17, Mr. Malmsten called in the liquidators. Later in the day, he gave a farewell speech to his staff in London, drawing an appreciative ovation. Now the buyer of Boo's remains, fashionmall.com, a portal through which e-tailers offer merchandise, is considering an online museum dedicated to the many looks and poses of Miss Boo.

Mr. Malmsten and Ms. Leander both call it "sad" that Boo failed. Asked how they feel about the $135 million of investor money that vanished, Mr. Malmsten says it's "not good that our investors lost money," though Ms. Leander adds that it's also regrettable that investors didn't stick with the company longer and give it a chance to mature. Mr. Hedelin, the CFO J.P. Morgan wanted out, says: "Of course I feel sorry for the investors. But at the same time, they're all qualified professionals and in the position to understand the risks in a deal."

Mr. Malmsten and Ms. Leander still appear to be in demand. Headhunters call to dangle offers, Mr. Malmsten says, "although I don't know if any of them are real."

Investment bankers still call, too, but for a different reason now. "They want to get the inside briefing." Mr. Malmsten says. "They want to hear how it all went wrong."

Anatomy of a Crash:
From an Awkward Kid To a Star of
Software to a Body in a Hotel

By Matt Murray
and Jeffrey A. Tannenbaum
Staff Reporters of The Wall Street Journal

Milwaukee—To his fans, Phillip W. Katz was a folk hero of the computer culture, a pioneer who set the standard for file compression, or "zipping." Employees at his company, PKWare Inc., found him a beneficent, if often absentee, boss. Friends knew him as a shy jokester who loved partying and picked up tabs with wad of 50– and 100-dollar bills.

But there was a darker Phil Katz, one only half-hidden from those who knew him. For years, he nurtured a serious, steadily worsening drinking problem. As it deepened, Mr. Katz spent more and more time drinking alone, often in strip clubs. He brushed off questions about his problem and fell away from his friends. Even his widowed mother, when she challenged him one too many times, was cut out of his life.

At the office, "it was well-known that you didn't mess with him," says Steven Burg, a longtime employee who left the closely held PKWare in 1997. The tacit understanding, he says, was simple: "Phil drinks, and there's nothing you can do about it if you want to stay employed here."

Eventually, Mr. Katz, while still nominally running the company, embarked on a strange underground life. He stopped coming to work and stayed in touch with the office only by fax and e-mail. Fearful of arrest warrants stemming from his drunk driving, he kept away from his condominium in a wealthy northern suburb and stayed in a series of South Side hotels.

In one such place, a maintenance man found the 37-year old Mr. Katz dead on April 14. He had checked in a week earlier, left instructions for housekeepers to bypass his room and hung a "Privacy Please" sign on his door handle. He was sitting on the floor by his bed in his underwear, cradling an empty bottle of peppermint schnapps in his left arm, with two other empty liquor bottles nearby. The official cause of death: acute pancreatic bleeding caused by chronic alcoholism.

A Man Alone

Mr. Katz had long been troubled, but few who knew him realized how badly. His image as a software pioneer masked a profoundly isolated man who was slowly killing himself. Largely outside his colleagues' view, a sinking Mr. Katz had gradually disassembled his old life and constructed a new one centered on his illness.

He made a serious effort to turn things around in early 1999, receiving about eight weeks of treatment at a hospital and staying sober through the summer. But he started drinking heavily again early this year, says a friend, Lisa Marie Marciniak. "This spun out of control within 90 days," she says. "He spiraled quicker than any time before. He went from fine to dead."

As a teenager, friends say, Mr. Katz was a skinny, mop-haired, asthmatic kid. Confident in a few arenas—he enjoyed motor biking with friends—he was awkward in social situations, especially dating. Shorter than most, he was nicknamed The Elf in high school and known as one of the "brains," says a friend, James G. Chizek. He avoided athletics, excelled at chess and perpetually ran late.

Death in the Family

When Mr. Katz was 19, his father, Walter, with whom he had spent many hours playing chess, died unexpectedly after heart surgery at the age of 55. Though he rarely showed much emotion, friends say the young man struggled with the loss.

After graduating from the University of Wisconsin in Milwaukee with a computer-science engineering degree in 1984, Mr. Katz moved through two jobs writing code. Well into his 20s, he lived at home with his mother, Hildegard, on a quiet street in suburban Glendale.

At home, Mr. Katz often worked late into the night at his IBM personal computer, recalls Brian Kiehnau, ex-husband of Mr. Katz's older sister, Cynthia. He quickly found a place in the growing network of computer hobbyists. Home computing was then a cloistered world of clunky personal computers with little memory. Users communicated through networks of bulletin boards, a chat-room precursor.

Mr. Katz became known for posting long, often witty messages online. He also displayed a formidable intelligence, spending his spare time tackling a sticky problem: how to compress information so that downloading could be faster and more data stored on computer disks. He ultimately produced a breakthrough program that combined several techniques then in use and automatically determined the best in any situation.

"He didn't do it to get rich," says Bob Mahoney, who then ran a big bulletin board system, ExecPC BBS. "He did it for himself."

Mr. Katz posted his code, which he first called PKArc, on Mr. Mahoney's bulletin board, using the "shareware" approach, in which users are invited to try a program and send money to the inventor if they like it. Almost overnight, dozens of people started calling and sending Mr. Katz money, recalls Douglas Hay, who with Mr. Burg shared an office with Mr. Katz at a small company called Graysoft inc.

"Here's Phil, making, I'm guessing, $30,000 a year or so, and all of a sudden he got a $10,000 check in the mail," Mr. Hay says. "Then he got another $10,000 check in the mail, and he had made almost a year's salary in two weeks. That's when he decided he could quit."

On His Own

In 1996 Mr. Katz started his own firm, PKWare, working from his mother's kitchen table and awarding her a small ownership stake. Mrs. Katz quit her job as a nurse instructor at a technical college to handle administrative duties, while he wrote code.

By the late 1980s, Mr. Katz had become a major celebrity around Milwaukee. Big companies such as General Motors Corp. sent checks for the code, which became the computing standard.

When the former market leader in compression software, Systems Enhancement Associates Inc. of Clifton, N.J., sued for copyright infringement, claiming Mr. Katz had issued a simplified rewrite of its original Arc code, it only burnished his legend: Admirers orchestrated a campaign painting him as a David facing a corporate Goliath. The case was eventually settled. Mr. Katz retooled his code and renamed it "PKZip," implying speed.

Though uneasy with his growing fame, Mr. Katz enjoyed the benefits of success. He bought a condo by a golf course in the exclusive northern suburb of Mequon and finally left home. He started driving a red Nissan sports car with PKWARE plates. He bought compact disks by the score and developed a taste for fine watches and other jewelry.

And rumors began to spread about late nights, women and booze. "Frankly, we were saying, 'Go for it, Phil,'" says Greg Ryan, a veteran of the Milwaukee computer scene. "It actually gave a lot of the other programmers inspiration to do other things. I kind of revered him, too."

A Growing Company

As PKWare grew, Mr. Katz and his mother added staff and set up shop in an office complex in Brown Deer, north of Milwaukee. At its height, the firm employed about three dozen people and had annual revenue of around $5 million, insiders say. Robert Gorman, PKWare's sales and marketing director, declines to comment on the figures.

The Katzes seemed happy just to occupy a niche. "It was always a very relaxed atmosphere. There was never any pressure to release software," Mr. Burg says. The Katzes cultivated a family feeling, splurging on dinners out, paying generous Christmas bonuses, and sometimes doubling contributions to employees' 401(k) retirement plan.

Mr. Katz never showed much interest in the mundane tasks of managing. While he ruled on strategic matters, he left duties such as licensing, payroll and managing employees to his mother, say current and former employees. They add that though she arrived early and demanded promptness from others, her son often didn't show up until lunchtime or later.

With time, the mother-son relationship grew strained. Some staffers complained to Mr. Katz that his mother was controlling and secretive, co-workers recall. His response was complicated, they say. He sometimes griped that she was domineering and was interfering in his life, yet he also leaned on her and castigated those who tried to go behind her back to appeal to him. To employees, Mrs. Katz seemed both fiercely protective of her son and frustrated by his seeming indifference.

Rather than assert more control, Mr. Katz started coming in later and later. He would go straight to his desk among the programmers—rarely using his president's office—and write code late into the night. While he didn't show much emotion, he liked hanging out, deconstructing "Star Trek" movies, telling jokes and competing in computer games such as Doom. "We almost lost a year of productivity playing Doom," says one employee.

"Anything that was related to paperwork, he just didn't care," Mr. Hay says. "He used to come in at, say 4 o'clock and his mom would be standing there and he'd be like, 'What?' You could just tell he was already irritated.

"She'd say, 'You need to look over these faxes,'" Mr. Hay continues. "He'd say, 'I don't have time.' She'd say, 'They've been there two days.' "He'd say, 'Put them in my in-basket.' She'd say, 'It's already an inch thick.'"

It didn't help that Mrs. Katz was increasingly pressuring her son to get help for his drinking and demanding to know more about the women she'd heard he was meeting at strip clubs, insiders say.

Mrs. Katz declined to comment for this article, as did her daughter, Cynthia Kiehnau. Asked in writing about several incidents employees described, the Katzes' attorney, Fredrick J. Safer, wrote that the questions contained "numerous inaccuracies" but declined to answer them or be specific.

Behind the Wheel

In 1990, Mr. Katz was charged with driving under the influence of alcohol. At least three other such charges followed, along with arrest warrants for driving with a suspended license and bail jumping. Mr. Katz lost thousands of dollars in forfeited bail but never served a 45-day jail sentence he had drawn in 1994 for drunk driving.

According to Milwaukee County District Attorney E. Michael McCann, Mr. Katz first delayed the sentence with an appeal, then twice failed to show up to arrange to serve the time. On his subsequent drunk-driving tickets and arrests, officials apparently didn't notice the unserved sentence. Mr. Katz usually just posted bond, often forfeiting it later by missing his court date, Mr. McCann says.

It isn't uncommon for traffic violators who jump bail to escape arrest, the D.A. says. The sheriff's office doesn't have the staffing to track many fugitives, and priority goes to serious offenders such as robbers. "I don't know any community of any size where there is a substantial effort to apprehend traffic offenders," he says.

The alcohol assessments that drunk-drivers must undergo in Wisconsin sometimes lead to mandatory treatment for alcoholism. Whether they did in Mr. Katz's case the records don't say.

Because he delegated many tasks, his alcoholism didn't much disrupt PKWare's day-to-day operations. It may have hurt strategically. Mr. Katz had always coded in DOS. But Windows was becoming the dominant operating system by the early 1990s. Mr. Katz, who couldn't write in Windows and dismissed it as a fad, didn't get a Windows product out until 1996.

Once, a staffer complained to Mr. Mahoney that Mr. Katz was delaying the release of a product and spending too much time away from work. To prod his old friend, Mr. Mahoney posted a notice on his bulletin-board saying that the release had taken too long and threatening to switch his files to another format, which he says he never intended to do.

In one way, the ploy worked: Mr. Katz released his new software within a month. But he never spoke to Mr. Mahoney again. "I've always felt bad about the incident," Mr. Mahoney says. "But Phil was losing his connection to the responsibilities of the real world. The threat was a last resort to pull him back."

One day late in 1994 Mrs. Katz, unable to reach her son by phone, called Mequon police and asked them to check his home, according to local officials and friends of Mr. Katz. A police officer broke into Mr. Katz's condo through a basement window. He found mounds of garbage stacked on the floor and furniture. Mr. Katz, who was home, was frightened, then livid at his mother. He agreed to call his mother only when the officer promised to leave.

Break With Mother

Not long afterward, according to David Siebenaller, then PKWare's chief operating officer, Mr. Katz left a letter instructing Mr. Siebenaller to kick Mrs. Katz out of the company. Mr. Katz's former brother-in-law, Mr. Kiehnau, says that a flustered Mrs. Katz left on her own and eventually her departure sent a message to others about the consequences of confronting Mr. Katz about drinking. By this time, "you knew that if you said anything like, 'Phil, you've got a problem,' it would be the end of your discussion for the day," Mr. Hay says. "He would just turn away. You really were on pins and needles the whole time you were with him."

In 1995, Mr. Katz's legal troubles worsened. At 3:24 a.m. one night in May of that year, he was again pulled over for drunk driving. Given three tickets, he faced, if convicted, anywhere from 30 days to a year behind bars. He once again skipped court dates, though, and warrants for his arrest began to pile up.

Police sometimes stopped by the office looking for Mr. Katz, but by the end of 1995 he wasn't coming to work at all, nor staying at his condo. Several colleagues say he feared jail and had told them he would disappear until his legal troubles blew over. Others say Mr. Katz, who was still drinking heavily, was simply ashamed. Though he continued to write code and make major corporate decisions, he stayed in touch only by fax and e-mail.

Days or even weeks could pass before he responded to messages. He began staying in motels and using a Mailboxes Etc. outlet. His $200,000 salary, plus other withdrawals he requested, was deposited directly into his account.

Day-to-day functions continued at PKWare. Mr. Katz laid out for his managers how far their authority went and when they needed to seek him out. "It still was a pretty fun place to work," says Travis Gensch, a former programmer there. "You got to do software which was used by the masses, which isn't too much of an occurrence in Milwaukee." Employees hoped Mr. Katz would someday sober up and return.

At the strip clubs where he drank, Mr. Katz rarely spoke of his company or his achievements. He was known as a quiet, very heavy drinker. He favored Bacardi-and-Coke and Rumple Minze, a 100-proof German liqueur that he drank in shots. He often chatted with the dancers but wasn't known to be pushy.

Dancer Friends

Chastity Fischer, a sometime dancer who met Mr. Katz in 1994, says she was one of his closest friends during the late 1990s. Ms. Fischer provided an account of her relationship with Mr. Katz to the *Milwaukee Journal Sentinel* last month. In an interview with the *Wall Street Journal*, she described him as sweet and naïve, often too generous with dancers who asked him for favors.

Several spent heavily on his credit cards. "You could almost just tell Phil what to do," she says. "People would go up and say, 'Phil, I need this right now. Could you please help me out?' I think he was like a little kid inside, almost childlike."

He bought Ms. Fischer a truck with the proviso that she chauffeur him on errands, such as to the liquor store, she says. He took her to movies, sometimes carrying a flask that he tried to hide from her, and on cruises and trips to Las Vegas.

When Mr. Katz talked about work, he complained that people took advantage of him, Ms. Fischer says. She says he confided to her that he liked himself only when he was drinking—that alcohol made him funnier and looser. Sometimes, Ms. Fischer says, he called her late at night and spoke into her answering machine, drunkenly moaning, "Chastity, I'm so alone." If she picked up the phone, he would hang up.

Occasionally he talked of his mother, with a mixture of bitterness and longing, Ms. Fischer says, and once or twice sent her e-mails. "He felt she was controlling, but when she wasn't there anymore, it was almost like he couldn't handle it," Ms. Fischer says. "He wanted her to be away, but I think when she really was, he almost freaked out. Real life was hard for him."

Ms. Marciniak, who met Mr. Katz a decade ago when she worked as a bartender and dancer, says Mr. Katz lived in fear of being sent to jail. He dreaded the memory of his previous short stays in cells while awaiting bail. One thing he feared was that his asthma inhaler might be taken from him in jail.

"He was on the lam," Ms. Marciniak says. When he was sober, "the reality of jail came to him," and that often started him drinking again. "You'd think he was a murderer," she says. "That's how he felt they treated him."

Mr. Katz spent long days in his hotel rooms watching CNN, taking naps, reading science-fiction magazines and astronomy books and playing games or logging on to his computer, says Ms. Marciniak. "He wanted to be out and about," she says. "He loved going out to eat and he was trapped in hotel rooms eating pizza or Taco Bell. I would tell him, 'Phil, if you could just get this out of your way.'"

In 1997, when PKWare was inducted into the ShareWare Hall of Fame, Mr. Katz skipped the awards dinner in Rhode Island. When his childhood friend Mr. Chizek, now an Air Force chaplain, e-mailed an offer to help, there was no reply.

Inside the Condo

In August 1997, Mr. Katz faced a crisis when neighbors complained of a stench from his condo. Local officials couldn't reach Mr. Katz and finally got a search warrant to enter his home. The garbage piles had grown. Insects infested his home.

"It was quite a scene: a beautiful neighborhood, a very nice building," recalls John DeStefanis, Mequon's city attorney. "The interior was unbelievable: knee-deep in trash and garbage. Papers, magazines, spoiled half-eaten food." Officials also found a collection of sex toys and videos.

The city cleaned up the mess, collecting $8,000 from him for its trouble. It did nothing for Mr. Katz. "You can't force anyone to get help unless he's a danger to himself or others," the city attorney says. But Mr. Katz told Ms. Fischer that the raid and local publicity about it made him feel invaded and embarrassed.

Until almost the end, Mr. Katz kept in sporadic touch with the office and occasionally saw his employees at computer trade shows out of town. He was involved in a breach-of-contract suit, now settled, that PKWare filed against another firm last year. A few months ago, PKWare released a software product Mr. Katz had worked on. But many of his oldest staffers say they saw him only a handful of times in the last five years.

Several say they considered calling the police and trying to find him and force treatment on him. "We thought, 'If we can get him into jail we can get this over,'" says Mr. Hay, who left the company last year. "But everyone said he would find out who called the cops and that person would be fired." They asked themselves if they would share the blame if their boss were involved in a fatal car accident and concluded that yes, they would.

By the last months of his life, Mr. Katz had lost most of his hair and developed a paunch, which he and Ms. Fischer joked about. She says that when she last saw him in 1999, he was drinking as much as three liters of liquor a day and hiccuping and belching uncontrollably. His teeth were rotting. He had the shakes.

"I told him, 'You just have to get some help,'" Ms. Fischer says. She says he told her on the phone that he had received a week's treatment, but then he stopped calling her. "I think he was more or less ashamed," she says.

Drying Out

His friend Ms. Marciniak says she and PKWare's Mr. Gorman escorted Mr. Katz to Charter Hospital in suburban West Allis at 4 o'clock one morning in February 1999. A doctor at the now-closed hospital told him he would die if he kept drinking, she says.

"He sat there and told me I saved his life," Ms. Marciniak says. "He did not want to die." Mr. Katz told her not to call his mother, she says.

Ms. Marciniak says that years earlier she had taken Mr. Katz to another Charter facility, in Las Vegas, and also to another Las Vegas hospital whose name she doesn't recall. Charter Behavioral Health Systems LLC of Alpharetta, Ga., a psychiatric-hospital network now in bankruptcy reorganization, won't comment because patient records are confidential.

In the latest visit, Mr. Katz stayed at the Charter near Milwaukee for about eight days, then spent about six weeks living with Mr. Gorman and attending daily sessions at the hospital, according to Ms. Marciniak. She says Mr. Katz stayed sober for as much as seven months after this treatment.

Last summer the two visited Mexico, whre Mr. Katz climbed hundreds of narrow steps on Mayan temple ruins. "He was looking forward to just hanging out for a couple of more years," she says. He wanted to run his company. He wanted his life back." She doesn't know why he eventually started drinking again.

When Mr. Katz's body was found in April, his mother said she hadn't seen him in five years, according to the medical examiner's report. Although she was notified within hours after his body was found, employees of PKWare say there weren't told until a few days later, after the funeral had been held.

Mrs. Katz, as next of kin under Wisconsin law, stands to inherit the company. Employees expect her to sell it. Their mood is somber, some expecting to lose their jobs when the firm is sold.

PKWare recently posted a brief remembrance of Mr. Katz on its Web site. "We will greatly miss his caring, generosity, help and kindness," it says, and "will always view him as a gentle and special human being who will be sadly missed."

Some nurse private regrets. "A few months ago, I was thinking about going out looking for him," Mr. Hay says. "I said one of these nights I'm going to go out and find him, see if he was doing OK. I didn't really know it had gotten that bad."

And Now the Big Bankruptcy

By Jim Evans, Los Angeles

Robert J. McNulty has struck again. Only last year the Southern California retailing impresario, who is known as much for his legal troubles and bankruptcies as his megamillion-dollar successes, quietly launched his latest venture. The BigStore.com, which followed the $220 million sale of his first Internet company, was going to hawk everything from top-of-the-line digital cameras to dog food.

But that grand ambition is now a remote dream. At the end of July, TheBigStore was forced into bankruptcy. While the company challenges that court order, the site has shut down. And it's beginning to look like this could be the ugliest of McNulty's failures to date—the fourth bankruptcy in a checkered career that has earned him a yacht and a $14 million mansion, in addition to the attention of federal regulators.

The BigStore's troubles are just a piece of the broader fallout in the Internet Economy as the e-commerce bubble burst. The failure stands as a stark reminder of the go-go months of 1999, when anything dot-com seemed like a winner, and even executives with questionable track records were given a green light to go full-speed ahead.

Now TheBigStore's critics are circling. After hiring as many as 220 employees earlier this year, the Santa Ana, Calif.-based retailer has laid off almost all of them, with at least some owed weeks of back pay. Suppliers are lining up to sue the company for millions of dollars. And about a dozen messages have been posted from people who claim to have been BigStore customers. The messages, posted on a Web site called The Complaint Station (dedicated to airing attacks against companies) allege that customers paid for goods that were never delivered.

McNulty, whom a company news release describes as TheBigStore's co-founder, did not respond to requests for interviews left with BigStore CEO Mike Skellern, as well as with Christopher Connolly, a lawyer who is listed in court documents as McNulty's attorney.

Despite the surprise now expressed by McNulty's partners, his past raises red flags that might have led his supporters to proceed with caution. Three companies he started in the 1980s—All-American SportsClub, Auto Giant and Auto Depot—went bankrupt. Then, in 1994, the Securities and

Exchange Commission ruled that McNulty defrauded investors by using the proceeds of securities offerings from three companies he headed to finance the operations of affiliated companies.

Five years later, McNulty left the first Web company he founded, Shopping.com, amid an SEC investigation of the manipulation of the company's stock, which had increased more than 250 percent over a few months. While McNulty escaped blame in the SEC's initial ruling in 1999 (the underwriter was tagged for the manipulation), the case is still open.

Even McNulty's founding of TheBigStore, soon after Shopping.com was sold to Compaq for $220 million, raises questions about his reliability. McNulty and a group of former business associates started the business, but his involvement in the project was kept quiet. Why? One reason could be the noncompete contract he signed with Compaq upon the sale of Shopping.com. According to SEC documents, this prohibited him from working for, consulting for or being more than a 5 percent investor in any company that conducts retail business on or through the Internet without Compaq's approval until June 2000.

Those who chose to work for TheBigStore can't be held entirely responsible for not knowing this background. Indeed, one employee, who insists that he not be identified, explains, "We were told that everybody was out to get Bob, so we should just be quiet about his involvement."

And there were good reasons to believe in McNulty, whose career includes some successes. In addition to his work with Shopping.com, he founded the Southern California discount retailer HomeClub, which he sold to Zayre for $151 million in 1995.

Some respected executives clearly had faith in McNulty, most notably Tracy Nolan, who left his job as Drugstore.com VP of operations to become CEO at TheBigStore (he quit in June and was replaced by current CEO Mike Skellern). Nolan declined to comment for this story.

Chris Hoven, TheBigStore's IT administrator, says that he took his job unaware of McNulty's background, but that changed quickly. "When I was first hired I didn't know anything about McNulty, but in the first three months I found out," says Hoven, the company's 15th employee, hired in April 1999.

Nonetheless, TheBigStore appeared on track for much of 1999. Sure, it was losing money, but what e-commerce company wasn't? Besides, employees were assured that there was $150 million in reserves, says one worker.

Only after the company missed its October launch did the mood darken as executives admitted they needed cash. McNulty then brokered an agreement with China.com that would see the Chinese portal take a 7 percent stake in TheBigStore, according to a news release issued Jan. 4.

Today, it's in dispute whether the deal ever happened. Craig David Celek, China.com VP for investor relations, says his firm never completed the investment, because it was disappointed with TheBigStore's merchandise. But TheBigStore CEO Skellem insists China.com invested in his company.

When the market for Internet stocks crashed in March and April, TheBigStore's cash problem became even more evident. Employees noticed that the company was struggling to pay suppliers.

Robin Smith, a customer from North Bend, Ore., also felt the change. She had successfully purchased batteries from the site in January without any problems. In April, she ordered a $877.99 Sony digital camera. Though TheBigStore cashed her check in May, the camera never arrived.

"I've done a lot of business online and this has never happened to me before," Smith says.

Employees also felt the pinch. On June 12, the company announced that about 75 percent of the staff would be laid off. The following Friday, the company missed its first payroll. Skellern promised that checks were on the way.

Two week later, the company missed its second payroll. Workers got more assurances and were told that an investor was close to signing a deal. After missing its third payroll, the company announced it would lay off the remaining staff.

Hoven says he's owed $16,000, but he, like another worker interviewed for this story, doesn't expect to get it.

At the end of July, the company was forced into Chapter 7 bankruptcy by distributor Ingram Micro, affiliate Ingram Books and another BigStore supplier, Page Digital.

TheBigStore filed a motion Aug. 30 to dismiss the bankruptcy. In court filings, it claims that Ingram Micro intentionally harmed TheBigStore's business because of ties to competitor Buy.com. Skellern says Ingram Micro tampered with a round of financing the company was negotiating with Red Dolphin Enterprises of New Mexico, and contends that Page Digital didn't live up to its contractual obligations.

In turn, Ingram sued TheBigStore for $3.28 million, claiming that McNulty personally guaranteed $1.6 million of the company's debt. All told, according to lawsuits and bankruptcy filings, TheBigStore owes about $8.2 million to supplies, workers and customers.

All of this could have been avoided, of course, had the company managed to close another round of financing. But it didn't, for which McNulty partly blames the critical missives about him and the company posted to stock message boards on Raging Bull, a subsidiary of CMGI-owned Alta Vista. On

Aug. 16 McNulty sued Raging Bull and Alta Vista, among others, for defamation and emotional distress.

"Each separate publication exposes plaintiff McNulty to unwarranted ridicule, contempt, hatred and obloquy," his complaint says.

It's a contempt, however, that at least one BigStore employee has developed without reading the site. Says Hoven: "McNulty will screw anybody for a buck."

What Price Glory?
Personal Tales of the Dot-Com Trenches

There is, of course, no single catalyst for a so-called midlife crisis—no matter when it comes. Sometimes an event can send someone soul-searching, such as losing a job, hitting a career stalemate or realizing that a chosen professional path is all-wrong. Or the trigger can be personal: A relationship dissolves, or maybe there's no relationship to lean on at all. The end result, however, often feels similar: "It's people being pulled apart limb by limb, and pretty soon they don't feel like there's anything left, and their core is burned out," says Ellen McGrath, a psychologist and executive coach.

For a segment of young professionals, the Internet boom-and-bust cycle has accelerated—and in some cases precipitated—this painful life awakening. A group of dot-com veterans tell their stories:

Seth Baum

Age: 29

Workplace War Story: A graduate of Harvard University and the son of an IBM veteran, Mr. Baum seemed bound for a traditional career path—until the Internet revolution struck. He was so anxious to get on board that he rejected a $150,000 consulting job and started at San Franciso-Based Petstore.com while finishing classes at UCLA's business school.

He says the decision to join a dot-com seemed like a no-brainer at the time: Not only did dot-coms hold out the lure of a quick fortune, they offered more responsibility and the promise of creating something new. "I interviewed for some normal brand jobs, but I just couldn't psyche myself up to sell bleach," Mr. Baum recalls, "I'm sitting there, and all I could think is how I didn't care about the differences between fresh-scent and regular."

But even from the start, Petstore was in near chaos, firing Mr. Baum's boss before he'd even reported for his first day of work. And as online retailers began collapsing, Petstore.com's volatile fortunes forced Mr. Baum to play by rules never taught in his management classes. He learned how to avoid calls from vendors to whom Petstore owed money. He acted as if his company was succeeding wildly even as it teetered on the verge of collapse. One day, he was behind his desk, cheerily persuading job candidates to join him at Petstore.com, even though he was uncertain about the company's future. "The people I was interviewing were more excited about the company than I was," he says. "I couldn't tell them I didn't believe in the strategy. I knew we weren't going to make it."

Two months later, Petstore.com eliminated its staff and closed its doors.

Current Occupation: Mr. Baum now runs his own Internet marketing consult-antancy, Feathered Fish Enterprises, out of his home in Presidio Heights, which he shares with his new puppy and two roommates. "I'm really content and happy where things are right now. I love the feeling of not being invested, not freaking out every night and waking up every morning in an environment that's so unstable," he says. "The last four to five months at Petstore.com were so depressing."

Personal/Professional Epiphany: Despite his disillusionment, Mr. Baum wonders whether he'll ever have a shot at so much responsibility and so much financial promise again. After the excitement and optimism of the boom, he finds the field of possible employers less appetizing: struggling dot-coms, big Internet companies filled with the lucky rich, and old-economy companies where he'd be relegated to minor-league status.

"My brother, who's five years younger, is working for a dot-com in Tokyo but doesn't have any expectations. His generation is going to be okay," he says. "Once you've experienced that high, everything seems grey and bland by comparison. How do you settle down to that for thirty more years? I don't know the answer. At some point you rearrange what you though was possible."

—Suein Hwang

Cecilia Pagkalinawan

Age: 32

Workplace War Story: In March 1998, when the dot-com world was still flush with success, Ms. Pagkalinawan opened a New York-based fashion e-commerce consulting firm called boutiqueY3K. Ms. Pagkalinawan, who was one of the Internet pioneers in the mid-90s, kept 18-hour days, networking late into the evening and struggling to stay positive when people around her lost their passion and left. "I thought burnout would be inevitable," she admits. Her boyfriend at the time was also a dot-com CEO and after a while, they grew apart. "When you are moving 500 miles per hour, it's really hard to find time to bond, relax, slow down and share your problems, hopes and dreams," she says.

Without realizing it, Ms. Pagkalinawan sacrificed in ways she never would have imagined to keep her business afloat. On the night of her sister's wedding in late August, she left before the wedding reception to fly to an industry conference the next morning. She ended up missing the plane and sitting in the airport alone, making neither the reception nor the meeting. Similarly, about that time, she was forced to turn down the prestigious Rockefeller Foundation Next Generation Leadership Fellowship because she was too busy trying to win a multimillion-dollar account for boutiqueY3K. "If I didn't win the account, I might have had to let go of staff," she says.

But the final blow came last month, when her sister died unexpectedly. "My sister had wanted more time to talk, to go do things together, and I was too preoccupied with my own problems to help her," she says.

Slowly, Ms. Pagkalinawan has begun to make changes in her schedule, keeping weekends to herself and limiting evening outings to one or two nights a week. Recently bankers have begun suggesting that if she doubles her financial projections, she might be able to take her company public next year. So far, she's putting them off. "It's too much pressure," she says. "I'm not going to put unnecessary stress on this company we've taken three years to cultivate."

Current Occupation: Still CEO of boutiqueY3K; salary $150,000 annually plus bonus.

Personal/Professional Epiphany: In a world where work can easily become your personal life, it's critical to keep a division between the two. "What's going on in this fast-paced industry is unnatural," she says. "You can have very little patience with family and loved ones, but they're not working on your time frame, and you have to adjust to theirs. We think everyone should understand what we're going through, but that's not necessarily the case. Sometimes it's perceived as arrogance and insensitivity." As for her next romantic relationship, she says, "I'm looking for someone who's not in this space so when I do have down time, I don't have to talk about work, which is foremost in the minds of other CEOs in this industry. It's very hard to get away from it. . . . You become very myopic."

—*Jennifer Rewick*

Theo Song

Age: 29

Workplace War Story: In December, 1999, Mr. Song jumped from his consulting job with Bain & Co. to a Silicon Valley technology-staffing start-up. At the start-up, "everybody had high expectations that it would be analytically driven and that we'd be able to run this place in a professional manner. But there was no 'adult supervision' in the firm," he says.

He put his personal life on hold while working at the start-up. After all, everybody else in the Valley was doing it, he explains, "I made a lot of sacrifices during that time in terms of lifestyle," he admits. When the startup was sold seven months later, an exhausted Mr. Song took a breather to figure out his next moves. After leaving the startup, Mr. Song's South Korean grandparents happened to be visiting him. "They don't know what the hell the Internet is. All they saw was that their grandson looked totally unhappy."

Current Occupation: Back at Bain & Co.'s Los Angeles office.

Personal/Professional Epiphany: Who you work with matters. While surfing at the beach, he happened to run into a Bain partner who had been one of his mentors. "He asked me, very informally, 'What are you thinking of doing next?'" recalls Mr. Song. "While sitting on the beach, that was kind of the 'aha' moment to go back to the firm."

At the start-up, he says, his mentality was to "defer a lot of the social things" and focus solely on work. "Everyone was working themselves to death," he says. "Now I think that model's ridiculous. It was really abnormal to be sleeping in a sleeping bag under your desk three nights a week."

—*Rachel Emma Silverman*

Jason Salfen

Age: 27

Workplace War Story: Last year, Mr. Salfen dropped out of the M.B.A. program at M.I.T.'s Sloan School of Management to pursue a dot-com dream. He was one of the founders of eDentalStoreInc., a Silicon Valley online dental-tool supplier. The company had difficulty securing a third round of funding and was sold to a competitor this past September. By that time, Mr. Salfen had already decided to return to business school. "I wanted a more structured learning process," he says.

Seeing the business fold "was very depressing," he says. "I think had we been able to execute better, had we had a more experienced team that understood the pitfalls that young dot-com entrepreneurs have, who knows?" Still his hopes were inflated beyond reason. "A year ago, I could reasonably say that my goal was to retire by 30 with $10 million to $20 million in the bank, and now that idea seems very ludicrous."

Current/Occupation: Second-year student at Sloan School of Management.

Personal/Professional Epiphany: Love what you do for the work, not for the money. Mr. Salfen remembers exactly when he realized that the dot-com bubble had burst. When his friend joined a dot-com in December 1999, "we all congratulated him as the half-million-dollar man," he says. Two months later, all of the friend's options were underwater. "It made me realize that you can't base your happiness upon the value of your stock. You have to be happy with your salary and love your job. Think about your options and your future potential, but if you don't get to strike it big, you still have to be happy with life."

—*Rachel Emma Silverman*

Jeanne Meyer

Age: 36

Workplace War Story: In August 1999, Ms. Meyer left a secure post at a well-established public-relations firm, Robinson Lerer & Montgomery, to sign up as senior vice president of marketing for New York-based Pseudo Programs, Inc., a now-defunct Web broadcasting company. Lured by the chance to cash in on the Internet boom and expand her job skills into more powerful-sounding sectors, such as "marketing" and "deal making," she made a lateral six-figure salary move in exchange for an equity state in Pseudo. "I knew heady days were coming to a close," Ms. Meyer admits, "but it would have been nice to have a big windfall and buy an apartment—and in New York that costs $1 million."

It wasn't long before disappointment set in. Early this year, with the market's dot-com love affair waning, her marketing budget was slashed as the company strove to tighten costs across the board. As such, long-term planning became difficult, and she found herself falling back on the same skills she'd used in her old job.

Meanwhile, as management struggled to find a survival plan, Ms. Meyer's staff grew demoralized, and she often put in 18-hour days trying to hold her group together. The final straw came in September when Pseudo.com closed its doors, and Ms. Meyer was laid off, her equity stake in the company worthless. At that point, Ms. Meyer decided to return to her blue-chip roots. She wrote down four things she absolutely wanted in a job: smart people, great business, great backing and a great brand.

Current Occupation: ToysRus.com, vice president of communications.

Personal/Professional Epiphany: Don't get pushed into a job that's the wrong fit. "I had an epiphany that corporate communications strategy is what I'm really good at . . . The other stuff was not as great as it was cracked up to be." After significant soul-searching, she realized "it was OK to downshift a little bit. . . . Why kill yourself when it's not really what you want?" For Ms. Meyer, it wasn't about going to a 40-hour week. "I'm a 70-hour-plus-a-week person no matter what, but I've learned to work a lot smarter and not obsess when I don't need to." Now, she says, "I'm at the top of my game at a point when I'm starting to think about settling down."

—Jennifer Rewick

Justin Boyle

Age: 25

Workplace War Story: In February, Mr. Boyle was bartending in Pittsburgh when he got a call from a friend who was helping to launch NetFlip.com, an incentive-based marketing network, in Palo Alto, Calif. Lured by the promise of wealth and the thrill of the Internet, Mr. Boyle abandoned his plans of going back to graduate school to study math and then teach, and moved across the country to join the firm. He received a $45,000 base salary, equity and a performance bonus target of $20,000.

After six months at the start-up, it became clear the high-stress, fast-paced environment wasn't for him. Eighty-hour weeks were the norm, as was working Sundays. He didn't like the "competitive, cutthroat environment" of big business and says he never felt a sense of completion at day's end. "It was an ongoing process; you never feel you're getting your head above water." He thought the company would hire more people and that would help alleviate his workload. That didn't happen and two weeks ago, Mr. Boyle quit. (Net-Flip says Mr. Boyle's decision to leave was based on his "passion" for teaching and adds that the company is not in "any financial difficulties and is always looking for talented people.")

Current Occupation: 7th- and 8th-grade math teacher making $36,000 a year.

Personal/Professional epiphany: It's better to try something new than to live with regrets. "I think this was a great experience for me," he says. "If I'd gone straight into teaching, I might always have wondered if I should have gone into business."

—Jennifer Rewick

What Goes Up:
For Some Executives, The Internet Dream
Has a Deep Downside

By Susan Pulliam and Scott Thurm
Staff Reporters of the Wall Street Journal

At the age of 36, after a career toiling mostly as a mid-level engineer and manager, Michael Donahue became a member of a very exclusive group: the Internet centimillionaire club.

The founder of InterWorld Corp., a business-to-business company in New York, Mr. Donahue saw his stake rise to $448 million last year as InterWorld's share price skyrocketed after an initial public stock offering in August 1999.

He then did what many red-blooded Americans would have done: He splurged, big time.

Mr. Donahue bought a $9.6 million second home in Palm Beach, Fla. A polo enthusiast, he ponied up $100,000 to help sponsor his own team there. He spent a bundle more sharing in the rental of a Hawker Sidney private jet, the better to whisk off to Palm Beach on weekend jaunts with his wife. "It was a lifestyle thing," he explains.

Another Club

Today, Mr. Donahue is a member of another club—call it the 90% club—of executives whose companies' stock price has fallen that much or more from their peak.

The value of his InterWorld stake has plunged to $12.6 million, as the share price has fallen 96.8% to $2.94 from a peak of $93.50 on Dec. 31. He was asked to repay a $14 million loan he took out with his InterWorld stock as collateral. And the Palm Beach house? To help satisfy his lenders, he has put it on the market for more than $13 million. "Going up was easy. But when it starts going down, no one wants to talk to you," he says. "It's been the most challenging personal experience of my career."

At least he has plenty of fellow sufferers. More than 60 companies—most of them start-ups that went public at the height of the Internet frenzy—have seen their stock nosedive 90% or more. They include such well-known names as eToys Inc., Webvan Group, Internet Capital Group Inc., Ask Jeeves Inc. and Priceline.com Inc. All told, according to market trackers Birinyi Associates, in Westport, Conn., about $114 billion in market value has been erased among the 25 worst-performing Internet stocks, which are down a staggering 95.7% on average from their highs this year. Like so many Humpty Dumptys, executives of those companies have had a truly, great fall, with the combined losses of the largest shareholder at each company adding up to about $14 billion.

Top of the Drop

Perhaps never before have so many been worth so much for so little time. At the top of the 90% club is Shelby Bryan, a former Wall Street investment banker who became chief executive of ICG Communications Inc., a fiber-optic telecommunications company. Thanks to a 99.4% decline in ICG's stock, to 25 cents from a peak of $39.25 in March, his stake in ICG, once worth $89 million, is now valued at just $550,000.

Jeff Dachis, the brash co-founder and chief executive of Razorfish Inc., a Web strategy and design company, had stock and options worth $281 million at their peak. When the stock was riding high , Mr. Dachis was quoted as saying, "there are sheep and there are shepherds, and I fancy myself to be the latter." With his stake now valued at only $24.8 million, Mr. Dachis is singing a different tune. "Anyone paying attention to short swings in a volatile market has their eye on the wrong ball," he says.

Candice Carpenter, founder of iVillage Inc., a Web site for women, had a stake once valued at over $100 million. It's now worth $890,000. Last month, she was forced to sell a block of stock to satisfy demands from Merrill Lynch & Co., which gave her a loan secured by her iVillage stock. And then there's James Cramer, who founded The Street.com. His shares, once valued at $235 million, are now worth about $10.5 million with the stock down 95%.

'Try to Not Focus'

Peter Jackson, founder and chief executive of Intraware Inc., which sells software over the Web, has seen the value of his stock shrink to roughly $22.8 million from $340 million. At Mediaplex Inc., an online marketing-services company, Chief Executive Greg Raiffman has watched his stake plummet 96.8%, to just $20 million from more than $700 million. "You try to put it out of your mind," he says. "You try to not focus on how much has evaporated."

Most Americans can only wish they were so unlucky. None of these Internet entrepreneurs is headed for the poorhouse. But there is more than a little gloating over their diminished fortunes.

Let's be honest: Even while Internet founders were lauded as poster people of the New Economy, they were also widely resented. Kevin Marcus, a 26-year old who helped found Internet software company InfoSpace Inc., recalls being viewed "as some snotty kid." At a neighborhood party he attended when InfoSpace stock was soaring—pushing the value of his stock over $100 million—a middle-aged man asked him sarcastically, "You mean you could write me a check for $1 million today?"

InfoSpace executives were briefly in the 90% club, though a modest recovery means the shares now are down just 86% from their peak. To help ease the pain, Mr. Marcus has a new home, a Mercedes and a Ferrari, with the help of cash from regular sales of some stock each quarter.

The financial losses of the Internet nouveaux riches have created a wealth of black humor. "B to B," the Web jargon for "business to business," has become shorthand for "back to banking," the industry that some Internet executives came from and now are returning to. The term "B to C," for business-to-customer Internet companies, now stands for "back to consulting." And companies such as Internet Capital Group—current stock price $10.25, down 95.2% from its peak of $212 last December—that were once referred to as "incubators," because they financed and nurtured infant companies, are known as "incinerators."

Many of the fleetingly mega-rich were wealthy only on paper, because they never sold a share of their company stake. In part, that's because so-called lockup periods require most insiders to refrain from selling any stock for six months after a company's IPO, to protect other investors from concerns about executives bailing out at the first opportunity.

'Balata' and Backspin

Mr. Jackson of Intraware has coined a phrase for the company's seemingly ever-shrinking stock price: the "balata," named after a golf-ball covering that helps golfers put backspin on the ball, making it roll back toward the golfer after landing on the green. But, he claims he has "not lost any sleep" over his declining net worth. Who needs a multibillion-dollar valuation anyway, he asks? "A year ago money grew on trees. It makes you think you can do anything. When money doesn't grow on trees a year later, you become very focused on what your competency is," he says.

Glen Ballman, the 29-year old founder of Onvia.com Inc., a Web portal for small businesses, also is publicly nonchalant about seeing his net worth tank by a little less than $800 million. Mr. Ballman's personal net worth soared to $827 million the day after the company's IPO in February, a development he couldn't have foretold only a few years before when he was traveling the world with "a pair of sandals, a T-shirt, a backpack, shorts and a camera." To celebrate, Mr. Ballman treated five childhood friends from tiny Wilcox in the Canadian province of Saskatchewan to steak dinners in New York City.

Today, Onvia's shares trade at $2.97 and Mr. Ballman's stake is worth about $31.5 million. "One day we didn't have a ticker [stock symbol]. The next day [the stock] was in the 60s and 70s, and a few weeks later it was in single digits," Mr. Ballman says. He wasn't able to sell any shares when the stock was higher, but he says he doesn't need the cash because he shares a Seattle house with three friends.

For others, even if their fortune was only on paper, losing much of it has been painful.

"Jeepers. Don't make me think about it," says Matthew Szulick, chief executive of Red Hat Inc., which offers services for the Linux operating system. Its shares are down 90.5%. At one point last December, Mr. Szulick's five million shares were worth $756 million. And now? About $71.5 million. The lockup period prevented him from selling shares anywhere near the peak.

Mr. Donahue of InterWorld was one of the biggest spenders among the now not-so-rich Internet entrepreneurs. He founded the company six years ago after working for PepsiCo and Citigroup, and then running his own consulting company, never earning more than $200,000 a year in salary.

As InterWorld's stock soared, he cashed out few of his 4.8 million shares. Although the lockup period had expired, he sold only several hundred thousand shares, keeping the rest because of the bad publicity that can be generated by insider sales by senior executives. Instead, he took out loans to finance his jet-setting lifestyle, using his stock as collateral.

Mr. Donahue agonized over the precipitous decline of InterWorld's stock, as it tumbled to $10 just before Memorial Day weekend. "I never believed it would get to $10. I was incredulous that we were that low." That weekend he skipped the trip to Palm Beach, working to concoct a plan to shore up the company. "The lower the stock goes, you have a series of events that begin happening and you are second-guessing yourself," he says. "It's a painful process."

The shares perked up, getting back to the high $20s in July, before descending even further. Things went from bad to worse for the company in recent weeks when it told investors it would report a worse-than expected loss from operations. With the shares under $3, the company hired Bear Stearns &

Co. to explore strategic alternatives. On Oct. 12, it announced that it had signed a pact with technology holding company Jackpot Enterprises for a $20 million private placement of convertible preferred shares. As part of the agreement, Jackpot said it would also assume Mr. Donahue's $14 million loan in exchange for some of any future gains from his InterWorld stock.

Versailles—With Golf Course

Another big loser in the tech-stock decline has been Michael Saylor, the flamboyant founder of Internet software concern MicroStrategy Inc., based in Tysons Corner, Va. With its shares down 92% since their peak in April, the value of Mr. Saylor's stake has plunged to $1.09 billion from $14.3 billion.

When MicroStrategy's stock was still up, Mr. Saylor bought a 50-acre lot on the banks of the Potomac River where he planned to build a mansion, modeled after the Palace of Versailles, with a nine-hole golf course on the grounds. Mr. Saylor declines to comment, but those plans are "on hold" at the moment, a spokesman says. He attributes the delay to demands on Mr. Saylor's time rather than the decline in his net worth. "At the moment, neighbors' horses are grazing on the land," the spokesman says.

Gone also are the lavish parties and events formerly bestowed on MicroStrategy employees. Last year, MicroStrategy booked a celebrity line cruise ship and treated all 1,500 employees to a week in the Caribbean at a cost of about $3 million, according to a person close to the company. The company had booked the ship and rooms for another free cruise this year, before MicroStrategy drifted into dire financial straits, now, employees will have to pay their own way—$1,000 and up per room, the spokesman says. "We're trying hard to get back to profitability," he explains. MicroStrategy was forced to restate its earnings earlier this year after it disclosed in March that it had misstated earnings and revenue for several years.

It's not just the founders and top brass who have watched their Internet-financed dreams fade. The boom in Internet stocks lured many executives from older companies, with promises of potential wealth from stock options.

A Surreal Spike

Peter Hutto, 41, left Electronic Data Systems Corp. in November 1999 to head the Southern California office of Lante Corp., a Chicago-based consulting firm for business-to-business companies. Though he walked away from soon-to-vest stock options that would have been worth several million dollars, it appeared initially that he had scored big by moving. Lante went public at

$20 a share in February, and jumped to $87.50 on Feb. 29, making his stock worth many millions (though he won't say how many). Since then, Lante's stock has plummeted to $3.94, making him worse off than he would have been had he stayed at EDS.

Mr. Hutto calls the spike in the stock price "surreal." He adds: "I no more believed that was going to last than I believe there's a man on the moon."

A mid-level executive who has seen his riches vanish is Jake Bramhall, director of client services at the once highflying web consultancy US Interactive Inc. based in Philadelphia. At the beginning of the year, when the company's shares peaked at $90, his stock was worth over $1 million on paper and he took the occasion to go with his wife to check out vacation homes at Point Pleasant, a beach town on the New Jersey Shore.

Now, with US Interactive's shares trading at a mere $1.21, down 98.6%, those plans are out the window. "The money we were using to buy it disappeared, and it became a stupid thing to do," he says.

Mr. Bramhall says he did make $100,000 cashing out some of his shares. "One day you're worth almost a million, another day it's gone," he says. "Easy come, easy go, although we kick ourselves...for not cashing out more of them."

Now, he must also endure the ribbing of his in-laws and other relatives who had also invested in the stock. "I get some teasing, but at the same time I bought some [stock] of my father-in-law's company, Xerox, so to hell with him," he laughs. Xerox Corp.'s shares are down 88% from their 1999 high of $63.94 a share.

Some executives are finding their celebrity status is diminishing along with their net worth. No one has run up lately to Gordon Hoffstein, chief executive of Internet marketing company. Be Free Inc., like the woman who had head about his company and who recognized him in a shoe store last year. "She said, 'You have the golden touch. What's the name of your stock? I want to buy it,'" says Mr. Hoffstein. His stock has sunk 93.5% since its peak, causing the value of his stake to fall to $14.6 million from $240 million at its peak. Mr. Hoffstein says he counseled the woman not to buy the stock if that was the extent of her due diligence.

He says now, "If she liked the stock at $60, she ought to love it at $2."

CHAPTER 5

Just Because It's the Dot-Com Era Doesn't Mean That There Aren't Other (Bad) Computing Failure Stories

I've always been a sucker for failure stories. I collect them, like some people collect baseball cards or caps or thimbles or (name your own collector's poison). I keep a file folder in my desk, and whenever I come across a worthy story in some part of the computing or popular press, I rip it out and chuck it in. Sometimes that file grows slowly, and sometimes it grows rapidly.

It's been growing astonishingly rapidly recently. When I published my most recent computing failure book (*Computing Calamities*, Prentice Hall, 1999), I figured that would be it for awhile. It had taken the better part of a decade to collect the stories that went into *Calamities* and its predecessor, *Software Runaways* (Prentice Hall, 1998), and—although I kept on ripping and chucking—I didn't expect to do another book very soon. Perhaps never (I am, after all, 68 years old as I write this, and definitely an Old Computing Fogy!)

Then came the spring and summer of 2000. Out of the Sky's the Limit era of dot-com history suddenly came the Sky is Falling era. There were tons of failure stories hitting the press, especially the computing press. And most of them, as it turned out, were about dot-com companies. Promises were suddenly no more important than profits. And a lot of companies big in promise but small in profit were falling by the wayside.

What an opportunistic little mind I have! This veritable blizzard of dot-com stories suddenly were enough to make a book on dot-com failure—something I hadn't even thought about before—become viable. That rapidly filling folder had suddenly and surprisingly become grist for another book. And this is it.

But there was a problem. There were plenty of dot-com failure stories, to be sure. A new periodical with what I think of as the strange title *The Industry Standard* (I.S.) had made that happen. (What industry? Standard how? They bill themselves as "the Newsmagazine of the Internet economy.") I may not have quite understood what this magazine was all about, but it rapidly became the primary source for these dot-com failure stories. They were being published, in I.S., at the rate of several per month, some of them in glorious, rich human-interest, fascinating detail. Well-researched, well-conceived, well-written. My folder filleth and runneth over.

Well, almost. There were plenty of dot-com failure stories. But not quite enough to make a full 300+ page failure book, the kind my publisher loves to slap a beautiful binding on and charge you $30-something to buy.

No worries, I told my publisher. I'm also accumulating some non-dot-com failure stories in my folder, I said to him, and we'll use those to pad out this book.

This is that padding chapter. I think the stories are good ones, mind you, but there's really nothing dot-com about them, no matter how hard I tried to wedge them into the book's theme. So I hope you enjoy them. They'll be coming at you thick and fast in what follows.

Failure From the Top

The dot-com failure stories that we have seen in our earlier chapters are almost always top-down failures. That is, something bad happened at the top of the company—the leadership domain—and as a result, the whole company tumbled, often to its death.

That kind of failure is more rare in the traditional company. Usually, in an established enterprise, it takes several bad somethings to pull the whole company down, and most companies—like most people—are a mix of bad somethings and good somethings. Complete and irrevocable failure from the top is uncommon in the bricks and mortar business.

But in the stories that follow, that's not the case. The whole company may or may not go under, but these stories are about a failure so profound, so thorough, that the effects continue to last to this day, the company either falling into the abyss or at least teetering on the edge.

For instance?

For instance, there's the sad story of the Amiga computer. This is a continuation of a story [Glass 1999] from one of my earlier books. In its heyday (and in that previous story), Amiga was the beloved technology of the computing elite, a computer so wonderful that, in the minds of its followers at least, it put the Apple Macintosh and the Windows Intels (Wintels) platform to technical shame. But Amiga died in the failure of the company that produced it, Commodore International. Some say that marketing naiveté did it in. It was heavily mourned.

When Gateway Computer made moves to resurrect the Amiga some years later, as the story to come tells us, the Amiga faithful could hardly wait for their beloved computer to rise from its ignominious ashes. Their hopes, as this book's story tells us, were to be dashed. Two and a half years after announcing Amiga's resurrection, Gateway made a total change of plans and decided that Amiga was to be a "software company" for "information appliance" devices. Why? It's hard to imagine why. The Amiga name stood for one thing—exciting, superb technical computing innovation, especially in its Windows-like GUI. What did the name bring to the software/appliance table? What could have crossed the minds of the key players at Gateway? Those questions, unfortunately, are not answered in our story.

From the glorious reality of the Amiga, which died in its first incarnation through a failure of marketing, we arrive at our second story. Transmeta was a company that promised a secret so dramatic that the business expectations were breathtaking. Employees, our story tells us, "couldn't even tell their parents what they did for a living," the secrecy was so intense. If mystery is good marketing, then Transmeta's marketing was as superb as Amiga's was not.

But the reality of what Transmeta finally announced resulted in a come-down so severe that it's hard to imagine what its future can possibly be. "I know the Amiga, Senator, and the Transmeta is no Amiga!" After all that secretive and suspenseful labor, Transmeta produced . . . a computer that would run the same software as an Intel chip! The anticlimax was astonishing! Now, is Transmeta a failure? As of the writing of our story, the answer was "not yet."

There's no doubt, however, about the fate of the final company in this section. InaCom, a computer sales enterprise once so successful that it had gobbled up some well-known key rivals, fell into a "tangled financial mess" that one industry observer called "as ugly a travesty as has ever occurred." The carnage of its collapse culminated in the firing of its 5,100 employees by an email message that pointed them to a toll-free telephone number ... where a recorded message fired them! It doesn't get much more graceless than that. Does it?

Reference:

Glass, Robert L., "The Rise and Fall of Commodore: Amiga Came, Saw, But Failed to Conquer," *Computing Calamities*, pp. 166-169, Prentice Hall: Upper Saddle River, NJ, 1999.

Adios, Amiga

By Greg Lindsay

Jim Collas, president of the Amiga computer company, was partying hard. It was March 16, and Collas, Bill McEwen, his marketing director, and a loyal following were rocking into the small hours at the Amiga99 show in St. Louis, Mo. Hotel security was on hand to keep the room close to fire code. The crowd had reason to celebrate. Two years earlier, PC giant Gateway Computers had snatched Amiga from the jaws of bankruptcy and promised its small legion of avid fans a new life. The plan, which the faithful were celebrating with such gusto, was already in place and might even restore Amiga to the spot it occupied in the '80s when the revolutionary, multimedia computer was considered best of breed, years ahead of its time.

Today, six months after the Amiga99 bash, the party appears to be over yet again. On Sept. 1, Gateway announced that Collas and McEwen were leaving the company to take advantage of "other opportunities." Collas disappeared, but McEwen angrily declared on Amiga-related newsgroups that the company had refused to renew his contract. "I did not leave Amiga," he said. "Amiga left me."

Once again, when Amiga was finally gaining some momentum, the earth shifted under the community's feet. Collas, Amiga's champion inside Gateway, was the guy who persuaded the company to release a long-awaited official update to the late-'80s operating system and to build an entirely new Amiga computer that would run a Linux-based OS with a new processor and hardware design. In July, he and Amiga unveiled mockups of the new machines. Amigaphiles rejoiced.

"When he came in January, I don't think he understood why people were using 10-year old machines and sleeping with them and kissing them," says Harv Laser, author of Amiga books and editor of *AmigaZone.com*. "He didn't understand why we hated Microsoft and laughed at the Macintosh. And then suddenly he changed and finally understood what the passion is, and then he was just gone."

Into his place stepped Tom Schmidt, Amiga's chief operating officer. But where Collas was outspoken, Schmidt has so far been silent. And so has the company. Officials from Gateway and Amiga declined to comment publicly about their plans for the Amiga. On Sept. 14, though—after Amiga removed

Originally published in Time Digital, November 1, 1999 (a supplement to Time magazine). Used with permission. Copyright 1999 by Time.

from its website all references to and photographs of Amiga OS 5.0 and the new boxes it would run on—Schmidt issued a statement: Amiga would henceforth be a software company. It wouldn't aim to put an OS on desktop PCs after all. Its target? The "information appliances" hyped as the next phase of computing.

Naturally, Amiga users were incensed. The debate between Amiga users and Gateway boils down to a single, metaphysical question: Can the soul of Amiga be reincarnated in other devices? Or is it a fixed identity residing irrevocably in its beige box? For Gateway, the answer isn't metaphysical at all; it's strictly bottom line. Gateway sees Amiga's value as a brand that still has an aura to be leveraged. "We realize," said Schmidt, in a follow-up posting to the company's website, "that this does not satisfy the desire of the Amiga community for a next-generation Amiga."

That's for sure. Impassioned users have called for community action, boycotts and even class actions to save the platform. One group, the Phoenix Platform Consortium, boasts a number of Amiga pioneers among its members and is mentioned by Schmidt as a possible outside partner for bringing plans for a new machine back to life.

Laser and others are skeptical. "I compare this to when Apple killed the Newton. Newton protesters gathered in the parking lot in [Apple's headquarters in] Cupertino, where Apple fed them drinks and cookies and patted them on the head. To me, Amiga's been a box. [Schmidt's statements] are the equivalent of Apple's handing out cookies and saying 'You've been good little customers, and we'll ship something new and better soon, but we won't tell you what, and we won't tell you when.'"

Some people say Amiga's curse is that it has always been someone else's technology to kick around. The computer was created by the late Jay Miner, revered by Amigans as a cross between Apple's Steve Wozniak and St. Francis. Miner drew up the plans for the original Amiga's circuit boards by hand while an employee at Atari in its 1970s heyday. (According to legend, Miner would consult with his dog, Mitchy, before finishing each page.) He sold the technology to Commodore in the early '80s after recognizing that he could organize neither the marketing nor the manufacturing muscle to build the machines. The Amiga was the first personal computer to boast stereo sound and thousands of colors, plus a genuinely fast, multitasking operating system. This was way back when PCs still ran on DOS and Macintosh screens were black-and-white. But Commodore's marketing efforts failed, and the Amiga languished as Macintosh and Windows machines battled for mind share through the early '90s. After Commodore went bankrupt in 1994, the Amiga division was bought by the German company Escom (Amiga has traditionally been big in Europe). But that proved to be only a temporary respite from financial uncertainty. Following Escom's escapades in the PC-cloning business, it went bankrupt in turn, and Gateway bought the entire lot for the garage-sale price of $16 million in 1997.

That was supposed to be the marriage with a happy ending. By the summer of '98, Amiga had mapped out a plan to transfer the essence of the Amiga operating system to a new computer and set-top box for Christmas 1999. The high-end computer would retail for the low-end price of $1,000, and the set-top box for only $300. As the story goes, sounding fantastic and paranoid enough to be something out of a Thomas Pynchon novel, both would use a radically new chip so secret that only 12 Amiga executives had clearance to see it. It was known in the Amiga community as the "magical mystery chip," Joe Torre, Amiga's senior hardware engineer at the time, claimed it was so powerful that "you could play games at high-definition television resolution, battling monsters that you designed with the real-time 3-D program that came with the box."

But the MMC never appeared. The company that made it—still unnamed by Amiga officials—died during the Asian financial crisis, according to Torre. While the search for a replacement was on, Collas was brought in as president. And the rest, as they say, is history.

Unlike Amiga's previous parent companies, Gateway has deep pockets, but it is unwilling to act as Amiga's savior. Groups like the Phoenix Platform Consortium may try to build a new Amiga for the new millennium, but Gateway CEO Ted Waitt holds all the cards, not to mention the patents. And who's to say the answer to the Amiga question isn't yes—that one can, in fact, port the soul of the old machine to a range of "smart" consumer appliances? In that case, the box's faithful will still cry out, "Farewell, Amiga, we hardly knew ye."

Breakthrough or
Snake Oil?

By Jason Krause

Back in the old days the wagon would roll into town and out would jump a fellow dressed to impress. An audience would crowd around and listen to a spiel touting the latest, greatest cure—all for what ailed them—rickets, consumption . . . server crashes. Some of these products worked miraculously well, some did more harm than good. Some did nothing at all.

The jury's still out on Transmeta. After spending years in complete secrecy—employees couldn't even tell their parents what they did for a living—the company finally revealed itself to the world in a blowout PR event that had journalists salivating for an invitation.

But now that the doors have been flung open the company has lost a bit of its allure. Transmeta is just one in a long line of Intel computer chip knock-off artists. Its chip won't kill Intel. It's not designed to be able to run any software on any operating system in the world. It isn't an open-source chip. Like other companies before it, Transmeta simply came up with a chip that runs the same software as an Intel chip. Its biggest selling point: The Transmeta chip promises to consume less power than comparable chips.

It could launch a whole new class of handheld devices. Or it could be a lot of hooey. One thing is sure: Transmeta used the chip—and the hype—to convince a lot of companies to send it a lot of money—$88 million in the latest round.

"The list of companies throwing money at them is pretty impressive," says Tom Halfhill, an analyst for the *Microprocessor Report*. "They must be showing those companies something impressive. But they still haven't proved to anyone I know that their chip can do all the things they say it can."

Transmeta chips are currently in production. IBM is doing the manufacturing. The company has announced only one partner, though Frank Priscaro, director of brand development, promises a bunch by midyear. "We'll have more than people think," he says. As for taking the company public, no date is set, but the latest round of financing puts it well on the way.

Transmeta made a name for itself by keeping its mission a secret and letting others build the suspense. Since it's had to sustain interest on its own, though, Transmeta hasn't done so well. Do its chips really outperform Intel's?

Will they consume little or no power? Will they be as cheap as the company promises? Those questions still dog the company. But by the middle of the year, when Transmeta has promised to deliver products, it will either be the real deal—or just another failed Intel wannabe.

Computer Crash:
How Shifting Forces In PC Business
Undid Top Dealer InaCom

By Gary McWilliams
Staff Reporter for the Wall Street Journal

At 3 p.m. on June 16, InaCom Corp., once the world's largest computer dealer, sent most of its 5,100 employees an e-mail directing them to a toll-free phone number. There, a recorded message fired them.

In the hours that followed, thousands of InaCom customers discovered that their computer-service contracts had been canceled, multimillion-dollar computer projects were on hold, and equipment being repaired was stranded. Many got the word from stunned InaCom employees.

The final, chaotic hours of InaCom capped one of the wildest rides in modern personal-computer history. During an industry growth spurt in the 1990s, the Omaha, Neb., company gobbled up rivals such as Sears Business Centers and Vanstar Corp., becoming a Goliath with $6.9 billion in revenue. It supplied PCs and related services to a third of America's biggest companies.

But as PCs changed from an adolescent business to a mature one, InaCom was left by the wayside like some summertime fling. Several big PC makers, trying to match Dell Computer Corp.'s astonishing direct-sales success, began to deal directly with customers themselves. In making the switch, computer makers created a Byzantine two-tiered pricing scheme that crippled longtime partners such as Inacom.

Down the Drain

Unable to adapt, InaCom found itself in a tangled financial mess. Its auditor never signed off on its 1999 numbers or a proposed restatement of 1998 results. Two "forensic" accounting teams are still working to unravel its twisted finances. A heartland company that prided itself on Midwestern values, InaCom now is being investigated by the Securities and Exchange Commission for possible accounting irregularities. A bankruptcy judge in Delaware is liquidating what remains of the business.

The carnage is widespread. Renowned technology investor Warburg Pincus Capital LLC had a 24% stake in InaCom, once worth $230 million and now worthless. Hewlett-Packard Co. says it is out $28 million. Compaq Computer Corp. has traded lawsuits with InaCom—the PC maker seeking $102 million of allegedly misdirected customer payments, and InaCom claiming Compaq withheld $43 million in service payments. Some of the fired workers complain that even before the company went into bankruptcy, they couldn't get health-insurance claims paid.

"This is as ugly a travesty as has ever occurred," says William Y. Tauscher, a director and former chief of Vanstar, who had a 4.3% stake in InaCom. Among those he criticizes is KPMG International, which certified and twice confirmed InaCom's now-disputed 1998 finances, but whose failure to sign off on the 1999 books added to InaCom's difficulties this year. KPMG declines to comment, citing client confidentiality and the SEC's InaCom investigation.

InaCom rose from humble roots, as part of the irrigation-equipment division of Omaha-based Valmont Industries Inc. In the early 1980s, the division started putting computer terminals in the offices of irrigation dealers. From there, it branched into providing computers to farmers and other small businesses. It became a separate company in 1985 and went on to acquire dealers that distributed many different PC brands.

William L. Fairfield, who founded the business, recognized PC manufacturers' obsession with ever-increasing sales. The more PCs they make and sell, the more cheaply they can buy parts such as chips and disk drives. And by lowering their costs they can reduce the prices for their computers, helping to sell still more of them. To keep this treadmill rolling, PC makers gave dealers bonuses, knows as soft dollars, for achieving sales targets and market-share increases.

The soft dollars were almost pure profit to the dealers, fattening their earnings. But the system became a trap as dealers grew to rely on the soft dollars. Pressed to keep their own prices down, dealers sometimes sold PCs at cost or barely above, depending on the manufacturers' bonus payment for their profits.

The soft dollars "were a narcotic and caused you to do unnatural acts," Mr. Fairfield says. Worse, they were a narcotic that could be pulled away if the dynamics of the computer business shifted.

And they did, thanks to Dell. It didn't sell through dealers but directly to the businesses that wanted the computers, building the PCs to order. Burdened with neither computer inventories nor dealer markups, Dell could underprice others by as much as 15%. Facing this price threat, Compaq, Hewlett-Packard and International Business Machines Corp. started to curtail their system of soft-dollar bonuses to dealers. In its place, a new, crazy-quilt pricing scheme emerged.

Under this system, when danger arose that Dell could win a large company's business, Compaq, IBM or H-P would make a "special bid," setting a price for that particular company below even the wholesale cost. The dealer had to deliver the goods. Then, to recoup the difference between the wholesale price it had paid and this low-low price to the ultimate customer, the dealer had to apply to the manufacturer for a rebate.

This demanded good bookkeeping. Sometimes manufacturers made more than one special bid, if Dell kept lowering its own price. Some of these bids might be in writing, some less formal.

Although dealers had to file rebate requests promptly, PC manufacturers had 90 to 120 days to process the claims and pay them. Moreover, manufacturers routinely rejected claims, citing missing or inaccurate serial numbers. That required dealers to track down field invoices and resubmit the claims. Then, it might take three to four more months before the claim was accepted or again rejected.

Some dealers, such as CompuCom Systems Inc., adapted to this squeeze by moving away from hardware distribution and into services, such as installation, support and network design. By contrast, InaCom sought greater volume (and rebate clout) through its Vanstar acquisition, according to a former CompuCom CEO, Edward R. Anderson. "InaCom and Vanstar hung on longer than anyone else to those vendor rebates," he says.

But InaCom had a hard time staying on top of all the paperwork. Its initial claims for rebates were rejected 60% of the time, a former executive says. Meanwhile, the old soft-dollar system continued to fade. InaCom collected only $90 million in such bonuses in 1999, down from $200 million in 1998.

The tightening economics conflicted with a generous corporate culture at InaCom. Mr. Fairfield treated employees as part of an extended family, whom he visited by crisscrossing traveling his empire in one of two company planes. As late as September 1999, Mr. Fairfield brought 50 executives and their spouses to a lavish five-day retreat at the five-star Broadmoor Hotel in Colorado Springs, Colo. Asked about this expenditure, Mr. Fairfield says the business was running fine then and he didn't need to sweat the pennies. "You can't cut your way to prosperity," he says.

Besides, InaCom eventually collected most of the rebates PC makers owed it, Mr. Fairfield says. "We always had good success in collecting those receivables. Up until the second or third quarter of 1999, we were collecting 96% or 98% of all the receivables due," he adds.

Squeezed Out

Other insiders say InaCom was developing cash-flow and accounting problems in 1999. Hewlett-Packard temporarily halted shipments to the dealer in the fall of 1999 for lack of payment, say InaCom financial executives. Such holds happened "all the time," says Greg Poole, a former InaCom product-marketing manager.

Mr. Fairfield came under increasing pressure from an InaCom director and Warburg Pincus executive, William H. Janeway, who led an effort a year ago to force him out. "The board was clearly reacting and responding to the accelerating deterioration of the business," Mr. Janeway says. He recruited Gerald A. Gagliardi, a 52-year-old former Unisys Corp. official, as chief executive in place of Mr. Fairfield, 53, who remained as chairman for a time.

Mr. Gagliardi brought a blunt, profane style that contrasted with Mr. Fairfield's one-big family approach—plus a new cost-consciousness. He pointedly criticized the Broadmoor retreat as an extravagance at a time when the company was financially pressured.

He brought in a new chief financial officer, Thomas J. Fitzpatrick, whose review of company accounting prompted directors to hire a law firm to investigate operations. The firm interviewed executives on everything from travel to the handling of rebates. Directors took no action but authorized the law firm to give the SEC anything it wanted.

Not Collectible

The new CFO, reviewing InaCom's bulging receivables, says he saw that many were aging rebate claims unlikely ever to be collected. He says KPMG approved an initial $80 million to $100 million write-off of such claims in February, and later began reviewing another set of possible write-offs.

Rich Smitherman, an InaCom manager, tells of one questionable item. Vanstar, shortly before its takeover by InaCom, had agreed to provide computers to a Lockheed Martin Corp. unit through a leasing firm. But the leasing firm failed just as the deal was to close, leaving Vanstar to carry the deal on its own. InaCom, after acquiring Vanstar, recorded shipments under the Lockheed deal as sales nonetheless.

"Internal auditors should have known from day one" that the deal wasn't properly handled, Mr. Smitherman says. InaCom ultimately booked $22 million in revenue from the deal, of which $15 million remained uncollected when the company filed for bankruptcy, says Mr. Smitherman, who now is shepherding the sale of some receivables for pennies on the dollar.

Shopping the Company

Mr. Fairfield says InaCom was aware of this problem and "it was on the verge of getting cleaned up" by late 1999. His successor as CEO, Mr. Gagliardi, says through a lawyer that he discovered after arriving that the vendor receivables had never been audited. Mr. Gagliardi didn't respond to requests for an interview.

The new CEO had begun looking for a buyer for the company almost from the time he came aboard in October 1999. One candidate was Compaq Computer. Compaq ultimately agreed to buy only InaCom's PC distribution business. The price was $370 million in cash, a $55 million line of credit and a commitment to deliver $430 million in computer-services business to what remained of InaCom.

In January, Mr. Gagliardi hailed the pending sale as signaling InaCom's rebirth as a service company. Instead, it triggered a crisis. IBM and HP—viewing InaCom as now part of a rival, Compaq—halted computer shipments. IBM demanded that InaCom repay money lent it to buy IBM computers. Customers, unsure of InaCom's future, cut back sharply on orders. Service revenue also declined.

Deutsche Bank AG, which was owed $188 million by InaCom, insisted it use much of its Compaq cash to repay debt. By April, InaCom's worsening prospects and still-uncertified 1999 financials led Deutsche Bank to refuse to make new funds available. Compaq's credit line wasn't available for another month, by which time InaCom's finances were so weak it couldn't be tapped.

New Talks

Unable to borrow, Mr. Gagliardi retained investment bankers to try to sell the service business. He began talks with CompuCom, the rival dealer that had switched its emphasis to service, and got so close to a deal that a draft letter was prepared describing the sale. It bore a date of June 19.

But five days before that target day, Mr. Fitzpatrick says, the talks collapsed. A key reason was that KPMG still hadn't signed off on the 1999 financials. InaCom board members say they stuck with KPMG because they thought it remained best-positioned to complete an audit in time to sell the company. But instead of being able to announce a sale, Inacom recorded the voice mail dismissing its work force.

A manager at Blue Cross Blue Shield of Michigan, David Doney, says he learned of InaCom's unilateral cancellation of a $30 million service contract when one of a group of InaCom employees who were working with the insurer told of the mass firing.

InaCom's message to employees also advised them to "make arrangements" for new health insurance, because theirs had ended with the bankruptcy filing. Some dismissed employees, such as Kirk Ransom of Eden Prairie, Minn., say certain already submitted bills weren't paid.

He and others flooded bankruptcy court in Wilmington, Del., with protests over a request to pay retention bonuses to Mr. Gagliardi and two other executives. "In this particular case the treatment of those employees has been just abominable," said the bankruptcy judge, Peter J. Walsh, according to a court transcript. "By any measure, I've not seen this kind of adverse treatment to employees."

Employees may yet receive some small payment. Next week, Judge Walsh is scheduled to consider a proposal that would pay employees as much as $4,300 each for outstanding health-care claims. Meanwhile, just 20 employees remain in an Alpharetta, Ga., office to oversee the sale of InaCom's final assets. The office furnishings and equipment will be the last items auctioned.

Failure at the Bottom

So much for top-down failure. It's time to get down and dirty with some bottom-up failure stories, failures in the small compared to the failures in the large we've been seeing. The stories in this section are about projects, not companies or business executives, that failed. What follows is a plethora of project failures. Sometimes they will even seem to be coming at you in blizzards!

In fact, the first four articles that follow each contain several failure stories. The first two collections are from the *CIO* magazine group (CIO stands for chief information officer, the usually accepted title these days for the head of the corporate organization that used to be called Information Systems). They are a particularly nicely organized collection of stories. Each has a section defining the project that failed, the problems with the project, and the recovery (if any—and, often, there was none). The second *CIO* article adds a fourth category, "Heavenly Hindsight"—the lessons learned on each project (you know, the ones the project manager wished he or she had known at project start?) The stories were all provided by various *CIO* readers, although several of the information providers (understandably) requested anonymity. Because of their source, they are a particularly credible collection of stories.

The third article from *CIO* fingers the Brits. It's not clear why England seems to have so many failure stories (there have been two books full of England-only computing failure stories written in the past several years), but these six stories are particularly wonderfully ugly.

The next story, from the Pacific Northwest, tells a strange tale of government failure. The county in question managed to blow $38 million while trying to put, of all things, a payroll system on the air. (What makes that an "of all things" story is that payroll is one of the first applications ever computerized, back in the early days of the computing field. People have known how to build payroll systems for well over 45 years now). The story has some other strangenesses. The county chose to use the megapackage vendor People-Soft* for its payroll system, a not unreasonable choice that coincides with PeopleSoft's best-known area of expertise, human relations systems. That in itself was not strange. But what made it strange was that the county also chose another megapackage vendor, SAP, to develop some accounting systems that had to interface with the payroll system. What is strange about that is that both PeopleSoft and SAP offer complete megapackages to handle all of these applications and more. Enterprises rarely bring in more than one megapackage, and even more rarely try to make them interface.

The final strangeness of the story is that one principle in the story said that the $38 million failure was not about "incompetent work or inadequate government requirements." It was, he said, "really about money." That is, the project was underfunded from the outset. Perhaps. But that certainly leaves us with enough finger-pointing in this story to last us for quite awhile!

The next story ventures from the Pacific Northwest to the state of Oklahoma for another tale of government failure. In fact, this particular story is titled "Double Jeopardy," and for good reason. As the story begins, the government agency is coming off one failure to produce a customer-billing system, and is about to embark on a second and completely different one. The first failure had involved the selection of both inadequate computer hardware and an inadequate code-generating software tool. The word "fiasco" leaps readily to mind. But the Oklahoma agency had only begun to encounter failure!

In Act Two of the story, trying to learn from Act One, the government agency insists in an RFP on a proven package to solve their problem. But somehow the winning vendor slinks through with a mere shell of a program that had not been fully tested or installed anywhere in the world. The struggles that follow to make a silk purse out of this sow's ear would be funny if it weren't for the fact that huge amounts of money were being wasted, and lawsuits were about to fly willy-nilly. Eventually, by hiring the programmers from the by-then-defunct software vendor, the government agency ends up with a working system—but one with no database! What's the good news here? Oh, the agency got back $6 million from its lawsuits.

The final story in this chapter is about yet another government agency, this one in the state of Virginia. Like the Pacific Northwest story, this one involves the use of the PeopleSoft megapackage, in this case for a human relations system (remember, that's precisely the thing PeopleSoft is best at). In this story the government agency found that it had to make "over 1,000 changes, including more than 100 to the core package," in order to even come close to making the system work. That's a more interesting problem than you might realize, in that people who know megapackage software know that one of its biggest no-no's is making changes of any kind to the code. The author of the story says that the changes were necessary in order to get the system to conform to some of the state of Virginia's unique laws. Perhaps. In any case, that problem eventually led to scrapping the PeopleSoft system and replacing it with a customized, phased solution. That's an interesting approach, in that it's the exact opposite of the way most enterprises are moving for this class of problem.

By the way, it's not too late for me to warn you that the material in this chapter is perhaps more technical than most, and may cause you problems if you're a nontechnical reader. The Virginia story is one which, in fact, you may want to skip if you're uncomfortable with the details of technology.

* These megapackage systems are often called Enterprise Resource Systems or ERPs, for reasons that are probably not worth explaining here and are subject to considerable controversy in the information systems field. In fact, to finesse the controversy, many people are beginning to call them Enterprise Systems, or ESs. The reason for *this* name? Because such systems are intended to solve all of the backoffice business system problems of the enterprise—like payroll and accounting and human relations and all the other types of problems mentioned in these stories!

To Hell and Back

CIOs Reveal the Projects That Did Not Kill Them and Made Them Stronger

By Tom Field, David Pearson, and Polly Schneider

You've all had them—IT projects that you've wholeheartedly sponsored, that you sincerely believed would fly. And then you've seen them stall and fall awkwardly back to earth, grounded by their inherent flaws.

You're not alone.

The Standish Group International Inc., a research firm in Dennis, Mass., has been tracking project failure since 1993. Its latest survey indicates that 46 percent of IT projects were over budget and overdue, and 28 percent failed altogether. Another of its studies cites even grimmer success rates—only 24 percent of IT projects undertaken by Fortune 500 companies in 1998 will be completed successfully. The problem has been going on as long as companies have been using information technology.

You may not be able to avoid them, but at least you can recognize them while they're still half-baked. To that end, a group of brave CIOs and IT staffers have granted us insight into the failures with which they've regrettably been involved. Our purpose in recounting these setbacks is not to focus on the failures, but to draw lessons learned and perhaps help other CIOs avoid the same traps.

Some of the CIOs with whom Senior Writers Tom Field, David Pearson and Polly Schneider spoke did so completely on the record; others requested anonymity either for themselves or their employers, and we've respected their wishes. Reading these case studies does not ensure that you'll never hatch another turkey, but the expert advice may help you avoid eating crow.

Lights Out on Lamp

The Project

In 1990 the Washington State Department of Licensing launched its License Application Mitigation Project (LAMP), a five-year, $41.8 million mission to automate the state's vehicle registration and license renewal processes. But when George Lindamood stepped in as director of the state's IS department in 1993, LAMP was hardly glowing. The budget had swelled to a projected $51 million, the legislature changed its schedule in the course of the project, and even if the project were completed, it promised to be a colossal money-waster. "It was like the Lilliputians dragging down Gulliver," Lindamood says. "The project was stopped dead in it tracks." And even had the project not stalled, he says, "it would have been much too big and obsolete by the time it was finished." Lindamood tried to save the project, but to no avail. In 1997, the plug was pulled on LAMP, but not before seven years and roughly $40 million had been wasted.

The Problem

The project's failure stems in part from bad project management, Lindamood says—the undertaking was too big with too few solid deliverables along the way. But the chief downfall was administrative meddling. From authorization to purchasing to quality assurance, LAMP was overseen by a mix of elected officials and political appointees whose agendas were more personal than project-driven, Lindamood says. He adds, "In government, it's almost irresistible for new people to get in [office] and want to stick their fingers into these things." By design, the project was inexplicably split between in-house developers and a private industry contractor, which led to poor coordination and delays. After Lindamood left, legislators diverted money from LAMP to fund construction of an offramp at a racetrack, and passed new licensing and registration laws that altered the project scope and caused further delays. "The real shame of the failure of a project like LAMP," Lindamood laments today, is that "the people who are ultimately responsible are the least likely to be blamed for it."

The Recovery

There was none. LAMP was turned off in 1997, after legislators calculated that the project ultimately would cost $4.2 million more annually to run than the state's $800,000 per year incumbent system. Before the plug was pulled, Lindamood washed his hands of LAMP and of his IS position, opting instead to be a consultant with GartnerGroup Inc., where he now is charged with (his description) "the care and feeding of CIOs." Asked what lessons he learned from the LAMP experience, Lindamood cites several:

- LAMP should have been bid entirely to a private industry contractor. "Government doesn't build [systems] well in-house," he says.
- The project should have been broken down into smaller, measurable chunks, rather than spread out over several years.

- Experienced quality-control personnel should have been hired from private industry and empowered upfront, as opposed to putting political appointees in charge during the project.
- Project managers should have expressed from the start exactly what conditions would necessitate shutting down the project rather than letting it limp along.

Looking back, Lindamood regrets that although he could see from the start that LAMP was headed for disaster, he couldn't save it. "The system doesn't want to hear [that a project is failing]," he says. "The system is the problem; it's the system that leads to the failure."

Sure Cure for the Blues

The Project

Back in the '80s, independent Blue Cross licensees around the country found themselves in a major consolidation mode. Big blues were swallowing up little ones, and the newly massive companies that resulted were having a difficult time merging disparate claims-payment systems. Inside one of the biggest blue sharks in the water, not to be named here, the time was ripe for a major new system—one that could grow along with the company, which was looking to expand beyond health care.

The company brought in a major consultancy, conducted a study, made recommendations and acquired a new claims system. And the $8 billion company got comfortable with the idea of spending $5 million to $15 million over two to three years to complete a project it saw as critical to its continued steady growth.

Chuck Southworth, an applications manager at the project's inception and CIO by the time of its demise, says that, looking back, the directive from senior management to "go get a new system, put it in place and make it work" should have tipped off the company's IT leadership to the problems that were soon to follow. "Things handed down from on high by fiat tend not to ever work," he says.

The Problem

Southworth, now CIO of the Martin Agency, an advertising firm in Richmond, Va., says the fatal flaw in the doomed claims system lay in executives' blindness to the human factors involved. Of an IT staff of around 400, 75 of the best and brightest were selected—ahem, make that encouraged—to "volunteer" to implement the new system. They faithfully stepped up and faltered.

"The big issue was backfiring," says Southworth. "You can't have people on two important endeavors at once, so who's going to do these folks' other work while they're concentrating on this big project?" The answer from all those good and talented individuals was that they'd work in two worlds at once. "It's a basic law of physics that you can't be in two places at one time," says Southworth.

Nor did it help matters that the staffers had been motivated to accept the new project largely out of job insecurity. They knew their employer was weighing outsourcing against in-sourcing on the project—and that, for them, the former choice might spell joblessness down the road. After all, the new claims system represented the future of the company. Their willingness to take on "extra" work convinced the company to keep most of the work in-house and provided management with a chance to cast a vote of confidence in its people. Then, too, good loyal "team players" will often take on more than they can handle. The consequence, revealed over the ensuing months, was constant conflict over priorities. "It scarred people really badly," says Southworth.

The Recovery

Southworth was promoted to CIO around nine months into the project. He labored to bring it under control until the end of the budget year, then approached the vice chairman of the company with the bad news. "I think you'd better sit down," Southworth told his boss. "We need to kill this thing now, before it gets any further out of hand." Southworth was surprised and relieved at the reaction his tidings elicited. After a brief denial—*What do you mean kill it? That's out of the question!*—he stepped back and let Southworth make the call. "The whole thing actually helped build my personal credibility in the organization," says Southworth. "They respected that I had the [guts] to come forward with something so painful, and to do it so forthrightly." The company abandoned the project, at a cost of millions. "We had moved people out, rented the space, bought the system, gone through all the planning, and it all wound up on the scrap heap."

Eventually, the company took up revamping its claims system once again, notes Southworth, and succeeded. What was different this time? Better dedication of resources.

Here's what Southworth took away from the experience:

- No matter how far your staff goes to convince you they're master jugglers, don't assign anyone to more than one major undertaking at a time.
- Downward buy-in means convincing staff that a new priority is more important than whatever they've been working on. To secure acceptance, stress ownership. "When the system was subsequently

deployed—successfully—it was because people believed and understood that it was really theirs" to bring to life, says Southworth.

- Don't let a doomed project run on—or die a quiet death. Admit it's failed and announce the failure.

Southworth says that, over the years, his few failures have taught him more than his many successes. "The key," he adds, "is never having to learn the same lesson twice."

Customer Disservice

The Project

Four years ago, a state chapter of a well-know national consumer group embarked on what was to be an 18-month, $1 million project to replace its customer database. The new system, to be designed, built and installed by the company's IS staff, would distinguish among different "preferred customer" levels, affording the appropriate products and levels of service on demand. The good news was that the company's IS team did deliver a new system on time. The bad news was that the system didn't work as promised, handling routine transactions smoothly but tripping over more complex ones. Within three weeks of throwing the switch, managers found that the new system couldn't distinguish among customers and that some transactions were being canceled while others were kept on hold. Immediately, the database was shut down, transactions were processed by hand and new IS leadership was brought in to rebuild both the system and the strained relationship between business and IS.

The Problem

IS couldn't—or wouldn't—say no. So eager to please their business partners, IS executives said yes, they could build this system, yes, it would be scaleable and yes, it would be Y2K compliant, on time and within budget. But in reality, IS could deliver on none of the promises. The other big mistake by IS was making this a date-driven project. There was no flexibility for mistakes or unforeseen challenges; developers simply kept their eyes on the calendar and failed to speak up about any glitches they saw along the way. "It was kind of like one of those horror stories you hear about," says the anonymous CIO who inherited the mess a couple of years ago, after more than a dozen people (including the former CIO) lost their jobs because of their roles in this disaster.

The Recovery

The new CIO immediately empowered "SWAT" teams to diagnose the problems and analyze whether the best course was to repair or replace the new database. "There wasn't enough good code there to repair," the CIO says, so plan B went into effect. IS partnered with two vendors—one to design and build, the other to oversee the first vendor's work—and a new multimillion-dollar database is projected to be installed sometime in 1999. But replacing the database is only half the battle. IS also must rebuild its fractious relationship with the business side, and that project has its own unique requirements. "I'm trying to dig out of a hole," the new CIO says. "Anything negative that happens now just reinforces the perception [among business people] that IS doesn't know what it's doing." But IS is making headway. The new CIO is making sure new projects are on time and within budget, and he is convinced that his organization's recovery from the database debacle will secure a new reputation for the group. Key lessons learned so far:

- IS must break its "code of silence" when working on challenging projects. "If [IS managers] had spoken up sooner, when things started to go wrong, 14 jobs might have been saved," the new CIO says.
- The best cure for failure is a good recovery plan. The new CIO gained his bosses' confidence quickly by stepping in, assessing the problem and developing a plan of action that stated clearly when the recovery would be completed and at what cost.
- You can't do too much too soon. Like the project itself, recovering IS's reputation is a slow process. "I'm trying to do things incrementally to restore customers' confidence," the new CIO says. "You can't do it all in a big bang—although you sure can tear it all down real fast." How long will the recovery take? Can the new CIO really pull it off? "Those are loaded questions," he says, "but I remind people that IS didn't get this way overnight; it won't get turned around overnight."

Too Many Cooks in the Kitchen

The Project

In 1996, a major San Francisco bank was poised to roll out an application for tracking customer calls routed to its "elite" group of customer service reps who handled problem cases. Reports provided by the new system would be going directly to the president of the bank and board of directors. An initial product demo seemed sluggish, yet the consultants assured both IS and the telephone banking division managers that all was well. They were wrong. "The source code was so bad it took 20 minutes to load the program on the

PC," recalls Jim Daviner, the systems analyst on the project, now a business systems manager for marketing at The Gymboree Corp. in Burlingame, Calif., a children's retail chain.

The Problem

The system crashed constantly, could not support multiple users at once and did not meet the bank's security requirements. IS hired a new consultant to help rewrite the application, but after three months the project was killed—resulting in a loss of approximately $200,000 in staff time and consulting fees, and a bad rap for IS.

According to Daviner, the first mistake was the bank's failure to check references and work samples of the consulting firm. Daviner caught a major flaw in the database design in time, but as the project progressed, the programming team became increasingly isolated and hard to work with, refusing to release the source code to the project managers. Daviner says the programmers didn't want the bank to find out that they were, in his words, "pretty inept."

But the root of the project's failure was a complicated reporting structure that left no clear line of command. Between Daviner, the lead analyst from the business side, and the four consulting programmers located in Arizona, there were two other layers of management from IS. Another layer, Daviner's boss, was the lead project manager and sponsor—yet she had no direct contact with or control over the programmers and left the company in the middle of the project. Worse, the project correspondence was lost in the process of cleaning out her PC, Daviner says. At the same time, the bank's IS department was being reorganized. One of the two IS managers on the project resigned to go to another company, and the other was restructured out of a job after the project's problems came to light. In late 1996, with no leadership or business sponsor to rescue a coding disaster, Daviner had to mop up the mess.

The Recovery

The project was never revived, and Daviner says the biggest loss for the bank is not having access to valuable customer information the system was to deliver. On a positive note, the business units are getting rid of unnecessary layers in projects. Today project managers have direct oversight of the programming consultants and approve all hiring of IS personnel. "Things happen more smoothly now," he says. Daviner (who, as an aside, says his reasons for leaving the bank were not related to this project) shares the following tips:

- Institute a formal review process for hiring consultants.
- Require change control documentation so those managers can see what changes were made during development, when and why.

- Ownership is essential. When sponsors or top players leave the company or the project, new owners should be identified immediately and supported with documentation.
- Assign a central manager for the project team who is the conduit for communication and decisions. Result: Everyone is on the same page rather than working in parallel and reporting to different managers.

In the end, a disorganized project team with unstable leadership wrought the ruin of an important customer application. Unfortunately, due to the ongoing IS reorganization at the bank, Daviner says that IS has not improved its project management practices—a clear example of chaos breeding chaos.

Payroll on the Loose

The Project

The night before the launch of a new payroll system in a major Boston health-care organization, project managers were sweating. During a sample run, the off-the-shelf package began cutting checks for negative amounts, for sums larger than the top executive's annual take-home pay, and checks that incorrectly matched employee numbers with names, recalls a former director of systems analysis who asked not to be identified. Called in to review the project before the launch, he wound up sitting in the payroll department for six months to help fix the problem.

Payroll was still delivered on time, and out of 7,000 employees, the fiasco affected the checks of only roughly 50 to 100 people. Still, the payroll office had to pull the bad checks and rerun them manually to create new ones every payday until the application was debugged. The incident damaged the relationship between IS and the payroll and finance departments, and the programming manager resigned in disgrace.

The Problem

"It became apparent the entire system was never tested or run in parallel" with the old system, says the director of systems analysis. IS did not check to ensure that an existing human resources database was compatible with the new payroll system software; the problem was that limit controls on hourly rates were not in place. An entry of 8.0 dollars per hour could be read as 800 dollars per hour if the user did not enter the decimal point, which revealed another problem: No one had been adequately made aware of the differences between the old system and the new one. "There was no turnover between development and production," the director says. Business managers were signing off on the system without really understanding how the people in their department would be using it, he recalls.

"A lack of clear leadership was a problem from the beginning," says the director of systems analysis. The main sponsor, the payroll director, suffered a heart attack three weeks before the launch date and was placed on disability; he was gone for months. Throughout the course of the project, the organization's top IT director was "uninvolved," the director of systems analysis reveals.

The Recovery

The organization hired a consultant to help and provide support, and eight months after the implementation date hired a new director of IS. An administrator who oversaw all IS-related projects was transferred to another area of the company altogether. With the new management, IS established a more formal reporting methodology and some ground rules. Outside consultants would be used on every major project, and business units had to identify a project manager for every project and provide adequate training for the staff. Overall, project managers began to forge better partnerships with users. "The effect was really a mandate to change," says the director of systems analysis. "It created the demand for a more professional way of managing projects." The director of systems analysis (who subsequently went on to become CIO of this organization and others) has a few lessons to share from the experience:

- Test, test and test again: "It's much harder to fix things afterward."
- Hire an outside contractor to complete an independent project review.
- Communicate with the business: Send a monthly letter to senior management with updates as the project progresses.
- When buying off-the-shelf software, hire a consultant who understands how the application will run in your environment. The former director says that this is the puzzle piece software vendors often can't deliver.

Looking back, the director-turned-CIO says that the bungled project was a blessing because it helped raise awareness of the company's growing dependence on IT. "Without a major catastrophe, there was a perception that IS didn't affect operations."

The Plan Man Learneth

The Project

You do the math: Anticipating growth, a $100 million division of a $740 million manufacturing business earmarks $5 million for a new distribution and customer service system to replace its old, sputtering setup. The project is to take a year and a half to complete, involve 20 business and tech staffers, make up for 20 percent of the missing source code, and set the division in good stead for Y2K.

Two years later, the CIO is fired. A knight in armor, an IT executive with years of experience fixing troubled projects, is brought in to save the day. He's informed that the challenge ahead is serious, but he's kept in the dark as to how goofed up things have gotten.

The Problem

"This project had the two deadly sins built in," reflects the old pro, who's since changed jobs and agreed to share memories of his nightmare under cover of anonymity. "They'd chosen the wrong software solution, thanks to a terribly naïve RFP process, and they had no project plan." Worse still, no one owned the project. "IS thought the business users owned it, the business users thought IS owned it and the CEO thought the vendor owned it." There was an unwritten project plan with five or six major milestones, but not a single one of those had been met and no one on the project team could say when they might be met.

The new IT boss pulled together all hands and, in just two days, orchestrated a 2,000 line-item plan. Three months later, with the company's best IT talent and the software vendor's consultants busting their chops, the system broke down altogether. "It was supposed to be the show-stopper for us," says the source, "and we couldn't get customer orders through the system." Internal users began panicking; customers began complaining about incompetence. "We were sending people the wrong stuff and sending everything late."

The Recovery

Finally, three years and $4 million into the project, the CIO polled the 20 players anonymously. Eighteen said they thought the project was beyond saving. The two who held out were the project manager (a business-side person) and his boss, the VP of manufacturing—apart from the CIO, the two whose necks were most at risk and, in the end, the only two to lose their jobs.

The CIO approached his boss, the CEO. "It was kind of like telling him a relative had died," he recalls. "First he denied it, then he went through a grieving process, then he accepted it. It was just so much money for a division that size to wave in the wind." A settlement was negotiated with the software vendor, and corporate IT stepped in and assumed direct control of all IT operations in the division.

For the CIO, it was time to leave—and to reflect on some hard lessons:

- If you don't have extensive experience with the RFP process, get help from someone who does.
- Decide upfront how decisions will be made through the duration of the project. "An essential aspect of good project management is a consistent approach to the inevitable forks in the road. You can't decide by show of hands at one turn, edict on another and a secret ballot on the third."
- Look before you leap into a new career "opportunity," and don't be afraid to conduct due diligence if you're taking on a project that's already underway.

Before I accepted that job, I should have talked to the project manager, asked to see the project documentation, studied the RFP, spoken with the software vendor, and talked to some internal users," says the CIO. "Had I known how amiss this project was, I would not have joined that company."

Another Trip to Hell

By Polly Schneider

The time for a project blowup could not have been worse. In the summer of 1999, Hershey Foods suffered a glitch in a $112 million new enterprise system built to automate and track every step of the company's candy-selling business. Just days before Halloween the problem was still unresolved, and business took a scary turn for the $4.4 billion candy-maker. The lost orders, missed shipments and disgruntled customers that resulted from the company's systems woes were well publicized in both the trade and business press. While Hershey would not reveal its losses from the glitch, third-quarter revenues were down $151 million from 1998.

What happened to Hershey can happen to any company, any time of the year. Unexpected changes in management or business direction, or the loss of key staff members, can send high-profile projects into a tailspin. Many problems are preventable, and yet the same ones seem to crop up time and again. The horror stories below tell of out-of-control consultants, project managers who've never managed an IT project before, and sponsors who disappear until the product is finished and then report that it's absolutely nothing like what they had in mind.

CIOs can minimize the risk by clearly defining leadership roles, getting commitment of sponsors from the business, and securing executive support and participation. Other steps are less obvious. Not all of the CIOs who agreed to share their stories felt comfortable disclosing their companies' names or their identities. However, the lessons they've painfully learned have helped them become better leaders today.

THe SCouRGe oF ISoLaTioN

If you suspect IT is working in a vacuum with no help from the business sponsor, pull the plug—lest you care to witness 11th-hour scope creep.

The Project

In 1995, Omni Hotels, a small, struggling hotel chain based in Hampton, N.H., decided a snazzy guest recognition system would boost customer loyalty and drive repeat sales. Omni's executive team, desperate to improve the company's lackluster performance, pinned the company's financial future on the project. Hotel employees would reward repeat guests with gifts or room upgrades as they checked in, and note guest preferences for future visits and promotions. The marketing department happily promoted the loyalty program to customers and hotel managers, but, when the system went live a month behind schedule, the hotels hated it: It had little business value, was difficult to use, and ran slow as molasses. "It was a joke," says Thomas Murphy, CIO at Royal Caribbean Cruises in Miami, who was Omni's vice president of IT at the time. The system was yanked just six months later.

The Problem

Early on, Murphy tried in vain to get the company's vice presidents in one room to define the system requirements. The executives couldn't be bothered with the details, however, and sent their underlings instead. When IT presented a demo to the business units, all hell broke loose. Managers from marketing, sales and operations began fighting over functionality. Lacking input from the business units, the system had been designed without any rules for granting the rewards. No one could agree on when and how guests would receive gifts. The hotel managers—who had never been consulted about the project—were hardly thrilled about making room in their budgets for bottles of wine and other pricey gifts. Worse, the marketing department had kept the CEO in the dark from day one. "When we sat down, his expectations were wildly different from what was being developed," Murphy recalls. "That was a gut-churning moment."

Murphy admits that the lack of a business sponsor was the ultimate oversight. The business units couldn't decide among themselves what they wanted, the CEO had a grandiose vision of a dynamic system that would never happen in the allotted time frame, and the hotel managers who had to implement the program wanted nothing to do with the whole mess. Politically, it was impossible to pull the plug—yet deep down, Murphy knew the system was going to be a sham.

Murphy and his team raced back to the drawing board and spent a month frantically reengineering the system in an attempt to placate the various warring parties and meet the CEO's desire to get the application up and running ASAP. The laundry list of requirements included ease of use, speed, improved reporting capability, and interfaces to other legacy systems—among other surprise requests. Oh, and make it sexy, they added. On top of that, there were drastic technical problems to address. The software had been developed on a Microsoft Access database rather than on a relational database, which could have scaled to the requirements of Omni's 40 hotels. Further, users had to access the software through sluggish dial-up networking since Omni did not yet have a wide area network installed. Updating the database each morning tied up a PC at the front desk for an hour. Finally, no formal training or documentation was provided to the hotels. First-time CIO Murphy candidly admits, "My relative inexperience certainly did not help the situation."

The Recovery

There was none, and the company lost $250,000 in the process. Murphy says the failed project succeeded only in further exacerbating internal conflicts between business units that had been brewing for some time. Years of turnover in senior management had created a rift between long-term Omni middle managers and the autocratic executive team. Not long after the system went live, TRT Holdings of Irving, Texas, acquired Omni, and Murphy decided not to join the new company.

Heavenly Hindsight

1. Sponsor, sponsor, sponsor! And it's never enough just to assign the role—CIOs have to be sure of commitment. Eventually Omni's VP of Rooms Operations became the official business sponsor, but Murphy says his travel schedule kept him out of the office most of the time.

2. Insists on a well-defined scope. Require participation from business sponsors and users—even for the mundane technical details. "The business did not want to hear about technical challenges," Murphy says, remembering that the reigning attitude was that IT ought to be able to make anything work.

3. Do your infrastructure homework. Will your network and database support current and future demand and usage patterns for the system you're building? Do whatever you can to assess the situation, even if it means bringing in a consultant from the outside.

4. Choose technology, not skills. If you don't have the right skills for the project, hire them. Murphy admits that he used Microsoft technology simply because those were the skills he had on staff.

THe CoNSuLTaNT aS RoCK STaR

Pity the company that lets a star consultant take over. Like good government, every project needs a system of checks and balances.

The Project

Big egos are no big deal in Hollywood, yet one studio didn't foresee the consequences of allowing an egomaniacal consultant to control a royalty project. The bread-and-butter accounting package in music studios, a royalty system calculates and tracks payments to performers and helps studios avoid lawsuits over contracts. While these systems often cost upward of $10 million to develop, *this* studio had determined it could develop one for $7 million in 18 months, says the former IT director of the studio's music division (still working in Hollywood, he requested anonymity). Its secret weapon, he says, was a savvy designer who had created a stellar royalty system for a competitor.

Before long, the project began to hit sour notes. The studio's lawyers protested how much the system would automate the contract process. Studio vice presidents stepped into the ugly fray and delayed the process further. Finally, the designer ignored everyone and began creating the system he had envisioned from the beginning. When the IT director left the company in 1997 (out of general frustration with the studio's divisive culture), the project was still under way, having racked up $10 million in costs with no completion date in sight.

The Problem

There were too many stakeholders who wanted a say in the outcome, and no strong sponsor who could mitigate the factions and get things back on track. The executive in charge of the project was a senior user with no experience leading such a project, which only contributed to the politics. "He was far more concerned about spinning the right message to the executive committee than he was about applying good oversight," the IT director says.

This left the designer—in whom the vice presidents had placed the utmost confidence—with the power to take the project where he pleased. "From the beginning, he became almost unmanageable," the IT director remembers. "He refused to share design and analysis concepts with the rest of the team. He refused to be beholden to budgets and schedules. He basically said, 'That's not the way my mind works.'"

For the IT staff, the studio's closed corporate culture made frank discussions nearly impossible without screaming matches. "There was never an atmosphere of low-penalty information flow," he recalls. "No one was allowed to take the authority to make decisions, and yet no one was comfortable making decisions as a committee."

The Recovery

Again, there was none. A consultant who also worked on the project confirms that the studio is still developing the system. The executive user in charge of the project was replaced with another senior vice president, who applied even less budgetary and scheduling discipline to the project.

Heavenly Hindsight

1. **Emphasize team, not individuals.** Not only is playing favorites bad for team morale, but it gives too much control to one person.

2. Appoint an experienced IT project leader. "If you have a $10 million project, don't put it in the hands of someone who has never managed a $50,000 project," the studio IT director says.

3. Don't kill the messenger. Project leaders and other participants need to feel comfortable waving a red flag without jeopardizing their career.

DiD SoMeBoDY SaY INFRaSTRuCTuRe?

Few CIOs neglect infrastructure planning today, yet for urgent projects it's easy to minimize network needs and focus on the application. The oversight can be costly in more ways than one.

The Project

In 1992, a California pharmaceutical company yearned to reach new levels of productivity in an industry where it usually takes $500 million and between eight and 12 years to bring new drugs to market. The company hoped a new global knowledge sharing application would cut its eight-year development cycle in half—and presumably, the associated costs. The multimillion-dollar project was a combination of custom-built and off-the-shelf application software. To further complicate an already complex system, the development was split between IT and a "major" consulting firm. Nine months into the project, the network lab tested the system and found it suffered from sickly response time. "It was so poor it was unusable at first," says Jeff Lucchesi, formerly a network manager at the pharmaceutical company, now CIO at DHL Airways in Redwood City, Calif. The system and its software components had, inexplicably, not been designed to run over a wide area network.

When the application was finally released, it was eight months late, $1 million over budget and lacked the functionality promised to its users. "The only thing on time," Lucchesi asserts, "were the consultants when it came to getting their checks."

The Problem

The first mistake IT made was leaving its infrastructure group out of the project until the testing stage. "IT didn't have time to scope it out well," Lucchesi remarks. "We were designing and building it at the same time." Second, no single person was accountable for the project. The consulting firm had its own project manager, as did the pharmaceutical company. To add to the confusion, each division in the company had its own IT director, and not all of them reported directly to the CIO. Consequently, when it was apparent the design had fundamental flaws, the fingerpointing and sidetracking began. "That was when the CYA ["cover your ass"] really kicked in," Lucchesi smirks. The consultants wedged themselves between IT and the business, taking advantage of the company's decentralized IT structure to win the trust of the business.

There were other problems with the consulting relationship. The contract was designed as a time and materials (T&M) agreement, which means the consultants billed as they worked rather than agreeing to a fixed cost based on deliverables, upfront. This contributed to scope creep, worsening the network problems, Lucchesi says. Today Lucchesi won't even entertain a T&M contract.

The Recovery

In the end, R&D users did not get the system they wanted because pieces of the application had to be stripped out to improve performance. To no surprise, IT/business relationships suffered measurably as a result. Lucchesi applies the lessons he learned from this story to his current job at DHL, where he's proud to report he's never had an infrastructure problem. He recently completed an 18-month enterprise system project under budget and on time.

Heavenly Hindsight

1. Commit time upfront for project planning. If that's not possible, IT needs to inform business sponsors of the risks (software bugs, deadline extensions). Require the involvement of those responsible for infrastructure, development and project management during initial meetings with the sponsors.

2. Test the network end to end. Do this testing before you start development and before purchasing additional bandwidth or making network upgrades. If you don't, Lucchesi warns, you'll wind up spending too little, or too much, on bandwidth.

3. Hire the best project manager possible. Lucchesi uses professionally trained project managers rather than shoehorning a technical person into the role.

4. Avoid T&M contracts. Since the experience, Lucchesi insists on a fixed-cost relationship with consulting firms. However, he adds, "It takes a lot of upfront work to really scope the project and put in contingency plans."

THaT DaRN CuLTuRaL THiNG

The time to learn that your company is adverse to big change is not midway through an enterprise system project. It's wise to assess business goals and cultural readiness before purchasing any technology.

The Project

In 1995, mass confusion reigned at an Atlanta-based manufacturer of forestry products. Its 12 divisions were running separate back-office systems, and financial reporting was a nightmare. For instance, $7 billion in sales invoicing was actually internal billing between divisions that exchanged goods and supplies. To simplify, the CFO and CIO jumped headfirst into the zany world of SAP. At first, the various business VPs and stakeholders were all for centralization. On paper, it sounded like the right thing to do.

But 11 months into the project, trees began to fall left and right. Once the vice presidents realized they would soon lose their respective empires for the sake of centralization, they revolted. The project was stopped dead in its tracks before the pilots had begun, according to Dan Sheehan, a former senior IT manager on the SAP project, now CIO at Atlanta-based staffing firm Acycs. As a result of the project, the company had to write off $120 million in software development losses in 1997.

The Problem

In Sheehan's view, the biggest gaffe was the classic IT mistake of choosing the tool before understanding the business problem. There were no frank discussions with the executive team about the company's long-term strategy and goals until after the contracts were signed and the project team was well under way. This leads to another issue: cultural readiness. The CIO and CFO, who were champions of the project, did not consider whether the company could handle such sweeping change all at once. The plan was a big-bang approach of launching pilot projects in two divisions on five SAP modules simultaneously, followed by the rest of the company.

And to pick up a common theme, consultants got in the way. The company used four consulting firms at various phases of the project, all of whom bickered among themselves over how to approach the project. "SAP didn't have their own methodology at the time, so we were taking all the advice from third parties—who were probably making it up as they went," Sheehan observes. Furthermore, many of the consultants were more interested in controlling the project (and overstaffing it, he adds) than partnering with the company. The project was eventually shelved.

The Recovery

Once the project was killed, senior management gave division vice presidents the choice to implement SAP or not, and not surprisingly, only one did. Sheehan says the company's systems are still not integrated, and little has changed. Sheehan left soon after to take a senior IT position with another major manufacturing company in Atlanta, where he experienced yet another trying ERP experience resulting from a change-averse culture.

Heavenly Hindsight

1. **Help people feel comfortable with technology.** With his current employer, Sheehan takes "road shows" to the business to demo products and discuss new technology concepts like ERP.

2. **Make business needs a priority.** Sheehan says he strives to be a resource to his current CEO rather than touting his own agenda.

3. **Proceed with caution.** At the forestry company, Sheehan says they should have opted for a slower, phased-in approach for SAP, launching the product in just one division initially.

4. **Don't let consultants rob you blind.** Some consulting firms employ a "pyramid" approach, where they involve many people in order to rack up fees. During the SAP project, Sheehan recalls how discussions between consultants and their managers were invoiced as billable time.

Her Majesty's Flying I.T. Circus

By Malcolm Wheatley

Even traditional British stoicism has a breaking point—and for more than half a million British citizens, that breaking point was sorely tested last summer by the introduction of a £120 million ($180 million) computer system at the country's Passport Agency. Processing times for passport applications stretched to eight weeks instead of the normal 10 days. As telephone calls went unanswered—over a million in May 1999 along—people began turning up outside the agency's six regional offices to request their passports in person.

In Liverpool, the queues stretched for more than 100 yards. In Glasgow, over 500 people queued for 150 yards, In London, thousands queued up in the rain, forcing the agency to purchase hundreds of umbrellas to loan to angry would-be-travelers. Television crews descended in droves.

In contrast to the United States, where many people don't have passports, Britons' annual hot-spot vacations in France, Greece, Spain and Portugal are an institution. Passport renewals are a must. Adding to last summer's urgency, as it unveiled the new passport computer system, the United Kingdom also began requiring that children travel on their own passports, rather than as add-ons to their parents' papers. Consequently, the problem for many citizens was that their vacations appeared to be more imminent than the arrival of their passports: At its height, the backlog of applications reached 538,000.

For the long-suffering British public, the debacle was yet another in a long string of IT failures. Undaunted, the Blair government has embarked on the United Kingdom's highest-profile public sector IT project to date—e-government, where citizens and companies transact most of their business with central government through the Internet. The problem? IT's a huge hostage to fortune. Past government IT failures have rarely touched individual's lives: E-government will. And, as the passport fiasco showed, if it goes wrong, then the British bulldog possesses a formidable bite.

And in the passport case, that bite reached the Parliament. Senior government ministers were forced to make lengthy explanations in the House of Commons. A change in the law was rushed through, giving two-year, free of charge passport extensions at any post office. As hapless ministers bungled explanatory media appearances, mass-market newspapers like *The Daily*

Express called for cabinet sackings—an unusually forceful terminology to use in a country where the correct protocol requires unfortunates to be called on to "consider their position." Compensation was announced for those whose travel plans were thwarted by the nonarrival of their passports.

And outside passport offices, a triage system was put in place, with agency officials scurrying along the lines dispensing advice and prioritizing people into "urgent," "non urgent" and "awfully urgent indeed, old chap" categories.

Home Secretary Jack Straw announced the recruitment of additional staff—this for a system that was supposed to reduce administrative head-count, not increase it—and promised that the situation would return to normal by September, an assurance that came as little comfort to those who had July or August vacation plans. At its nadir, Straw personally promised to move "heaven and earth" to get a passport to a woman going abroad for her honeymoon after her angry member of Parliament raised her case in the House of Commons.

The Ministry of Silly Lines

For both Siemens Business Services—the computer contractor that had developed the system—and the U.K. government's Home Office, the passport debacle bore an awful similarity to the shambles that had occurred a few months before. That was when Siemens' £77 million ($115 million) computerization of the Home Office's Immigration and Nationality Directorate (IND) ran into the buffers. This system was designed to handle applications for asylum, extended stays and citizenship. Instead of processing 3,000 applications a month in fall 1998, the period prior to implementation, the number of applications processed had dropped to 995 by January 1999. The legal status of thousands was unclear. Again, queues of applicants formed—stretching for hundreds of yards on some mornings—while telephone calls went unanswered and newspaper reports spoke of sacks of unopened mail piling up in the IND's corridors in the south London suburb of Croydon.

And while the problem's initial public perception revolved around hapless refugees from conflicts overseas, the economic reality was far worse. Foreign nationals working in key jobs all over the United Kingdom were affected—the country employs a lot of software engineers from the Indian subcontinent, for example—as were the top executives of incoming foreign companies intent on establishing a British subsidiary. Media coverage quickly refocused on lost jobs and lost opportunities for investment, forcing Home Secretary Straw to add several hundred employees to the IND's staff.

For a system that was supposed to process more applications, faster and with fewer people, the awful reality was that the new system was taking longer, requiring more people to administer, and processing fewer applications. Not surprisingly, the government's National Audit Office and Public Accounts Committees, the two watchdogs that monitor government spending, duly lambasted both Siemens and the civil servants in charge of the project, with Siemens being fined £4.5 million ($6.8 million) for its role in the disaster. (In fairness to Siemens, the penalty levied on it in the aftermath of the Passport Agency implementation was much smaller and reflected the role of the government's own rule-changing in exacerbating the shambles—a fine of a mere £66,000 ($99,000), despite the fact that the new system resulted in the rising cost of processing passports from £12 to £15.50 [$18 to $23.25].

Yet spectacular though the Passport Agency and IND failures were in terms of their public profile—there's nothing like queues of people on the television news to alert media and opposition members of Parliament (MPs) to savage the government—the system' difficulties were relatively small fry in the fast-growing pantheon of British government computer fiascoes. In fact, one of the real surprises in both imbroglios was that opposition MPs and media commentators still had the energy to lambaste the government for its information technology record—or, indeed, that they could come up with new and different synonyms for *shambles*, *disaster*, *fiasco* and *bungle*.

Curiouser and Curiouser

Take a look at some other recent British government computer fumbles. After massive computer failures in a new Social Security system installed by Andersen Consulting, for example, some 400,000 people received compensation payments of £10 ($15) each—a National Audit Office investigation had reportedly found no fewer than 1,900 separate failures. The system, which was supposed to track Social Security contributions and calculate benefits owed to widows, pensioners and the unemployed, crashed within days of its debut in January 1999, resulting in 17 million contributions being unprocessed and forcing civil servants to guess at the benefits payments due to people. Even so, 160,000 pensioners were out of pocket by up to £100 ($150) per week, newspaper reports claimed.

Or consider the continuing saga of the new national air traffic control computer system being implemented by Lockheed Martin, the cost of which will have tripled in the seven years it has been in gestation, and which was deferred yet again in 1999, with the result that it may not come online until winter 2002-03—or even later. Or the high-tech system that bar-coded patients' clinical notes in Britain's National Health Service. Implemented only in 12 hospitals (after eight years of work), the costs of the project spiraled over £32 million ($48 million) by 1998, attracting criticism from the Public Accounts Committee in a report published in January for "almost unbelievably weak management."

Or the even more expensive cancellation of a system that was to have automated benefit payments by issuing claimants magnetic swipe cards, usable in the U.K.'s 19,000 post offices. The project, which started in 1996, was finally canceled in late 1999 with just 205 post offices converted to the new system after an estimated expenditure of £1 billion ($1.5 billion). Far from fining the outsourcing contractor in question—ICI, a subsidiary of Fujitsu—the government promptly awarded the company a contract to automate the operations of the post offices themselves, figuring that the company must have learned something about them in the three years it spent working on the project.

But best of all, according to aficionados of the British government's forays into computing (of whom there are many: One of the country's IT magazines, *Computer Weekly,* even has an annual award for the biggest government computer foul-up—competition is reportedly fierce), was the 1999 House of Commons report that acted as the obituary on a top-secret defense system buried deep in a war bunker beneath London's Whitehall.

Apparently code-named Trawlerman (government officials aren't exactly forthcoming with details), the system first began to run into difficulties when officials realized that the only access to the underground bunker was through a small hatch. Everything—even mainframes—had to be built, tested, dismantled, taken through the hatch, rebuilt and tested again. And the problems meant that by the time the plug was pulled, says one long-standing critic of the British government's approach to IT, the computers were operating to a specification so loose that it did not include a requirement that they do the job for which they were installed.

Nor were recent breakdowns isolated incidents. "[Although] 1999 was a bumper crop of IT failures in the U.K. government," says the University of Manchester's Richard Heeks, author of *Reinventing Government in the Information Age,* "a number of those turkeys were eggs laid by the previous Conservative administration and which merely happened to hatch under the [present] Labor government."

Indeed, consider the following damning indictment from *The Independent* newspaper: "Problems with the Department of Social Security's multimillion-pound computer project is the latest in a string of similar disasters. Hundreds of millions of pounds have been wasted on computers in the public sector, and the mismanagement appears to continue. Two months ago, it was revealed that the department had wasted about £35 million ($52.5 million) on rework—dealing with mistakes. Sources within the department put the latest losses as high as £125 million ($187.5 million). The National Audit Office and the House of Commons' Public Accounts Committee have been frequent critics of computer management by civil servants."

The problem is those words were written in 1994, and the Department of Social Security's computer system referred to was the system that the current bug-ridden one replaced. In other words, these problems with government IT in the United Kingdom are not new, and they aren't getting any less frequent. As *The Independent* article went on to observe, the fact is that the U.K. public sector's history of flawed IT implementations stretches back many, many years.

The Inquisition

But the problems that bog the systems down don't appear to be radically unusual or different. As Heeks says, the National Audit Office and Public Accounts Committee have for years been looking at the failures as they have occurred, and have generally come up with similar reasons for them. Heading the list: a failure to set clear objectives, a lack of senior management support, and taking on projects that were technically overambitious. Coupled to this list, Heeks points out, the challenges facing public sector projects are usually larger than those facing typical private sector projects; staffing and skill levels are lower because of the private sector/public sector remuneration imbalance; and government organization structures are more conservative and less flexible than in the private sector.

Apart from better public relations management of the fiascoes as they happen, there are few if any signs that the British Government is learning from its experiences, Heeks adds. (Coincidentally, the interview with Heeks took place May 5, the day that the British media was reveling in still another high-profile problem: the delays in the ballot count for London's first-ever elected mayor, as hundreds of electronic vote-counting machines, being used for the first time, broke down from ingesting dust coming from the green baize tables on which the ballot papers were stacked.)

But for many weary British taxpayers, the best government IT-related news in 1999 was that the civil service Central Information Technology Unit was launching a no-stone-unturned review of government IT practice, headed by an IT expert seconded from the Australian civil service, Anne Steward. In contrast to previous blame-pinning exercises, ran the hype, this analysis would actually try to formulate some best practices.

Well, good news for everyone except the hapless outsourcing and contracting community, perhaps, whose trade organization, the London-based Computing Services and Software Association, promptly announced in December 1999 the launch of its own review of what went wrong—fearing, possibly, that its members would find themselves smeared with others' failures. "We're certainly concerned about the number of projects that don't go as well as they should," concedes the association's director in charge of the review, Charles Hughes. "When things go wrong, it causes problems for the client, the general public and of course the suppliers." In particular, he notes, problems absorb association members' management time as they try to correct them, add to costs, and create bad publicity.

According to Hughes, the high-powered team that the association has gathered to investigate the causes of failure includes a general who headed up the Ministry of Defense's information systems (and who now works for defense contractor British Aerospace); a former computer expert from GCHQ, the government electronic spying bureau (who now heads the IT function at Clifford Chance, one of the world's largest law firms) and a professor who has worked within the Cabinet Office. Together, they are taking testimony submissions from contractors as diverse as Andersen Consulting, EDS, IBM and Sun Microsystems.

Although its findings have yet to be released, says Hughes, the finger from his group's preliminary inquiries firmly points to basic project management principles as the main shortcoming—especially within the civil service. (Now there's a surprise.) "There's oodles of good practice about, but all too often it isn't followed—many of the problems would be avoided if the government merely followed recognized good practice," he says. What's more, he adds, there's often a focus on the computer aspect of the project to the detriment of the change management aspect of the project. "There's no such thing as an IT project in isolation," says Hughes. "It's the business activity that needs to be understood and specified—the IT project is just a part of this. And it's essential to focus on the business objectives and outcomes, not just the IT outputs."

Something Completely Different

Reassuringly, this turned out to be one of the principal conclusions of the government's own findings, contained in a report published May 22. "A change of approach is needed," recommended the authors. "Rather than think of IT projects, the public sector needs to think in terms of projects to change the way government works, of which new IT is an important part." Officials declined to comment further, pointing merely to the views expressed in linked pronouncements by MP Minister of State, Cabinet Office Ian McCartney, in which he acknowledged that harnessing the power of IT is not always easy. "The tasks involved are very complex and fraught with risk," said McCartney. "The government has already successfully implemented a range of complex projects. However, we still need to improve performance and avoid the mistakes of the past."

Apart from the "think of the project, not the IT" recommendation, the report also suggests an organization change: the creation of a single responsible person to oversee each project rather than the management-by-committee approach that had preceded it. Changes in the procurement process were also suggested. Startlingly, these included the importance of suppliers understanding the requirements for a new system—and only promising what they could deliver—and a firm vow by the government to manage suppliers better. "This government will not tolerate failure and repeat the mistakes of the past," said McCartney. (For its part, Hughes' industry group, the Computing Service and Software Association, says it agrees with the government's findings.)

Not tolerating failure is a laudable goal but one that could prove tricky to achieve. Experts such as Marcus Pollett see the review as a welcome step in the right direction—providing that deeds follow words. And that could be difficult to determine. Pollett, a London-based writer and commentator who has followed the U.K. government's IT projects for some years, is scathing about both the review itself and the culture of secrecy that shrouds it and much else in the British civil service. "It's tremendously difficult to get any useful information at all from these people," he complains, referring to the Central Information Technology Unit and the Cabinet Office that oversees it. "There's a real control-freak mentality: Things do leak, but it's a tremendously secretive culture."

All of which bodes ill for e-government, a bold bid to deliver all services online by 2005. "One of the key ways to which businesses have applied e-commerce techniques is in managing their relationships with customers and suppliers," says an official in the Cabinet Office. "Public sector bodies must do the same if they are to derive the same benefits in terms of reduced costs and better procurement. The effect of the public sector doing this as a whole will itself be a significant contribution to advancing e-commerce."

Not to mention cutting the cost of government. Neil Mellor, program director of the e-government division at British Telecom—to which the government is outsourcing some of the work—points to the significant savings. The savings could be as high as £13.5 billion ($20.3 billion), he estimates—equivalent to a cut in the income tax of between three and four pence in the pound. E-procurement and electronic service delivery alone could save £6 billion ($9 billion).

And already, points out a government official, work has begun on building the Internet portal through which citizens and businesses will communicate with government. Intended to be up and running this summer, it will provide relatively static information at first, but from a single source rather that multiple websites. Work on the second stage of the project—building links between the portal and government IT systems, so that, say, a change of address has to be communicated only once—will begin later this year.

But, ever accident-prone, the U.K. government soon slipped on yet another banana skin. Announced with a huge fanfare in April, officials forgot to check the name for the portal—U.K. Online. It's a great name for a portal, but it also happened to be the name of a middle-ranking Internet service provider, which was less than amused to find its name hijacked. Once again, awkward questions were asked in the House—this time from the member of Parliament in whose constituency the business is based.

An accommodation was apparently reached, and U.K. Online continues to be the name of the e-government portal. How? On what basis? Officials remain tight-lipped. Good lord, no, they say. We can't release information like that . . .

Lost in Chaos:
Chronology of a Failure

By Steve Adolph

One of my favorite TV shows when I was growing up was *Lost in Space*. I was particularly fond of the robot who would always warn the Robinson family about perilous situations with the now cliché phrase "Danger, Will Robinson, danger!" Today, I wish I had one of those robots standing behind me when someone describes a project to me using phrases like "It's an aggressive schedule," "It's a challenging project," or the ever-popular, "This project is on the fast track."

"Danger, Will Robinson, danger!" What these phrases really mean is "We don't have time, so we're abandoning any software development process and, therefore, our ability to control the project."

On the surface, the short-circuiting or total abandonment of process has a seductive appeal: no tedious production of requirements documents, no boring review meetings, and no one telling you what you can or cannot put into the build. This approach to software development assumes that your project will never hit a crisis, no key personnel will leave, all third-party software will work as advertised, and the system will meet its performance requirements. Success is rooted more in faith and the tenacity of the developers than in a controlled, predictable process. This chaotic approach to software development is characteristic of immature organizations.

The Capability Maturity Model is a framework developed at Carnegie Mellon University in 1989 that outlines the elements of an effective software process. The CMM describes an evolutionary path from an ad hoc, chaotic process to a mature, disciplined one. It covers practices for planning, engineering and managing software development, which, when followed, improve the ability of an organization to satisfy cost, schedule, functionality and product-quality goals.

Unfortunately, many developers have a Pavlovian response to words like "process" and "methodology." They believe that process shackles their creativity and will prevent them from developing the creative solutions to the problems they have at hand. Often, the developers justify the belief that the CMM framework is not applicable by describing their project as different, too small or destined for an overly competitive market. After all, the CMM is for mega-programming ventures in the aerospace industry, not little applications like ours. Another popular justification is that, in the case of a legacy system conversion, a process is unnecessary because the legacy represents the company's core competency.

Although the CMM may originally have been adopted by large development organizations, its recommendations and goals are applicable to any development group. A software development group does itself a great disservice when it dismisses CMM out of hand.

Setting the Stage

Our story begins several years ago with a mobile dispatching business whose products were used by taxi companies, police and fire departments, and utilities, for dispatching their fleets.

The product for utility companies was nearing the end of its useful life and was therefore too expensive to maintain, modify or enhance. At the same time, the company had won an important contract to supply a dispatch system to a large utility company. We had a choice to make: Upgrade the legacy system to handle the customer's requirements, or take this as an opportunity to create the next-generation utility dispatching system. We decided to build the next generation. I had recently been hired by the company because of my technical expertise in UNIX software development, and it was going to be my job to serve as the team's technical leader.

The Legacy

The system that was about to launch us into chaos was in fact very simple. A dispatcher sat at a terminal and would receive a phone call from a client who might require, for example, a furnace repair. He would create a work order by entering the customer's information and a description of the required work into the system. The work order would be prioritized by urgency (from emergency calls to routine maintenance), and a service technician would be assigned to the work order, either by the dispatcher or the system. The service technician would receive the work order in her service vehicle on a mobile terminal, which she also used to report her status and request more information.

The system was based on UNIX System V and was written by a group of former mainframe programmers who did not trust UNIX. The original authors had decided to handle threading, file, terminal and memory management themselves rather than relying on the UNIX system services.

This was one of the finest examples of spaghetti code ever created, packed with hardware dependencies and corrupt with several years of undocumented enhancements and bug fixes. It was not unusual to fix a bug in one subsystem and have a completely new bug suddenly appear in an unrelated subsystem.

The programmers who maintained the system didn't enjoy the task; as a consequence, turnover was high. This threatened our ability to deliver because we could not keep our staff long enough for them to become experts in the system.

The system, the code and the programmers' disdain for the legacy were not our only problems. Our company was developing its next generation of mobile terminals, and many clients were clamoring to get them. However, the legacy system could only operate with one type of terminal, which meant all the existing terminals would have to be replaced with new ones. This was not an option that our existing clients would consider; they wanted to keep their existing terminals and add new ones as their fleets expanded.

Justifying Replacement

Our normal procedure for system delivery was to customize the software on a standard system. The customization requirements were usually straightforward: Configure the system to operate with the specific type of mobile terminal used by the client, customize the menus with the customer's name, and adapt the host interface to match the communications requirements of the client's mainframe.

Our standard customization process had worked fine until an existing utility dispatch client requested new features that went well beyond our standard customization. The customer wanted to move to a client/server architecture with automatic fail-over for high availability, and the incorporation of a commercial off-the-shelf relational database.

It should be clear by now that our utility dispatch product was old, limited and difficult to modify. Therefore, after estimating the cost of incorporating these new features into the legacy system, the decision was made to replace the legacy with a new system.

The Project Mandate

Management was not enthusiastic about replacing the legacy system (management never is)—and with good reason. Despite its technical flaws, the legacy was generating revenue for the company, and there was a great deal of reluctance to replace the product simply because programmers found it hard to maintain.

Management was concerned that the justification for the legacy replacement was being driven strictly by the technology rather than by business objectives. They were concerned that we were risking proven—albeit archaic—technology with a promise of wonderful vaporware. Our group was given a strict project mandate: Re-engineer the utility dispatching system to create a client/server architecture, operate with multiple mobile terminal types, decouple application functionality from the hardware, incorporate a commercial off-the-shelf database, and add a high-availability feature.

We had 18 months to deliver a new architecture that combined the services of the legacy system as well as the new required features. In everyone's opinion, the project goals were aggressive but achievable.

Our team consisted of a very aggressive and capable hands-on project manager, two senior designers including myself (a contractor who frequently worked with the company), and four junior-to-intermediate developers, one who had good experience implementing the company's proprietary communications protocols, and others who had customized the legacy system extensively. The team members were enthusiastic and got along famously.

One of the first warning signs should have been our cavalier approach to schedule estimation. We estimated a multi-million-dollar venture the same way three engineering students in college might estimate their term project. The senior developers simply met with the project manager and within two hours decided that we required six people over 18 months to satisfy our contractual obligations. This approach to estimation is typical of an immature, or CMM level one, development organization. What influence could following the CMM framework have had on this estimation effort if we had decided to move to at least level two in the maturity hierarchy?

One of the key practices of a level two organization is the tracking of project costs and schedules. This information forms a historic database that can be used in subsequent estimates. Of course, our software development group didn't have any historical data for making estimates, so the wet-finger-in-the-air approach was about the best we could do. However, we could have established short-term milestones—a key practice in many of the modern interactive software development processes—and then frequently compared our actuals to our estimates. That way, as the project progressed, we could have begun to use the historical database to produce higher-quality estimates.

Unfortunately, not only did we not follow this approach, we also set our project milestones too far apart: every six months. In other words, it would take that long to accumulate enough objective data to indicate whether the project was on or off track. For a project of our size, we should have set monthly milestones that would have forced us to compare our actuals to our estimates much more frequently.

Analysis or "We Don't Need No SRS"

The next warning sign should have come during the analysis phase, which, for all practical purposes, was skipped. Our wet-finger-in-the-wind style of estimating had almost panicked us into believing that we were under a great deal of schedule pressure. The approach to mitigating this risk was to abandon what we perceived as unnecessary steps in the software development process.

Having come from a very disciplined software development environment, I recommended the creation of a software requirements specification (SRS) as part of the requirements analysis process. This was rejected by the project manager for two reasons: First, it was considered unnecessary because the company had expertise in the field of mobile dispatching, and second, the schedule was the risk and all unnecessary activities—including the preparation of an SRS—needed to be pruned from the schedule.

There is a perception that creating an SRS is a time-consuming, paper-wasting exercise that doesn't contribute to a project. This perception is probably reinforced by published SRS standards such as the ANSI/IEEE 830 in the *1984 IEEE Guide to Software Requirements Specification.*

The ANSI/IEEE 830 provides a comprehensive and complete format for an SRS. There are seven major sections covering everything from the information model and functional models, to validation criteria. A complete SRS for a moderately sized project (moderate being about 15 staff-years) can be more than 100 pages long, and one for a defense system (approximately 100 staff-years in effort) was said to have been shipped in a panel van! While it is inappropriate to prepare such a comprehensive document for a small project, that does not justify abandoning a document or other artifacts that serve the purpose of the SRS. The usefulness of the SRS is not in the volume of paper produced, but rather in how well it communicates what the system should be to all project participants.

For a small project, the IEEE 830 standard becomes an excellent checklist for ensuring that all project participants know the functional requirements, the stored data model, and the constraints on the system. Often, the objective of the SRS can be satisfied with a few bullet lists and a couple of class diagrams.

Our project manager didn't want to produce an SRS because he saw himself as an expert in the legacy system and thought he had a clear vision of what the new system needed to achieve. Regardless of that fact, abandoning the analysis process altogether is not a justifiable project management practice; without it, we have nothing that states the requirements for our project and nothing constraining it, other than the whims of its participants.

When replacing a legacy system, software developers often underestimate the risk because they assume the legacy system is one of the organization's core competencies and that it represents a set of stable requirements. This perception is true only if the replacement project's development team understands the legacy system and actually uses it to reduce the risks associated with uncertain requirements.

In *The Mythical Man-Month: Essays on Software Engineering* (Addison-Wesley, 1975), Frederick Brooks called this the "second system effect," writing "the second is the most dangerous system man ever designs . . . There is a general tendency to overdesign the second system using all the ideas and frills that were cautiously sidetracked on the first one."

Unfortunately, we were destined to find out how accurate Frederick Brooks's prediction was.

Design or "I Like This Part Best"

Based on the assumption that we were experts in the domain of mobile dispatching and that the majority of our functional requirements were captured in our legacy system, we short-circuited the analysis phase of our project and moved quickly into high-level design.

Our goal in the design phase was to create an executable architecture: a foundation for our new system that we would grow by adding new functionality as we went along. To satisfy our project mandate, the senior designers reorganized the monolith into a textbook three-tiered client/server architecture. This immediately satisfied our project mandate because it provided a clean separation of our business rules from our device interfaces for both dispatcher and mobile terminals.

The new architecture supported a variety of mobile terminal types. Now, all that was needed to add a new terminal type to the system was to write a device driver for it and add an entry for that terminal type to the configuration table. Unlike the legacy application, the system no longer had to be recompiled to add a new terminal type.

In design, we once again avoided the formal process, opting instead for having a couple of programmers confer with the project manager and sketch system components on a whiteboard. The programmers would write the code and rely on the project manager for midcourse corrections. Once the code was complete (that is, when a clean compile had been obtained), we would have a normal code walkthrough. The project manager, a senior designer, and the programmer whose code was under review, participated in the walkthrough.

There was one glaring exception to this informal process. Because the senior designers had placed a lot of emphasis on the communications backbone for the new client/server architecture, we published a formal document describing the APIs for the communications backbone and also created a guidebook to help the other programmers use the backbone's services.

As a result, the backbone was beautiful, heavily overdesigned and a reinvention of the remote procedure calls (RPC), a service readily available on most flavors of UNIX. There were several justifications for this reinvention, but the one that kept resurfacing was performance. High performance was necessary, and it was believed that our design had less overhead than the RPC.

The excessive attention paid to the design and implementation of the communications backbone was a result of what we had perceived as the risks to the system—probably diverting our attention from handling the true risks—and also a result of the fact that the senior designers found it interesting.

The First (and Last) Milestone

The departure of one of the senior developers, a contractor on the project, was the first blow. Suddenly we had no one with experience in the business services the system was to provide; without the de facto expert in the legacy system, it was extremely difficult to read and understand the legacy code. So, rather than trying to continue to recover the application logic from the existing code, we began to recover it from the only documentation we had—the user manual.

At this point, the legacy code was lost as a risk-reduction mechanism.

Six months into our project, at our first milestone, we were able to successfully demonstrate the executable architecture to our marketing group and corporate executive. It satisfied the mandate given to us by management, featured a client/server architecture that was nicely layered to decouple application functionality from the hardware, and the system used a commercial off-the-shelf database. The system was dynamically reconfigurable, and management was extremely impressed when we could change terminal types on the fly during the demo.

Our executives were happy. The demonstration gave them confidence in the system. Better yet, it boosted the confidence of the team. We started to become arrogant and forgot that this little performance had only demonstrated approximately 10% of the functional capability of the system—while we had used up 33% of our project time.

The second blow to hit the project occurred when the project manager left the company. He had acted as a living SRS and had often scrubbed feature changes recommended or desired by the project team. Under the fast-track process (or lack thereof) we were running, this was the fatal blow, although it would be another six months before anyone would notice the symptoms.

A former employer was brought in on contract as the new project manager. His management style was quite different from our previous manager. He believed strongly in employee empowerment, and he let the development team manage itself. One of the key requirements of empowerment, however, is that empowered employees must clearly understand what the project objectives are—and those had gone out the door with our living SRS. In the absence of well-defined goals, staff members created their own, based on what they thought important, rather than what was important to their clients.

Beyond its spaghetti architecture, the legacy system had numerous technical and application problems. The design team often chose to invent new strategies rather than reuse techniques from the legacy system. There were good technical and application reasons for these new strategies. However, what was unseen was the element of risk these new strategies introduced.

Let's take an example. The unit of work assigned to a service technician was a work order. Only one service technician could be assigned to a work order; however, many of the tasks required more than one service technician, and each of the attending service technicians would be on the job for different periods of time. The legacy system handled this by linking work orders together so one work order became a kind of primary work order, and other work orders became secondary. There were numerous problems with this design, especially when trying to determine when the work order was complete.

We viewed the linking of work orders as a hack; it offended our collective sense of good design. We came up with a better idea: the concept of a job as a unit of work that a service technician performed on a work order. A work order was a set of one or more jobs. Now, knowing the work order, you could find the service people and their jobs.

The only problem with this beautiful scheme was that it completely changed how the system operated. It changed the user interface for both the dispatchers and technicians, which meant that all the documentation had to change. Furthermore, our field-service people would have to be retrained.

Nevertheless, the development team aggressively sold this idea to the new project manager, who approved it. Indeed, the new project manager endorsed most of the design team's suggestions and improvements without question. This led to situations where the design team would implement a feature and then decide later there was a better way to re-implement that feature.

The existing code would be ripped out and an improved feature implemented. In all cases, there were good technical reasons for rewriting the feature. The problem was that the technical justifications conflicted with schedule requirements and, in some cases, caused the project to actually slide backward. Without a requirements scrub process—a hallmark of developmental maturity—and without a single clear vision for the product, we began to suffer feature creep on a monumental scale. The worst part was that this feature creep was self-inflicted.

Curtains

The legacy replacement project was canceled a year after it was started. Six months after the highly successful first demonstration, at our second milestone, management no longer clung to the hope that the development team could deliver the new system on time. We had less than 30% of the legacy system's functionality incorporated into the new architecture, despite the fact that we had expanded nearly 70% of our project's allotted time and resources.

In retrospect, it's amazing that the team could let the situation deteriorate to the extent that it did. We were all too interested in how to make the system technically perfect to notice that we were in serious trouble. I had received praise from my manager and from my team for the architectural elements that I had created for the system. Unfortunately, I let these technical achievements delude me into believing that our project was well on its way to success. I had lost sight of the project mandate originally specified by our corporate management.

This is all too common an occurrence in immature development organizations. People have an amazing ability for denial, which is abetted by an absence of objective data. Perhaps this is the ultimate purpose of a software development process: to shake us out of complacency by pushing the hard facts right into our faces. If the project had been reviewed early and frequently, we would have had the opportunity to take remedial action.

The development team was redeployed to create wrappers around the legacy system so that it would minimally satisfy our client's requirements. Within two years of the legacy replacement cancellation, the company was out of the business of supplying application software for its mobile terminals.

The Final Analysis

Without a defined process, the project relied entirely on the first project manager's ability to maintain the project vision. When he left, all control was lost.

Our justification for not applying a disciplined process was the tired cliché that our project was somehow different. We deliberately chose a chaotic approach to software development because of the belief that following a process would bog us down in miserable details.

Following a process does not mean turning a fast-moving software development organization into a plodding bureaucracy. The CMM provides a tailorable framework that shows progressive levels of process maturity, with the goal of improving an organization's ability to meet goals for cost, schedule, functionality and product quality.

Each maturity level has a set of process areas that an organization should have in place to help it achieve the goals of the CMM. The mere production of documents does not satisfy the requirements of a process area. Therefore, it is more important to understand the risks that the process area mitigates rather than the format of an industry standard document for that area.

Had we made a commitment to improving the maturity of our development process and at least borrowed some elements from the CMM, we might have had a successful project.

For example, the first key process area of level two is requirements management, which establishes a common understanding of the requirements. We never produced a requirements document, assuming instead that our project mandate and the legacy system represented our requirements. As a consequence, there was no way to control changes to the requirements after the first project manager left.

Other level two process areas include software project planning, tracking and oversight, which establishes visible milestones to compare estimates to actual progress.

Finally, level two's emphasis on quality assurance gives management visibility into the process. This helps prevent long periods of developer denial due to the lack of objective data to shake them.

In retrospect, the task of maturing into a level two organization wouldn't have been very onerous, entailing perhaps the creation of a few short documents and the implementation of regular reviews. Perhaps we wouldn't have won the heart of an ISO 9000 auditor, but we might have succeeded in delivering our project.

County Blew $38 Million:
Here's What Went Wrong

By Roberto Sanchez
Seattle Times Staff Reporter

The managers of King County's unfinished $38 million financial computer system didn't take into account basic computer and business procedures, forced part of the system online before it was ready, and spent the rest of their budget trying to fix problems that followed, leading to the cancellation of the project last month.

County records, and interviews with the people in charge of the Financial Systems Replacement Program (FSRP), show that the project to replace the county's ancient accounting and payroll systems failed mostly because of delays and cost overruns in one of its components, a payroll system for the county's 19,000 employees.

In the end, the county's investment—including an extra $3.7 million approved this week to shut down the project—will only return a payroll system for a third of the employees.

A bank of computers and software that would have gone online this month sit idle on the 24th floor of the Key Tower; boxes of unfinished records lie uncatalogued a few blocks west. All will be mothballed until the county figures out how to revive the rest of the canceled system.

Managers of the payroll project and the county Finance Department defend their work, saying that they made the right decisions and managed to install a complicated payroll system on time, a rare feat in the industry. But records and interviews show that the county rushed the installation of the first part of that system, serving about 6,000 employees, despite evidence that important features were not finished and the knowledge that people in critical jobs were not trained to use it.

E-mails and consultants' progress reports at the county also show that the people in charge of the payroll project, and of the whole computer project in general, refused to acknowledge for most of 1999 that there was a crisis, despite thousands of errors in paychecks produced by the new system after it went online.

They also ignored detailed written warnings in May from the county auditor, in July from Chief Accountant Rudy Caluza and in October from a consultant hired by the council to keep track of the project. All of them said serious problems with implementation of the payroll system threatened the rest of the project.

Instead, project managers at the county and their chief consultant on the project, the accounting firm KPMG, chose to push back some deadlines and increasingly rely on expensive consultants—some earning more than $300 an hour—to fix bugs, train employees and, eventually, to run part of the county's payroll.

By the end of 1999, the county had practically drained its budget for the entire program, forcing King County Executive Ron Sims to cancel the project last month.

Those managers, however, say they did the best they could under extremely difficult circumstances, and managed to install a complicated payroll system in time to beat Year 2000 bugs in the old software. They also said most of the problems in payroll, then and now, are from human mistakes, not software or design errors.

"I think the system needed to be implemented, and it is paying 6,000 employees every two weeks," said Acting Finance Director John Amos.

Amos, former Finance Director Brad Duerr, former payroll project manager Cindy Lee, and a representative from KPMG, all said that what seem like excessive expenditures are actually the real costs of installing a new system and changing the way people do business with it.

"You have to ask whether the original budget was sufficient," said Peter Julicher, a director at KPMG.

"This is really about money, not about incompetent work or about poor requirements, or bad business-process definitions," Lee said. "It's about, did we have enough money to do all of what we had to do?"

Move to Modernize System

Since the court-mandated merger of King County with the old Metro agency in 1996, agencies and employees have used separate computer systems for finance and payroll, some using 20-year-old software.

In 1997, the county set out to replace those systems, selling $32.7 million in councilmanic bonds, which the council can issue without a vote of the people and then pay off from the general fund.

In December 1997, county administrators chose a software package from PeopleSoft, based in Pleasanton, Calif., to handle payroll for both county and Metro employees.

A year later, the county decided to buy an accounting package from SAP, based in Walldorf, Germany, to run general finances for both Metro and King County. In May 1999, the German firm BrightStar was hired to manage that side of the project.

In April 1998, the county hired KPMG to do the project management for the entire computer replacement. That involved reviewing budgets and schedules and preparing regular progress reports.

The schedules for the two projects were separate at first. Because of Y2K problems with the old computer for the former Metro employees, payroll would replace that system by June 11, 1999. The rest of the county's employees would be switched to the system by September 1999.

The finance package would go online by May 2000, since it depended on accurate data and other information from the payroll side to function properly.

Though there were no obvious problems with either change in 1998, a May 1999 audit of technology projects by the King County auditor suggested the project didn't have detailed cost estimates. That meant it "had a high level of risk with regard to being able to complete the project within the stated budget," according to Harriet Richardson, a county auditor.

Tests, Little Training

Through much of 1998 and part of 1999, the payroll-project team, led by Lee, worked on transferring data from the older county computers to the new PeopleSoft program, and testing to see how the program behaved. They were also responsible for getting county employees trained to use the system.

As the deadline of June 1999 approached, the team scrambled to finish that work. By late May, payroll team members had done six practice runs with the PeopleSoft package, comparing the results with the old software. It was about 98 percent accurate, Lee said. Amos and Duerr joined Lee in saying they thought the program was ready.

The people working on the payroll say that in the months before going live, they had few contacts with people running the project, and that tests of the software didn't include all deductions taken from most checks. Most importantly, their staff was not getting training on the PeopleSoft system. Even the five people who would process the actual checks in the end had not been trained.

"When we became vocal about it, they asked us to come in on a weekend [for training]," said Sue Constable, an accounting technician at the county. "They had us do menial jobs like cutting and pasting paper."

Caluza, chief accountant at the time and ultimately in charge of payroll for county employees, said he told Lee he was concerned about going live. Lee now says that if Caluza had concerns, he didn't tell her. But she said she knew people were not trained. She felt that her project team, which included people borrowed from the payroll department, would be able to help process payroll and teach the staff by doing.

"The efforts were made to not necessarily train them but to mitigate the risk," Lee said. "We'd help them run their payroll, we'd help them do research . . . the idea was to go live and then to provide support."

Immediate Headaches

On June 11, the county switched 6,000 employees to the PeopleSoft system. Within hours, people knew something was wrong.

"We were overwhelmed," Caluza said. "We couldn't balance payroll; we couldn't determine retirement benefits."

Caluza said his staff worked 12 to 18 hours of overtime per person that week to correct errors before checks went out.

Even so, once they received their checks, employees flooded payroll phone lines and e-mail to complain about mistakes. The payroll system had sent direct deposits to accounts that didn't exist, retirement accruals were wrong, child-support payments didn't get to their destinations. An inventory of the errors filled more than six pages.

Still, Lee felt these were expected.

"We are live with PS [PeopleSoft] and it's going. We had a few problems, but all were human errors. It's a terrific system, and I just love it," Lee wrote in a June 29, 1999, e-mail to a PeopleSoft representative.

Caluza didn't think so. After three payroll cycles, on July 26 he sent a confidential memo to Duerr and Amos outlining problems. He felt many of these were the result of poor planning and showed that the software package and the team running it weren't ready to meet county needs. He felt KPMG was not overseeing the project well and not meeting the terms of its contract with the county. He also asked them to remove Lee from the project.

Duerr told Caluza in person that he was keeping Lee on the job and didn't respond to the other concerns.

For the next 10 months, the payroll-project team had many of its members doing the grunt work of payroll: entering data and checking for bugs; and still paychecks were riddled with mistakes. This delayed work on installing the rest of the payroll system, pushing back the September 1999 deadline. More significantly, it created such a tense situation in payroll that the county lost key employees, including the payroll supervisor.

The response from management was to hire more consultants, many from KPMG, including a database administrator and, eventually, a temporary payroll supervisor at $217 an hour each. The management team eventually decided to push back the implementation dates for both the second part of the payroll project and the SAP finance computers to July 2000.

Delays Meant Budget Danger

The payroll project, which had a total budget of about $11 million, had already spent about $9.5 million by Sept. 30, 1999, according to a progress report by KPMG. By contrast, the other side of the project, the SAP financial system, had spent $4.7 of its $14 million.

Pacific Consulting Group (PCG), a watchdog hired by the King County Council to keep an eye on the entire computer project, rang the alarm in an Oct. 13, 1999, memo to the County Auditor. Bob Fuller of PCG said the entire project was in danger because delays were about to bust its budget.

The next six months were spent trying to figure out whether the existing budget was enough to fix the problems with payroll and complete the SAP finance-computer project. In February 2000, Cindy Lee was moved to another position in finance; Duerr announced plans to retire in May. On March 23, Caluza announced his resignation to take a job with the Port of Seattle.

By May, county executive Sims and his new system project managers, Caroline Whalen and David Martinez, suspended work on the project and fired KPMG as the project-management office. To date, the county has paid KPMG about $4.4 million, according to Martinez.

KPMG is still working for the county to fix problems in the installed payroll system, for $1.7 million. The County Council has asked that the contract be renegotiated.

In June, the new project managers canceled the entire project and focused on saving the pieces. The project had nearly gone through the $38 million in its budget. By some estimates, it would have cost an additional $30 million to complete it.

To this day, the Metro payroll system is plagued with errors. The state has routinely rejected retirement-account data from the county, at one point creating a nine-month backlog of data. It still requires overtime and a team of consultants to put out checks every two weeks.

In March, the county hired a payroll supervisor at $65,000 a year. By contrast, the temporary KPMG consultant who did that job earned $217 an hour—that's $6,944 for a 32-hour week, according to the KPMG contract with the county.

The county will spend $3.2 million of the money authorized this week by the council to "stabilize" the payroll system—training people to use it and fixing the bugs in how it processes information.

The cancellation of the project effectively killed most of the work done on the SAP finance-computer system. That side of the project had been on budget and, until the PeopleSoft project went sour, on schedule. Some of its elements were almost done, but now that there is no money, they will be mothballed.

Because software is a fluid product, some feel that all the work done will be obsolete by the time the county chooses to revive it.

"A project that was going well, pretty much on time and on budget, has been wasted," said Casey O'Connor, an SAP team member.

Who's to Blame?

Who or what is to blame for the failure of this project?

KPMG was the overseeing consultant for the county, and it was fired in May. But Peter Julicher, the only director commenting for this story, said the consulting company's contract didn't give it authority to make decisions; its job was to advise.

"Our client was the director of finance," Julicher said. "Ultimately, the business people who were in charge decided which risk to take and which not to take."

Brad Duerr, the former director of finance, said you can't blame one person or one event for the problems. He said it was a likely a combination of a tight market for specialized labor and a budget too small for the project. He said he was forced by circumstance to rely on consultants.

"I wonder what people thought I should have done. I thought I took the only action I could. I got somebody in there who, though expensive, knew PeopleSoft and knew payroll," Duerr said.

He said Cindy Lee was a good, tough manager for the payroll project, but in retrospect, "I think sometimes she didn't tell me the whole story."

Lee also says the budget was too small for the job. And she says that in an organization as big as King County, where people have used the same business systems for decades, there are inherent flaws nobody could have predicted that slow down changes.

"Sometimes a new system brings out the flaws in your organization that you haven't been aware of before," she said.

Executive Sims, in his June news conference announcing cancellation of the project, said he would not blame anyone, that ultimately he was responsible because it happened on his watch.

Still, in an interview last week, he said his office has to "rely on department heads and division heads to implement these projects." He said he reacted as quickly as he could, once his staff knew the project was in trouble. He said there was no clear information to make a decision about the project until May. He also said it was time to move on, fix what's wrong with the project and find a way to finish it, rather than place blame.

"Who are you going to go after now? All of the individuals around this project have either left or moved on with their lives. Who would you hold accountable?" he said.

That's not good enough, according to critics and people involved in the project.

"The county needs to end this whole conspiracy of silence around failure," O'Connor, the SAP-team member, said. "If you look at private enterprise, you see a failure like this, you see that people in charge would be held accountable, and that's not what's going on here."

Double Jeopardy

By Christopher Koch

Ernie Aschermann is a good software salesman. He knows how to pitch and he knows how to write code—a rare combination of talents in the software industry. On Jan. 16, 1992, he had a rapt audience in the managers of the Oklahoma City Water Utilities Trust, the public corporation that sells water to the citizens and businesses of Oklahoma City.

Desperate to replace its antiquated customer-billing system, the Trust had invited Aschermann and his sales sidekick, Steven "Pax" Darlington, to give a demonstration of a utility-billing program developed by their company, Network Computing Corp. (NCC). In a small conference room at the Trust's headquarters, Aschermann delivered an impressive presentation. He practically finished the Trust people's sentences for them, showing off his knowledge of the water utility business and his software know-how.

After building up the Trust's expectations, Aschermann finally hit a button on his laptop and the screen filed with arcane references to utility-billing functions. "What I want to show you now is Affinity Revision One," he said. "I'm going to show you this because number one, I don't want you to go away with the impression that there's anything that doesn't exist—any smoke or mirrors." Then he drove the "trust me" point home with a bit of self-deprecating humor. "What's that joke about computer salesmen and car salesmen? At least the car salesmen know when they are lying?"

During the disastrous software project that followed, questions arose as to where Aschermann and Darlington fit in that sales spectrum. Allegations of misrepresentation and fraud would land NCC in court a few years later, where a jury decided that the two men might, in fact, have made great car salesmen. Even within the Charlotte, N.C.-based software company, Aschermann's colleagues had their doubts about his Affinity sales pitch, referring to it from the beginning as "smoke and mirrors." George Mackie, who was president and CEO of NCC at the time, charged that Aschermann "was stretching the truth to his favor."

Unstretched, the truth was that Affinity Revision Two (or Affinity 2.1), which the Trust would later buy from NCC for $1.3 million, was far from being fully developed, contrary to the impression left by Aschermann and Darlington that day. The Trust became an unwitting beta site for a desperate, financially troubled software company that needed a big sale to stay afloat.

Ironically, the ensuing catastrophe was not the first of its kind for the Trust. As the NCC salespeople spun their tale in the Trust's conference room, across town the Trust's hired-gun lawyers were busily preparing legal documents for the Trust's case against Peat Marwick Main & Co. (now known as KPMG Peat Marwick LLP), the accounting and consulting firm that had tried and failed to develop a custom-billing program just a few years prior. Like the NCC debacle, that case also involved an unproven software product encased in a sweet, candy-coated sales shell. The complex software overwhelmed Peat Marwick's well-meaning software developers and the Trust's expensive new computer system dissolved—like the project—leaving a bitter taste in everyone's mouth.

That's why Stacey Davis, utility customer services superintendent for the Trust and the lead business person on the utility-billing system project, decided to videotape (with the vendors' permission) the sales pitches from NCC and the three other vendors who came to the Trust in early 1992 offering to pick up where Peat Marwick had left off. Davis was prescient, it turned out. A five-minute "highlight tape" from NCC's presentation became one of the most powerful pieces of evidence during the Trust's second civil trial against the unfulfilled promises of software vendors and consultants.

The Trust's 10-year saga of failed software projects and legal wranglings is a cautionary tale for any company contemplating a large, complex software installation using consultants. The story of the Trust shows just how easy it can be for these projects to go horribly wrong, and how bittersweet revenge can be when administered through the courts.

Even more disturbing is the fact that Davis and his colleagues at the Trust are not naïve. Most had been through software implementations before the big troubles began. In both projects, the Trust took the standard precautions to avoid disaster: clear, detailed requests for proposals (RFPs); exacting contracts that outlined specific deliverables, milestones and dates; full-time project staffers from the business and technology sides of the Trust; and high-level project steering committees that met regularly with the consultants on both projects. Nor were the consultants evil charlatans. Most were dedicated, experienced, talented people. And still both projects ended with unworkable software and angry recriminations on both sides. The Trust's story is a shocking testament to the ravages of complexity and to the need for businesses to impose radical, almost irrational, levels of control over the management of these projects to avoid major delays, cost overruns and breakdowns.

Act One: A Big Eight Blunder

The Trust's painful saga began in 1987, when it resolved to find a replacement for its already obsolete '70s-era mainframe computer. The Honeywell-Bull system was an expensive technological antique that cost $30,000 or more per month to maintain, according to Davis, and cost Trust staffers precious hours of lost productivity. It was impossible to look up customers by name in the system, for example. Any problems not linked to an account number meant a walk to the research desk, where a massive printout of the Trust's 170,000 customers sat waiting to waste everyone's time.

That's why the Trust decided to bring in Peat Marwick to help figure out what to do with old Bessie. After scanning the software landscape for options, Peat came to the fascinating conclusion that the best software solution was its own. On the surface, Peat's proposal did indeed look good: a custom-developed software program that would have all the functionality the Trust needed and then some, as well as a fancy new Digital computer, all for $2.6 million. Even better, if Peat could sell the new software to other utilities around the country, the Trust would receive royalties to help defray project costs.

Yet behind the scenes, all was not well with the proposed project, says Ralph Shay, who would become Peat Marwick's first manager on the project. Shay had heard rumblings within Peat Marwick that the computer Digital had recommended for the project, the VAX 6220, would not be able to handle the large, complex application being proposed to the Trust. The computer choice was critical to the success of the project, because the software did not yet exist and therefore could not be tested to see how much processing power it would consume. But the Trust could not afford to wait before buying a new machine, says Davis, since it did not own a computer powerful enough to handle the software development project, let along run the finished software. The computer and the software would need to run together seamlessly; the Trust was on a fixed budget and could not afford to swap out the computer for something more powerful (and expensive) once the project got going.

But the Trust had reason to believe that the 6220 was the right machine for the job. Before it became the project consultant, Peat had been hired to coordinate the Trust's formal search for new hardware and had recommended Digital, which proposed the 6220. Peat Marwick tried to distance itself from that recommendation during contract negotiations with the Trust, but things only got muddier when both sides' lawyers got involved and inserted a murky accountability clause in the heart of an otherwise clear contract. The Trust bought the 6220 at the same time it signed on with Peat in November 1988. Both parties forged ahead blindly, each assured that the other was legally responsible for any computer problems that arose.

But those who worked on the project for Peat Marwick say the company's project leadership was more aware of the potential for problems than it let on during contract negotiations. Shay says he made his concerns clear to

Larry Lott and Thomas Gorley, his project superiors at Peat Marwick, in a series of meetings in Lott's Dallas office before the contract with Trust was signed. "We discussed quite a bit the fact that only one of us on the project team had experience with the combination of hardware and software we were proposing," he says. "That combination represented an unknown and a risk."

The new technologies didn't bother him so much as the computer. "We could learn the new software, but there was a lot of risk in proposing a system that had already been locked into a processor," he explains. "We felt we could make it work, but there was still a lot of risk." In sworn depositions taken in 1993, both Lott and Gorley would deny that they had spoken with Shay about the ability—or lack thereof—of the 6220 to run the proposed software prior to signing the contract with the Trust.

Peat was also having problems with its new computer-aided software engineering (CASE) tool, Goldrun, that would generate the computer code for the Trust's software program. The lone Peat Marwick developer on the Trust project who had experience with Goldrun, Bill Blessing, claims that before the contract was signed, he warned Lott, Gorley and the Trust that Goldrun used bytes like a Sherman tank uses gasoline. During a prior project at an insurance company in Kansas City, Blessing says the application that he helped develop with Goldrun consumed so much processing power that the client had to trade in its Digital 6000 series computer for a 9000 series machine, which was roughly five times as powerful and almost three times as expensive as the 6220. "I knew [the application] would never run on the 6220, and I told many people on both the [Trust] and on the Peat Marwick side my concerns," says Blessing. Those concerns went unheeded.

To Davis, the hardware dance was irrelevant. He focused on the "acceptance testing" portion of the contract that bound Peat to explicit software performance requirements. Peat was obligated to provide a software program capable of getting information from the 6220 to the terminals of his customer service representatives in two seconds or less, and the system needed to crunch through its load of daily transactions during nighttime batch processing in five hours or less. To Davis, it was Peat Marwick's responsibility to meet these promises, including buying the Trust a faster computer if that became necessary. Davis says that he confronted Lott and Gorley about Blessing's warnings but was told not to worry. "They would say the Kansas City system was that system and this is this system and they would reassure us that this was going to succeed," recalls Davis.

Those assurances became less frequent and less reassuring in April 1989, three months after work on the project began, when Larry Lott sent a letter to the Trust's MIS director, Jana Bagwell, expressing Peat's opinion that the 6220 was inadequate for the job. Davis went ballistic. "In steering committee meetings we'd have Gorley saying, 'That's a hardware problem, you need to talk to Digital.' We said, 'No, it's your problem. If you want to call Digital in you can, but you are the ringleader here so you are responsible.'"

While the computer issue became public knowledge fairly early in the project, Peat decided not to send a letter to the Trust about the problems with its Goldrun tool, problems highlighted in internal memos written by the project's technical lead Steward Nazzaro. "The Oklahoma City engagement has a number of requirements which we are finding impossible to meet with the features currently available in Goldrun," he wrote in February 1989. In December of that year he criticized the "inefficient code" being generated by Goldrun. Although he declined to be interviewed directly for this story, citing a confidentiality agreement signed by the Trust and Peat in their legal settlement, Lott started in his court deposition that Gorley told him that Nazzaro was "overreacting."

Nazzaro may have been understating the problem, as it turned out. During performance testing in December, the new software posted an absurdly long batch processing time of 91 hours with just one terminal attached to the system (the Trust would need 65 to 80 terminals), and typical information request response times of 11 to 17 seconds. "I told them batch processing would have to be done in Alaska because there they have nighttimes that last six months," deadpans Davis in his Oklahoma drawl.

Even if Goldrun hadn't been a bust, there were other signs that the project was in trouble. There was constant turnover among the Peat staff on the project (which Lott characterized in his court deposition as "normal for a project of this size and scope"), and Peat consultants bickered openly with each other in front of Trust staff about the plan for developing the software and the schedule for testing it. But mostly they argued about Peat's decision to put them up in a cheesy motel. The techies wanted apartments.

Peat Marwick management didn't do much to quell the project turmoil; of the four project managers assigned to the Trust, three had no prior project management experience.

Things finally came to a head in 1990, when the Trust realized that the project could not be salvaged without going back to the City for more money. Despite well-meaning efforts from all the vendors and the Trust, which agreed to trim its functionality requirements, there was simply no way to bridge the performance gap with the equipment on hand. And no one was willing to chip in the extra $2.5 million for a 9000 Series VAX computer. With all sides clinging to their own versions of project responsibility and accountability, the Trust declared Peat in breach of contract in late 1990, and Peat walked off the project soon thereafter. The Trust would file suit against Peat almost one year later, in June 1991.

The Trust decided to abandon everything that had been developed to that point. "This isn't like buying a badly built house, where at least you have something to live in despite all the problems," Davis says. "When Peat Marwick left we had nothing we could use. Nothing."

Peat would eventually settle with the Trust in August 1993 for $1.8 million, about the cost of Peat's services. But that did not cover the time spent by the Trust's staff trying to help develop the new system, nor did it cover the cost of the Digital computer, which was eventually used by another City department. Even with the successful settlement, the Trust still didn't have the billing system it desperately needed.

Act Two: The Vaporware Fiasco

Davis says he was still licking his wounds from the Peat Marwick debacle in late 1991, when he received a phone call from Deniece Chaplin, Digital's sales representative to the City. "I believe I have found a solution for you," she said. She told Davis that Digital had just purchased 10 percent of a software company called NCC that offered packaged applications for utilities. This was the first time that Digital had gotten so cozy with a software company, and Davis took that as a good omen. He agreed to consider NCC during his renewed efforts to find a utility-billing system.

This time, the Trust decided to write its own RFP, which was lengthy and went into great detail explaining the Trust's specific functionality and performance requirements. One of the most critical requirements for Davis was that vendors show up with a proven packaged software application—no custom coding for incomplete "vaporware." NCC was able to present a proven product by affixing the Affinity 1.0 name to a separate program known as Flagship, which was already in use at several U.S. utilities. NCC could then represent Affinity 2.1 as an 'incremental upgrade" to Affinity 1.0, rather than an entirely new and separate development effort. By sending the Trust to Flagship reference sites and showing off the Flagship software, NCC avoided the uncomfortable truth about the Affinity product: it was a mere shell of a program that had not been fully tested or installed anywhere in the world.

NCC's struggle to stay afloat led the company to take desperate measures to win the contract. When Terry McClure, NCC's project manager, reviewed the Trust's RFP, he gave NCC management an estimate of 2,800 person hours to customize the base Affinity product (which was still not complete) to meet the Trust's RFP requirements. He says NCC management then told him and his technical colleagues that "we needed to go back throught the [RFP] and not analyze it so closely, I suppose, or words to that effect," McClure got the message and lowered the estimate by nearly 1,000 hours. He says he believes NCC intentionally "underbid" the project in order to win the contract, something he says is common practice in the cutthroat world of software development.

Davis got his own glimpse of that cutthroat world when a competing bidder sent him a letter warning that no one had Affinity up and running and that one of NCC's "current" (i.e., Flagship) customers, the public utility of Fayetteville, N.C., kicked NCC out and wrote a new RFP stipulating that "any product proposed must have at least a two-year installation history."

Davis remembers the "sour grapes letter," as he calls it. "The software business is a tough business where vendors do a lot of rock throwing," says Davis. "We called the utilities mentioned and asked what had occurred and we tried to draw a parallel where we could." He says he couldn't find many. Besides, he reasoned, the Trust was buying Affinity, not Flagship.

To Aschermann, who still inhabits that cutthroat world as an independent software developer and consultant, pinning the project problems to the Flagship versus Affinity debate is a cop-out. "The basic structure that was started with to develop [Affinity 2.1] was very much the core structure of Flagship," he says, although NCC developers who worked on the project assert that Affinity was completely new and separate from the Flagship development effort. Aschermann adds that during his videotaped presentation, "I believe it was fairly clearly described that [Affinity 2.1] was not running anywhere although it was being benchmarked at the time." He is less clear about his videotaped description of Affinity 2.1 code as having been "finished" in November 1991. "I was not in a position to know whether what I was being told by NCC [about the state of the Affinity code] was accurate or not accurate," Aschermann says. "Was I aware that it was not 100 percent complete? Yes. Was I aware of where it stood exactly? No."

After signing a $1.3 million contract with NCC in March 1992, it didn't take long for the Trust to find out exactly where Affinity stood. Nor did it take long to discover that NCC was in such deep financial trouble that it could not afford the computer and people resources necessary to support the development effort for Affinity—which it had agreed to install by April 1993. Soon after the project began, overwhelmed developers at NCC's Charlotte headquarters began shipping raw, bug-filled Affinity code to Oklahoma City, where the Trust's programmers took on the burden of testing the rough stuff while McClure and his programmers focused on repairing and installing the code.

Despite the obvious difficulties, McClure remained mum about the true state of Affinity. In an April 1993 project steering committee meeting, McClure even denied the assertion by City Auditor Brenda Carpenter that the Trust had become a beta site for Affinity. What he knew, but didn't tell the Trust, was that in order to meet the standard definition, the Trust would have had to *know* it was going to be a beta site and agree to it before the project started. Asked why he decided not to reveal the truth about Affinity to the Trust, McClure replies, "Just didn't seem to be in the best interest of the project to indicate that they had bought something that wasn't there."

Strange though it may seem now, the company man McClure managed to maintain the respect of the Trust despite all the broken promises from NCC. It had been clear from the beginning that he and his programmers were dedicated to making Affinity work. It's a good thing, too, because they would need every ounce of sympathy they could muster in September 1993, when NCC's owner and primary backer, William Devers, decided to pull the financial plug on the troubled Affinity division. "I think it was a Monday," recalls McClure. "I had flown back from Charlotte to Oklahoma City for another week's work here on the project. And when I arrived, I couldn't get into the system. Kerry (Wagnon, the Trust's new MIS director) informed me that NCC was closing down the Affinity division of the company and the project. So that's how I officially found out." McClure had worked for NCC for 17 years. The rest of the Affinity staffers were laid off the same day.

NCC sold the dregs of Affinity to Digital, which promptly shelved it while refusing the Trust's pleas for help in finishing the project. Left holding the bag once again, Davis knew the Trust could not afford to walk away from yet another pile of dead software. With nowhere else to turn, Davis hired McClure and his former NCC programmers to finish the project, and filed suit against NCC and Digital in hopes of recovering some of the costs. McClure and his team would spend another year and a half getting the system to work (at an additional cost to the Trust of $2.6 million) before it finally went live in May 1995.

Davis says he is happy with the system that emerged, except for one major flaw: It lacks a database that would have let Davis run ad hoc queries about customer loyalty, complaints, or other vital questions he had about the Trust's customers. "That was the primary reason we chose NCC over the others," he laments. What Davis got was a new system that does its job well, but can't think too much about the people contained in its vast database.

At least it was cheap. In June 1997, an Oklahoma County District Court jury found Digital and NCC both guilty of breach of contract, fraud and misrepresentation, among other charges, and ordered the companies to pay the

Trust $4 million and $2 million respectively. Digital paid in full early in 1998, while a battered NCC is making time payments on a reduced settlement of $200,000, according to the Trust's lawyer, Eric Eissenstat, of the Oklahoma City-based law firm of Fellers, Snider, Blankenship, Bailey & Tippens.

Though the Trust had the last word legally, Davis and the rest of the project team received their fair share of criticism for the two failed software projects. City auditors called for more stringent testing of vendor's software functionality and computer performance claims in future City projects as a result of the debacles. And outside observers criticize the Trust for trusting too much and not taking a more active role in managing the projects. "You can't rely on the contract," says Christopher Hoenig, former director of information management and technology issues at the U.S. General Accounting Office and president of Solutions, a Washington, D.C.-based independent consulting and training firm. "You have to be able to technically assess the project and flag problems early and fix them yourself, if necessary. If you don't have people internally with the skills to be able to do that, then hire them."

Davis believes he and his project team did the right thing by focusing on the agreed upon contractual requirements. "[In both projects] we found that sticking to our requirements was crucial," he says. "Any time the consultants strayed from meeting their requirements we knew something was wrong and we told them so." He adds, poignantly: "I also don't believe it's good to go around mistrusting everything someone says. That's just not a healthy way to live."

Though Davis feels vindicated by the successful legal cases, he looks back on those eight years of lost productivity and broken promises with a kind of pragmatic horror. Through all the pain, he and his staff endured and eventually prevailed. Davis approaches the triple-digit heat of an early June afternoon in downtown Oklahoma City with the same sort of doggedness. "When you live here a while," he says, "you just learn how to sweat."

Virginia Team Stops "Giant Sucking Sound" With Web

By Don Hutcheson

Buy or build? It's rarely that simple. Sometimes you need to modify what you buy so much that it becomes even more work than building from scratch. And while building from scratch can make for a monumental project, you can carve a middle course where you buy a little, build a little, use what you can from what you've already got, and move forward in manageable steps. In other words, using EAI as your vehicle can pay off—even if you've already spent nine million dollars trying to make the ERP you bought work. And that's just what happened in the Commonwealth of Virginia.

The *Richmond Times-Dispatch* said it best: "Taxpayers to pay for $9.4M goof," the headline screamed. The comptroller, William E. Landsidle, offered the accurate (if evasive) opinion that "It wasn't pretty. Mistakes were made."

To explain what happened, I have to take you back to January 12. On this day, the state legislature met for the first time in this millennium year. And it was Steve Long's deadline. He's the CIO for the Commonwealth of Virginia's Department of Personnel and Training (DPT). He's also the program manager for the state's Integrated Human Resource Information System (IHRIS). IHRIS is a crosscutting program running under the watchful eyes of the Secretary of Administration (Long's direct boss), the Secretary of Finance, and the Secretary of Technology (the first high-tech cabinet-level position of any state).

IHRIS gets this kind of visibility because it's both a development program and the outcome of a piece of legislation—a law mandating the migration of DPT's several HR applications off the mainframes. But Long is calm. As he says, "I am a fireman. I am used to fires."

Arriving on the scene in January 1999, he inherited a 15-year old homegrown HR information system based on a UNISYS mainframe running OS 2200, the UNISYS DMS-2200 database, a bunch of Cobol programs, and UNISYS's proprietary control language ECL. He also inherited the heir apparent: an unfinished PeopleSoft enterprise resource planning (ERP) implementation of IHRIS that had been in the works for five years, running up a close to ten million dollar tab. To add to the joy, it was of course the year of Y2K. Lastly, he received his marching orders: Virginia's aforementioned IHIRS legislation. As a consequence, most people figured he'd focus on getting the PeopleSoft project out the door as quickly as possible.

On January 12, 2000, I sat in on a meeting of the Commonwealth's Human Resources Leadership Council, comprising human resource directors from 17 agencies and DPT. Long and his team were showing off their Web-based ad hoc reporting capability. It was the first in a series of capabilities Long is planning. But the People Soft ERP was nowhere to be found. What happened?

Back in 1995, when the IHRIS legislation was passed and the PeopleSoft project began, conventional wisdom said the mainframe was a costly dinosaur, soon to be shouldered aside by client/server systems with pleasingly plump clients. Who had heard of the Web? PeopleSoft had a proven track record in private industry HR applications. It was the logical choice.

But the devil was sure in the details. Supporting the Commonwealth's HR and payroll policies and practices required over 1,000 changes to People-Soft's ERP system—including more than 100 to the core package. Ouch. It's one thing to alter screens and workflow elements. It's something else to do the major surgery needed to change the primary business rules and processing. Not to mention what ensues when the vendor upgrades the core product.

Canned Apps for Canned Needs

In the world of ERPs it's not unusual to need, say, a half-dozen core-level changes. Yet in my interviews of many public sector entities (I'm doing a best practices study), I've found that the Commonwealth's story isn't unusual. In the public sector, legislation and unions drive the business rules. And both of these forces can and will change the business rules at any time. Which requires changing the software accordingly. Neither legislatures nor unions spend much time worrying about what those changes will do to you and your developers.

And neither mainframe systems nor client/server ERP systems like PeopleSoft have ever really supported the flexibility requirements of public sector requirements like IHRIS. ERP systems certainly try to capture best practices in their code, and PeopleSoft had done so for private sector practices. But best practices for the public sector were virgin territory. And no wonder. Even in that sector, practices vary a lot from state to state. For example, the Commonwealth of Virginia is a right-to-work state with no state employee unions, while Maryland next door has a multitude of them.

The real way to implement a commercial ERP system like PeopleSoft successfully is to use the vanilla system pretty much as is, changing the business rules to match the software. Not so easy when some of those business rules are also state laws. And because DPT's IT staffers couldn't bend the rules in this case, they kept trying to bend the tool. As a result costs kept soaring, yet production kept slipping.

Within two weeks of his arrival, Long discovered that in just three more weeks the PeopleSoft consultants would drain his IT budget completely. So he cut off funding, stopping the IHRIS project in its tracks. This alarmed the legislators who had mandated the project, but they took a wait (for a little while) and see attitude because Long had the backing of his immediate superiors.

Looking at a track record of four years and over nine million dollars spent without even one module in production, Long suspected there were challenges within the program unrelated to technology. Over the next three months he gathered support from his higher-ups and the legislature to set a new direction for the IHRIS project.

A Webbed Feat, Step by Step

That direction was a produce a new custom built (using components wherever possible, of course), 100 percent Web-enabled HRIS. Moreover, the program would be done incrementally, in planned, controlled phases, rather than following the previous "all-at-once" strategy.

Everyone agreed that a phased approach had a much better chance of succeeding, and of providing more functionality more quickly. As for "buy versus build," it was also agreed that a custom system would have a much better chance of delivering an integrated HR system that met the requirements of the Commonwealth's HR laws, policies, and practices, as implemented by 264 highly autonomous agencies, and that could be changed as required, often with short timelines.

Meanwhile it was, as I said, the Year of Y2K. Resources were tight. The legacy systems remained while the talent pool for UNISYS OS 2200 and DMS 2200 continued to die off. And the legislature wanted results. Y2K was the priority, but Long couldn't let IHRIS go for another year without results.

Long looked for a way to quickly save people time and the state money. That turned out to be reports. As is so common with mainframe systems, reports took weeks to produce following an end user request.

He found a preexisting SAS Institute implementation on the mainframe, along with one SAS expert already on the payroll. The mainframe SAS program supported as many as 20 agencies, but it wasn't Web-enabled. Ad hoc reporting over the Web provided just the high-value, low-cost project Long was seeking.

SAS offered Web tools that were a logical extension of the current capability. A Cobol program on the mainframe was already generating the 250MB ASCII files (80,000 records per month) needed to populate the SAS multidimensional database (MDDB) every month. Long was able to take advantage of SAS's then-new state and local government practice, including a jumpstart program comprising one short proof of concept, one fixed price, and a one-page proposal. In three weeks, SAS came in and built the online analytical processing (OLAP) model (in the form of MDDB cubes) to support the monthly transaction data and a snapshot of the personnel data. Within those three weeks, SAS also built the SAS translation/mapping program, loaded the first snapshot and transaction files into the OLAP cube, and tested the app.

The SAS ad hoc reporting tool for the Web is a ready-to-run HTML implementation. Although there's some look and feel customization possible, no mods were needed. With minimal training, HR specialists were quickly using their Web browsers to point and click their way to the reports they needed. SAS came back and added an 18-month historical cube with another week's effort.

Rollout of the app has been incremental and "on demand." As word-of-mouth spreads or as requests for a report come in, Long's staff visits the person making the request and shows off the app's capability. No formal training is needed or given. In 80 percent of the cases, the ad hoc reporting capability fulfills the request. That 80 percent achievement has cost just $250 thousand—a bargain as such things go. The remaining 20 percent requiring custom implementation should cost about $1 million.

SASsing the Query from Hell

During that period, Long and his team took advantage of the SAS team's presence to transfer as much knowledge as possible. Two of Long's programmers will be trained on SAS. Other departments have decided to use SAS as well, along with a number of business analysts, who will use the SAS GUI-based tool.

The SAS implementation has had its wrinkles, of course. Security is a problem. After all, this is employment data; the problem is who has access to which rows and columns. Should the Governor's salary be accessible? The inelegant (but effective) solution has been to partition the OLAP cube by agency, along with modifying the SAS program that loads the partitions. This means that security has been pushed to the agency level.

So the needed security has been built using a combination of data structure, operating system, and application hooks. The data structure trick was to have OLAP code create a cube for each agency. Because parent/child relationships existed within the user base, the SAS team had to use a combination of systems and applications security along with data design to satisfy the security mode. In essence, an OLAP code was created for every group of users. An agency defines a group, so a unique cube is created for each agency. If an agency must see multiple agency data, this is handled at cube creation times. Data for that agency plus the multiple agencies is included in the cube. This also helps performance. The agency group defines which data an end user can see, along with which SAS application server is hit when requesting data.

The operating system trick was to place the cube into an agency file directory that could only be accessed by that agency's personnel. The last part of the trick is to use the Apache Web Server security to challenge the Web user for a valid ID/password combination. The Web user's rights are found on the Sun Server, and the app redirects agency personnel to the appropriate SAS application code that points to only that agency's cube. If an individual needs access to two or more agencies' data, an ID/password combination is mapped into multiple agencies.

Long's team is also working on a problem common to most out-of-the-box business intelligence systems: ad hoc queries from Hell that could hog the system's resources for days. The OLAP tools place no limits on the amount of data that can be requested. But the code structure is a summarized structure; it inherently minimizes large queries. Plus the SAS ad hoc query tools include some governors for limiting very large query pulls. This is done because the end users can query against the detail data. So if someone wants to see 100,000 records, he would only see a portion at a time. This is accomplished by dividing the query into multiple queries behind the scenes but transparent to the user. If a bad query is generated, then the user gets a message saying no records were selected or that the SQL isn't correct. It's also possible to add some canned reports to gently point users in the right direction.

Ad hoc reporting against an OLAP helps users, provides tangible results, and is true to the spirit of the IHRIS legislation—even if it doesn't abide strictly by the letter of that law. And it helps change the culture of the users and their agencies, making people comfortable with the technology.

SAS is taking on a life of its own in the Commonwealth's agencies, with more and more information being extracted and used. For example, benefits and payroll information can be mined along with HR information: EEO/AA compliance, metrics, and health benefits retention, participation, cost, and turnover. Virginia residents benefit from state agencies making better decisions faster.

Now that the technology is no longer the bottleneck, deciding what gets implemented next can go by what the state needs most instead of what the technology will permit. Meanwhile, Long must comply with The Law by migrating the functionality off the mainframe. But instead of using the "Big Bang" approach of the PeopleSoft project, he's bringing in an open systems architecture, on an incremental and phased basis.

Following SAS product directions and planning "to keep on relieving the most pain for the least cost," Long is looking forward to doing some screen scraping off the mainframe. It should be possible to integrate some of the mainframe's green screen I/O at the Web UI level. The Web UI acts as a unifying medium or "portal" for diverse back-end apps and platforms. As the Web UI gains acceptance, the back end system scan gradually move from the mainframe to Oracle servers. Users working at their Web UIs won't notice a thing.

At press time, Long is in the middle of choosing development platforms and tools. Because one of the primary mandates for IHRIS is to migrate off the mainframes, his group has to write new code. So he doesn't have the option of using Cobol programs that provide wrappers to the existing code.

Given the parameters of the environment, Long has made the strategic choice of an EAI approach featuring message-oriented middleware (MOM), which suits the inquiry-based (rather than heavily transactional) applications that DPT mainly needs. The combination of BEA WebLogic Enterprise Server and the SAS tools appear to provide this EAI platform. At the time he first looked at BEA, they were still talking about Iceberg and M3. But as Long understands it, BEA has since repackaged WebLogic Enterprise with Tuxedo, replacing the M3 component.

From what Long has seen, BEA WebLogic Enterprise Server and the SAS tools seem to provide a broad range of capability to integrate systems at the data layer and at the transaction layer. This doesn't change his long-range objective of migrating his legacy system, and then integrating with other systems. Once DPT is on an open system architecture, integration with other systems will become even easier. While the system migration is occurring, SAS tools can be used to begin collecting and exploiting data from the 70 personnel systems in use in the Commonwealth.

Platform and tool decisions have to be considered together, and for the toolsets he's looking at three possibilities: Java servlets, Microsoft ASP et al, and BEA WebLogic. This is still a work in progress, but it's worth noting that many of the products he's using are Javacentric or at least support Java. These include SAS AppDevStudio, BEA WebLogic, Verity Information Server, Rational Enterprise Suite, IBM VisualAge for Java, Symantec VisualCafé, Nuance speech recognition system, and Blaze Advisor.

As DPT moves forward, the Web will be the primary interface across the Commonwealth, though many nonwired employees will get interactive voice recognition (IVR). Administrators, employees, retirees, dependants, and other citizens can access services through a Commonwealth portal. And besides effectively disseminating HR information, DPT is also tasked with collecting consistent, accurate data from all agencies and institutions in the Commonwealth. The new systems will face that challenge as well.

During 1999 Long's staff tackled Y2K with over 2 million lines of new code, while at the same time carrying out the $250 thousand SAS project, which in a few weeks delivered a capability that satisfies over 80 percent of the HR queries of 90,000 employees in over 150 state agencies. Pretty good ROI.

Seeing what Long's group has done has convinced me that the "Big Bang" development is dead. As Long puts it, "Business is changing at the pace of technology." And that includes state business.

CHAPTER 6

Viruses:
Failure With a Cause

It's time for a left turn in our collection of dot-com and ordinary computing failure stories. By now, you may have this glazed-over, please-don't-hit-me-with-another-failure-story, look on your face. Each individual story in this book, I believe—and I hope you believe it, too—is fascinating, but the aggregation of all of them soon begins to be (a) too much more of the same, and (b) ultimately depressing.

So, to help ward off the depression of all those computing failure stories, I want to bring up another subject—viruses. Unless you've been doing a Rip Van Winkle on another planet for the last 20something years, you know that a virus is a mechanism for making a deliberate attack on a computing system, and that all too many of them hit the nightly news with a big, destructive splash.

I struggled for awhile with the question of whether a virus story is a suitable inclusion for a book on computing failure. After all, most failure stories are in some sense self-inflicted. Someone on project Y at company X takes on too ambitious a project, or doesn't understand the role of achieving profit in a business plan, or hides major problems from a higher-rafter-bat (*), and before you know it project Y at company X is in deep excrement—and maybe company X is, too.

Viruses, though, are different. It's this creepy breaking-into-the-house-in-the-middle-of-the-night kind of failure. The kind of failure that leaves you feeling violated, without even having a clue as to who has done the violating. Viruses are the very opposite of self-inflicted failure. They are failures done unto you. Oh, you may have left the figurative front-door unlocked, but basically you didn't cause yourself to be inflicted by a virus. Someone anonymous did it to you.

Okay, so viruses are a very different kind of failure. And yet, they are indeed failures. Astonishing numbers of viruses silently swirl about our systems all the time, seeking vulnerabilities. If they find their way in, damage may range from captured critical data, to destroyed critical data, to denial of service to your valuable users on the computer on which that critical data rests.

In the end, what swung me over the brink toward including a virus story in this volume was one of the most proactive pieces of computing journalism I have seen in a long time. *The Industry Standard*, a major source for the dotcom failure stories in this book, but a relative newbie in the field of computing journalism, assigned someone to track down that infamous Love Bug virus that crippled many of the world's computer networks. Tracking it down meant visiting the key players in the story, and the key computing school in the Philippines where the story began. The result is an exciting human-interest story that helps us readers have a much more clear picture of the what and why and how of the Love Bug.

To set the stage for the *Industry Standard* story, we first take a quick look at its bottom line. In "Love Bug Case Against Student Gets Dismissed," we learn that the long arm of the law simply wasn't long enough to reach the Love Bug perpetrators. It's a case of the United Nations having asked its constituent members to solve the legal aspects of the virus problem, but specific countries—like the Philippines—simply never having gotten around to passing the necessary laws.

Then comes the "Cradle of Love" story itself, the inside view of what happened in the Philippines. It's the story of a legitimate but second-rate [academic] institution, a surging demand for tech workers, and a student whom some admire to this day for his programming skills (if not his judgment).

One of the interesting peripheral thoughts in the Love Bug story stems from the remark by an administrator of the Philippine computing school to the effect that someone "in the U.S. or in the UK [should] come up with an antivirus." Well, that challenge has been met—that's the good news—but there's bad news, as well. There are such things as the antivirus programs the Philippine administrator wished for. But the bad news overwhelms the good, experts tell us (e.g., Berinato 2000) such software produces so many false positives—indications of a potential hack that are wrong—that many of its users simply turn it off so they won't have to spend the huge amounts of time needed to separate the virus chaff from the virus wheat. And even if users leave it on and do the resulting required research, one expert quoted

in [Berinato 2000] tells us, "there's no real science" to antivirus software—
"all the products," he says, "are faking it."

So, that's our chapter on viruses. Does it really belong in a book on computing failure? You know my answer—now it's time for yours!

* In the bat world, bats—as you no doubt know—sleep suspended from the ceiling. What you may not know is that leader bats sleep higher up in the rafters than their underlings, which turns out to be important because bats release excrement while they sleep. The analogy of leader bats doing their droppings on lower-ranked bats is too obviously similar to the typical behavior of a hierarchy in a corporation to be ignored.

Reference:
Berinato, Scott, "The Software That Cries Wolf," *eWeek*, Aug. 7, 2000.

'Love Bug' Case Against Student Gets Dismissed as Laws Lag

By Robert Frank
Staff Reporter of the Wall Street Journal

The Philippine Department of Justice dropped all charges against a Manila college student accused of releasing the "Love Bug" computer virus, citing a lack of applicable laws and evidence.

The move, which highlights the inadequacy of computer laws in many developing countries, brings a likely end to the case and to potential prosecutions in one of the world's most-damaging computer viruses. The "ILOVEYOU" virus, released in May, reproduced over e-mail systems and crippled many of the world's computer networks.

Philippine prosecutors said that since there were no specific laws against computer-hacking in the Philippines at the time the virus was launched, they have been forced to dismiss all charges.

Police had been seeking to charge Onel de Guzman, a computer-college student, with a related crime of credit-card theft. But the Department of Justice said the credit-card law doesn't apply to computer hacking, and investigators didn't present sufficient evidence to support the theft charge.

Police initially traced the computer virus to the phone line of an apartment occupied by Mr. de Guzman, who had written his college thesis on a password-stealing program similar to the one used in the virus. Mr. de Guzman acknowledge during a May news conference that he might have released the virus by accident but said he meant no harm.

Neither Mr. de Guzman nor his attorney, Roland Quimbo, could be reached for comment late yesterday.

"This shows how far the Philippines and other countries lag the U.S. in terms of electronic laws," said Rey Buzon, president of AJO.net Holdings Inc., an Internet incubator in the Philippines. "These laws are important not only to protect against crimes like this, but to protect technology investors and companies in the Philippines."

The United Nations adopted a universal law on e-commerce in 1996 and urged its members to accept the law in 1997. While most developed countries accepted the law, or cited adequate legislation of their own, dozens of developing countries have yet to pass the bills, according to legal experts.

Spurred by the "Love Bug" attack, the Philippines in June passed its first e-commerce and computer law. The new legislation, however, can't be applied retroactively to the "Love Bug" virus. Officials said the lack of computer laws in the Philippines will also make it difficult for another country such as the U.S. to seek extradition.

Cradle of Love

By Joanne Lee-Young, Manila

Once you get to the Philippines chain of islands in the South China Sea, finding Manila's AMA Computer College takes some looking.

Go down a residential alley where traffic is clogged with garbage trucks, follow the telephone poles with small, laminated signs.

Past several winding turns is a drab, six-story warehouse that's been converted into classrooms. This is Amable Mendoza Aguiluz Computer College, where investigators are searching for the origins of a computer virus that earlier this month crashed e-mail systems worldwide with a flood of messages that read "I love you."

Thirty or more AMA students, including Onel A. de Guzman and Michael Buen, are being questioned about their possible involvement with the creation and launch of the virus. And while the investigation twists and turns with odd clues and unanswered questions, the spotlight on the "Love Bug" mystery is revealing a class of young Filipinos who are embracing technology as a way to advance themselves in a country where the average annual income is only about $3,500. Graduating from AMA and other technology vocational schools, these new workers are filling jobs ranging from computer programmers to call-center attendants.

Sandra Blanco, 29, is a member of this new tech generation. Working in the hip basement offices of Summit Interactive, her current life seems a world away from her days as a student at the dreary AMA campus. Summit Interactive is an online publishing company, a recent spin-off from JG Summit Holdings, one of the largest family-owned conglomerates in the Philippines.

Blanco takes a bus to work from San Pedro, her hometown in a province outside Manila, a ride that can take as long as two hours when traffic is bad. As a systems analyst for Summit's stable of Web sites like Candymag.com, a site for female teens, and Femalenetwork.com, a community site, she chooses and implements software programs, and works with a team of five others to monitor the company's computer networks.

Blanco originally was among the many Filipino youths that sought jobs that would take them overseas, where they can make more money and perhaps send some of it home. According to the country's National Economic and Development Authority, Filipinos working abroad in positions ranging from engineers to domestic workers sent home $6.8 billion dollars last year.

That was Blanco's reason for studying nursing in the late 1980s at Centro Escolar University. At the time, there was a huge demand in the U.S. for medical workers, and visas for foreign nurses were easy to get. But as that demand waned so did Blanco's interest in the profession. After two years at nursing school, she failed two courses and had to drop out in 1989. It was then that she decided to study information technology at AMA. Upon graduation, a nurse in the Philippines earns about $1,450 per year, estimates Blanco. The starting salary for a systems analyst is three times that.

The promise of a lucrative job in the computer industry is being lauded everywhere, from television ads to signs at the mall. In one recent campaign for AMA, a young Filipino actress and teen-magazine sensation, Jolina Magdangal, appeared in advertisements for the school. She was a student, too, studying simple programming with a tutor on the set of her popular television series. Her fresh face, which had already been used to pitch canned sardines and fruit juice, was now promoting technical education as a cool way to move ahead.

Enrollment jumped 20 percent in 1997 when the ads began for the school, which was regarded as a legitimate but second-rate institution for people who did not have the money or the smarts to attend one of the country's universities. Students were eyeing opportunities at multinational companies that had begun to send their back-office operations to the Philippines to take advantage of the low wages and widespread use of English. Companies including America Online, Andersen Consulting, Microsoft and Procter & Gamble outsourced jobs like customer technical support and transcribing audio tapes to the Philippines.

AMA and similar colleges expanded all over the Philippines, from Manila to far-flung locales like the islands of Cebu and Mindanao, in response to the surging demand for tech workers. In affiliation with large technology firms such as Cisco Systems, Hewlett-Packard and Microsoft, the schools aimed to package computer training for consumption by the mass market.

Now in 150 locations—many of which are franchise operations—the blue-and-white AMA logo is as likely to jut out from a window or a side street as is a sign for a fast-food restaurant. "It is similar to McDonald's," says Juanito G. Ramos Jr., a vice president of the school's business development group.

Other colleges that resemble the AMA model, including branches of the Informatics Computer Institute, are located in shopping malls and other places where kids like to hang out.

The demand for technological skills is growing as a nascent Internet scene emerges here. Traditional business families like the Gokongweis, who own JG Summit Holdings, are morphing their old property, petrochemical and retail interests, into dot-com companies. While many of these employers say they are more apt to hire talent for their Internet divisions from large universities such as the University of the Philippines and Ateneo de Manila, the best of AMA's 50,000 students are also finding jobs.

"It's a step up," says Blanco of her current position, which she started about seven months ago. When she first graduated from AMA, she worked for a semiconductor company in Binan, a small town in the Laguna province that borders Manila.

For the time being, Blanco doesn't have her eye on a job overseas. She feels strongly that she first wants to focus on improving her skills in the Philippines, where she is "used to everything. I don't want to go [abroad] and end up as an encoder. I want to work as a programmer, a manager or a systems analyst there," she says.

Back at AMA's corporate offices, furor over the Love Bug is keeping officials busy. Rushing from one meeting to another, a walkie-talkie in hand, Ernesto A. Rioveros, a senior vice president at AMA, says the school is investigating on its own and is considering disciplinary action against students involved in spreading the virus.

"We are not too happy," he says. "Creating the virus was smart, but we should not be proud of that."

The topic has local television talk shows hashing out a debate that has been argued on street corners and at dinner tables: Should the Love Bug be a source of pride or shame for the Philippines?

True, it has caused damage estimated in the billions of dollars of lost information and productivity. But de Guzman, one of the main suspects, says that his program was driven only by the most heroic of intentions: to steal ISP passwords from paying subscribers in order to give Web access to the ordinary Filipino for whom it is too expensive.

Even though the school rejected de Guzman's thesis submission because the computer code involved stealing Internet passwords, Rioversos, the school official, admits that there is some admiration on campus for de Guzman's programming skills.

"Why, in the U.S. or in the U.K., couldn't anyone come up with an antivirus?" he asks. "This makes this guy [look] very good. It's the dream of every hacker."

Magdangal, the actress, teen idol, and computer student, however, takes no pride in the scandal and makes it clear that she stopped representing AMA last month.

"I am just a student there," she says. "I study well, get good grades and don't want to say anything else about AMA." Her father and manager, Jun

Magdangal, says that with the Love Bug controversy, they are concerned about "maintaining her clean-cut image."

AMA also has reason to worry about its image. But if anything, attention from the Love Bug only seems to have put a positive spin on the school's mediocre reputation.

The school's current ad campaign features a slogan that indicates that AMA in particular and Filipinos in general feel that their computer skills now rank among the best in the world. It says: "Finally, no Juan will be left behind by any Tom, Dick or Harry."

Conclusions and Wrap-Up

There's very little that I remember about the movie *Zorba the Greek*. It hit the screen, after all, 40-something years ago, and hasn't been seen very often since.

But there are two things I will never forget about it. The first, of course, is that haunting Greek title song. But that's not what I want to talk about here.

The second thing I remember is the ending. The ending is so bitter-sweet, so poignant. What has happened all through the movie is that Zorba has been working on the construction of (if I recall correctly) an aqueduct. The aqueduct is complex and difficult to build, but Zorba seems to have it all under control. Until the very end.

And then, in that ending, the aqueduct collapses. It is a complete failure. Nothing can be salvaged.

But that's not what I remember about the ending. What I remember is that, when the magnitude of the failure is at its most inescapable, when the dust of the collapse is beginning to settle, when Zorba is at the depths of his personal despair, he begins to dance. Yes, he begins to dance. To that haunting title song. Slowly, at first. But then, caught up in the pace of the music, he dances more and more wildly. He is choosing, we realize, to dance his failure away.

Failure is difficult for most of us human beings to grasp. We know intellectually what has happened, of course, but we hardly know what to do about it emotionally. Some of us mope. Some of us lash out. Some of us hide from the world.

But not Zorba. He engaged the world, danced with a smile (not a mope) on his face, lashed out at no one. It was as if Zorba were saying to himself, and through himself to the rest of the world, "Life is made up of successes and failures. This has been a failure. But let me treat it like I would a success. This is, after all, a human condition to be celebrated."

Most of us, with the thin veneer of civilization masking our raw emotions from the world, would not be able to do what Zorba did. And yet, I suspect, at some level we must all envy him.

The analogy to the failed projects of this book is fairly obvious. Many of those caught up in an enterprise failure such as those in this book would be deeply down at the moment of failure. But one of the things about the startup world, including the world of startup dot-coms, is that it is entirely possible to rise from those ashes, join another enterprise, try it all over again. And, eventually, to dance. Perhaps not as literally as Zorba did, but, still, many of those who populated this book will dance.

In fact, as we said in one of the opening quotes of this book, "The paradox is that you have to experience failure to have success." Many of the failure stories in this book will lead to subsequent success stories. Zorba will dance yet again. As a colleague of mine once said (on another subject) many years ago, "Heads roll uphill in the dot-com business."

Don't cry for me, ComputingFailure.com. Dance for me instead.

Probably most of us are sufficiently unlike Zorba that we won't literally dance when failure catches us in its snare. But a sense of humor is something most of us *can* manage. That's what I like about the little news story that follows. Let me close this book with the following upbeat, humorous view of how some people have chosen to handle failure.

When the Going Gets Tough, The Tough Change Their Titles

By Pui-Wing Tam and Mylene Mangalindan
Staff Reporters of the Wall Street Journal

San Francisco—Tough times call for daring strategies, which helps explain Silicon Valley's growing use of this innovative business tool: the really weird job title.

David Roberts, for example, is now Chief Zaplet. Mr. Robert's title was president earlier this year when ill winds began blowing in the Internet world. Mr. Roberts decided it was time to replace himself with an experienced chief executive for his company, an Internet start-up called FireDrop Inc. But then he agonized about what to call himself.

Mr. Roberts, 36 years old, didn't want the usual kick upstairs to chairman, with its out-to-pasture connotations. So he dreamed up a title with more flair. FireDrop's main product is an e-mail program named Zaplet. "I don't really believe in titles," explains Mr. Roberts, who co-founded the Redwood Shores, Calif., company last year.

With the bursting of the dot-com bubble in Silicon Valley, a whole new class of job titles is emerging. In today's less-forgiving business climate, many founders of cash-strapped tech firms are stepping aside, often in favor of more-experienced and more profit-oriented executives. Not content to take on traditional less prestigious titles, some people are inventing new ones.

Other tech firms, to try to bolster company morale, are creating newly titled positions such as Chief Morale Officer and Vice President of People. Such folks are responsible for keeping spirits up and making employees feel that they are still in the business loop.

Some companies are letting workers dream up their own titles. "Our company was formed during the market correction, so everything we've done—including letting people pick job titles—is done to attract talent," says Sheri Falco, a founder of start-up Libida.com, where she has the title of Chief Catalyst (translation: president).

Employees at the San Francisco company, which will soon launch chat rooms for women to talk about their health and sexuality, printed business cards in April with titles such as Sex Librarian (a k a content manager), Chief

Dreamer (chairman and chief executive), and Minister of Six-Degrees, (corporate communications manager).

Weird titles have a tradition in Silicon Valley. At Apple Computer Inc., which pioneered the trend, former Chief Executive John Sculley kept a separate stack of business cards on which he called himself Chief Listener. Guy Kawasaki, now plain-old CEO of Internet company Garage.com, was famously known as Apple's Chief Evangelist.

But unusual labels had been rare and largely a whimsical thumb-your-nose-at-the-establishment gesture. Now, companies are using them for more mainstream ends.

"People in tech companies are working obscenely hard," says Jon Holman, a venture-capital recruiter at the Holman Group Inc., in San Francisco. "In an environment like that these days, anything you can do to give people greater control of their life has got to have a positive effect."

The tactic appears to have cheered up at least a few Silicon Valley engineers. Organic Inc., an Internet consulting firm in San Francisco, is one of the firms that encourage people to call themselves what they want to. Engineers there have settled on a grab bag of names, such as Dark Jedi, Sushi Engineer and Code Therapist.

Over the past six months, as Organic's stock has fallen from $40 to about $5, it has been "a little perk" to have the attention-getting title, says Marc Majcher, a content engineer there. "Better to allow us a little wacky outlet like this than to have to deal with a bunch of engineers who are really grumpy, possibly armed, and drunk more often than not," he says.

Picking a quirky title is a serious matter requiring much study. Fire-Drop's Mr. Roberts drew up an elaborate chart that listed what he thought his main duties would be after the new chief executive arrived. He figured his primary role post-new-CEO would include helping the company develop a strategic vision for FireDrop's e-mail system.

Mr. Roberts says that right away, he got a positive response from colleagues to his Chief Zaplet choice. "It sounded like a good founder's title," says Joy D'Amore, whose business cards for internal use truly do read Goddess of the People, and who is FireDrop's manager of strategic growth when she is dealing with the wider public.

At Scient Corp., a San Francisco Internet consulting firm, each of the company's branches appoints a Chief Morale Officer once every six months. Every morale officer takes on the burden of promoting colleagues' feelings of well-being via such duties as organizing social events and occasionally handing out beer on Fridays.

And Rayna Brown at Vividence Corp., a business-to-business Internet company in San Mateo, Calif., chose her new title after serious consultations with the company's CEO in May. Ms. Brown says she didn't want the more common label of human-resources manager because her job also involves coaching executives and directors on the company's "culture of growth, and personal development," so she has become Vice President of People.

"Some of the other titles out there are meant for shock value," she says.

Indeed they are. Mr. Majcher, the content engineer at Organic, and a gun enthusiast who has taken colleagues to a shooting range as a team-building exercise, adopted the title Gun-Toting Psycho when he joined the company early last year. It is on his business card.

About the Author

Robert L. Glass has meandered the halls of computing for over 40 years now, starting with a three-year gig in the aerospace industry (at North American Aviation) in 1954–1957, which makes him one of the true pioneers of the software field.

That stay at North American extended into several other aerospace appearances (at Aerojet-General Corp., 1957–1965, and the Boeing Company, 1965–1970 and 1972–1982). His role was largely that of building software tools used by applications specialists. It was an exciting time to be part of the aerospace business—those were the heady days of space exploration, after all—but it was an even headier time to be part of the computing field. Progress in both fields was rapid, and the vistas were extraterrestrial!

The primary lesson he learned during those aerospace years was that he loved the technology of software, but hated being a manager. He carefully cultivated the role of technical specialist, which had two major impacts on his career—(a) his technical knowledge remained fresh and useful, but (b) his knowledge of management—and his earning power—were diminished commensurately.

When his upward mobility had reached the inevitable technological Glass ceiling (tee-hee!), Glass took a lateral transition into academe. He taught in the software engineering graduate program at Seattle University (1982–1987) and spent a year at the Software Engineering Institute (1987–1988). (He had earlier spent a couple of years (1970–1972) working on a tools-focused research grant at the University of Washington.)

The primary lesson he learned during those academic years was that he loved having his head in the academic side of software engineering, but his heart remained in its practice. You can take the man out of industry, apparently, but you can't take the industry out of the man. With that new-found wisdom, he began to search for ways to bridge what he had long felt was the communication chasm between academic computing and its practice.

He found several ways of doing that. Many of his books (over 20) and professional papers (over 60) focus on trying to evaluate academic computing findings and on transitioning those with practical value to industry. (This is decidedly a nontrivial task, and is largely responsible for the contrarian nature of his beliefs and writings.) His lectures and seminars on software engineering focus on both theoretical and best-of-practice findings that are useful to practitioners. His newsletter, *The Software Practitioner*, and his SoftwarePractitioner.com web site, tread those same paths. So does the (more academic) *Journal of Systems and Software*, which he edits for Elsevier. And so do the columns he writes regularly for such publications as *Communications of the ACM*, *IEEE Software*, and ACM SIGMIS's *Data Base*. Although most of his work is serious and contrarian, a fair portion of it also contains (or even consists of) computing humor.

With all of that in mind, what is his proudest moment in the computing field? The award, by Linkoping University of Sweden, of his honorary Ph.D. degree in 1995.

(Note: the sketch at the top of the previous page is circa 1970. That may not be how Glass looks now, but it's the way he wants you to think he looks!)

Sources

Sources for articles in ComputingFailure.com (in order of their appearance in this book)

Source, followed by the articles from that source:

Barron's
For Dot.Coms, It's The Vision Thing

CIO
To Hell and Back
Another Trip to Hell
Her Majesty's Flying I.T. Circus
Double Jeopardy

Computerworld
The Banality of Failure
CEO: Partnership Hurt Toysmart

Enterprise Development
Virginia Team Stops "Giant Sucking Sound" With Web

Indianapolis Star
Hidden Past Sheds Light on Ex-IQuest Chief's Odd Ways

The Industry Standard
Take It and Leave It
Startup Meltdown
An American Dream Gone Bad
The End of the Line
Back in the Saddle
Edfex Misses a Meal or Two
Atomic Pop's Final Encore
Pop.com Goes Poof
Broken Wing
Why Pandesic Didn't Pan Out
The Foreclosure at Mortgage.com
The Great Internet CON
The Life and Near Death of Drkoop.com

And Now the Big Bankruptcy

Breakthrough or Snake Oil?

Cradle of Love

San Jose Mercury News
Interval: The Think Tank that Tanked

Seattle Times
County Blew $38 Million: Here's What Went Wrong

Software Development
Lost in Chaos: Chronology of a Failure

Time Digital
Adios, Amiga

Wall Street Journal
The Color Green: The Internet Bubble Broke Records, Rules, and Bank Accounts

Angels of Death: Reality Bites Hard as String of Dot-Coms See Funding Dry Up

Pets.com's Demise

In Foundering Swedish Dot-Com, a Cautionary Tale

After a Life at Warp Speed, Netscape Logs Off

Dot-Com Liquidator

Spooked: Money Men Liked Boo and Boo Liked Money

Anatomy of a Crash: From an Awkward Kid to a Star of Software to a Body in a Hotel

What Price Glory?

What Goes Up...

Computer Crash

'Love Bug' Case Against Student Gets Dismissed as Laws Lag

When the Going Gets Tough, the Tough Change Their Titles

·

Index

A

Adobe, 61
Adornis.com, 107-108
Advanced Equities, 123-129
Affinity, 249-257
Aleshe, John Paul, See Hoquim, Robert
Allen, Paul, 52, 53, 91-101
Alta Vista, 35, 172-173
Amable Mendoza Aguilez (AMA)
    Computer College (Manila),
    270-273
Amazon.com, 14, 15, 17, 18, 27, 56-57,
    59, 109
America Online (AOL), 17, 85, 147-148,
    150, 153
Amiga, 189, 191-193
Apartments cats- 95-97
Ariba, 19-20
Ashford.com, 108
AskJeeves, 181
Atomic Pop, 70-72
Audible, 13
AudioCafe.com, 58-60
Autoweb.com, 13

B

Bain & Co., 176-177
BankOne.com, 75-81
Barron's, 23-25
Baum, Seth, 174-175
Beautyjungle.com, 83
Be Free, 185
BigPrizes.com, 60
BigStore.com (The), 170-173
Blue Cross, 207-209
Bokus, 156
Boo.com, 27, 34, 64, 89, 113-114,
    155-160
Boyle, Justin, 179
Bricks and mortar, 12, 39
Bringthenoise.com, 72
Broadcast.com, 123
Business to Business (B2B), 16, 19, 23-24,
    32, 67-68, 182, 278
Business to Consumer (B2C), 23-24, 39,
    182
Business to public sector (B2P),
    24
Business Week, 12

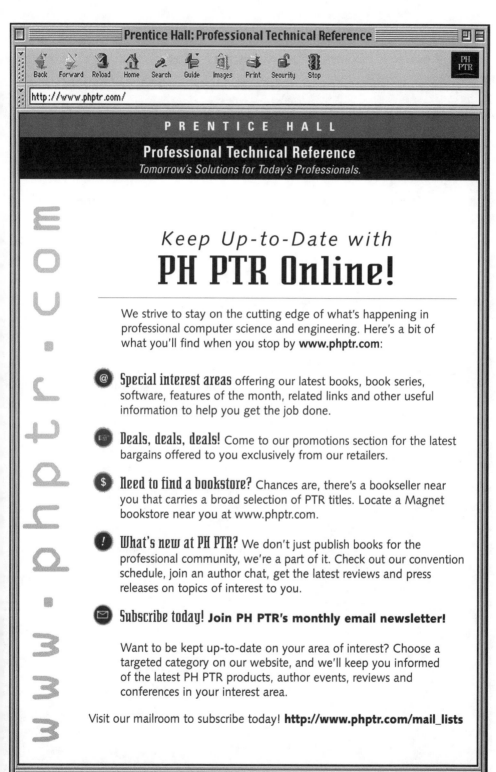

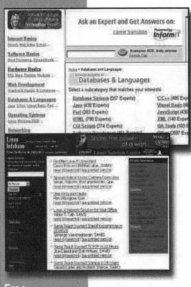